The Legacy Family

The Legacy Family

The Definitive Guide to Creating a Successful Multigenerational Family

Lee Hausner
and
Douglas K. Freeman

Foreword by Jay Hughes
Author of *Family Wealth-Keeping It in the Family*

First published in 2009 by
PALGRAVE MACMILLAN®
in the United States—a division of St. Martin's Press LLC,
175 Fifth Avenue, New York, NY 10010.

Where this book is distributed in the UK, Europe and the rest of the world,
this is by Palgrave Macmillan, a division of Macmillan Publishers Limited,
registered in England, company number 785998, of Houndmills,
Basingstoke, Hampshire RG21 6XS.

Palgrave Macmillan is the global academic imprint of the above companies
and has companies and representatives throughout the world.

Palgrave® and Macmillan® are registered trademarks in the United States,
the United Kingdom, Europe and other countries.

ISBN: 978–0–230–61892–3

Library of Congress Cataloging-in-Publication Data

Hausner, Lee.
    The legacy family : The Definitive Guide to Creating a Successful
  Multigenerational Family / Lee Hausner, Douglas Freeman.
      p. cm.
    Includes bibliographical references and index.
    ISBN 978–0–230–61892–3
      1. Family. I. Freeman, Douglas. II. Title.

HQ519.H38 2009
306.85—dc22   2009011691

A catalogue record of the book is available from the British Library.

Design by Newgen Imaging Systems (P) Ltd., Chennai, India.

First edition: December 2009

10 9 8 7 6 5 4 3 2 1

Printed in the United States of America.

CONTENTS

The Legacy Family—A Family for the Generations

During the past thirty years, a new multidisciplinary field has emerged to serve families whose "business is the family" and its long-term flourishing. Prior to this time the few families who had sold their enterprises and become financial families had very few advisors committed to their sets of transition issues. Perhaps it was natural that a family with a business enterprise could attract many professionals to serve it, since business management and branches of the law and accounting are areas of academic graduate specialty. Unfortunately, for families who had sold their enterprises there were then and are now no academic graduate programs devoted to their issues exclusively. Even more unfortunate for them is that frequently their most trusted advisors found it and continue to find it financially advantageous to stay with the business and serve its new owners. The families who sell their businesses suffer a double trap:

- the loss of their gifted counselors and their experience of how their families' system works; and
- often no continuing trusted advisors to pick up the families' journey, now as a financial family, who have any real experience of serving families whose business is their family and the goal its long-term flourishing.

As this new professional field of serving the issues of the "business of the family" developed, a small band of professionals began to study how to practice in this field. Very quickly it became clear that no one academic or professional specialty could meet the multiple qualitative issues these families presented. No such family fit into an attorney's practice since most of its questions were those of intra- and interpersonal communication and governance. There were no forms that fit these cases as they were all about function. In fact, many practitioners found that they had to relearn that form follows function if they were not to do harm. These are systems issues for which a quantitative law practice offers no preparation for developing the critical capitals of such families their human, intellectual, and social capitals. Similarly, those most gifted in the psychological, cultural anthropological, sociological, and organizational dynamics specialties often had no quantitative experience to bring to bear on the financial capital and its system of dynamic preservation of financial assets. Essentially each discipline had something to offer, but no one discipline offered all the wisdom and skills the business of a family required.

Enter Freeman and Hausner. Doug Freeman is an attorney who has practiced extensively with financial families and their philanthropies. Lee Hausner is a PhD psychologist whose two books *Children of Paradise* and *Hats Off to You*, coauthored with Ernest Doud, are required reading for all practitioners in this field. Both have long years of counseling experience, counseling some of the financially wealthiest dynastic families in the world. Their partnership now conjoins their multidisciplinary experiences to enlighten *Legacy Families* on how to see 100 years ahead and to imagine how to be flourishing families when they get there.

Freeman and Hausner, as they craft their chapters on the critical issues for these families and the skills they will need to develop for their successful resolution, show us why the family systems, communications, and governance issues that a "Legacy Family" presents cannot be remedied by one single discipline. They evolve our understanding, through examples, of the reality that the most important issues such families face are qualitative—issues of human intellectual and social development—not quantitative. They seek to help such families appreciate that the successful 100-year stories they are beginning will be ones that document the transitions that each generation of the family will help gently nurture to assure that each family member successfully fulfills the work of each stage of his or her life. They help us appreciate why each member's dream is precious and creative. They teach the age-old truth that a family's long-term happiness, thus its flourishing, lies in its capacity to adapt, its capacity to be resilient, and its capacity to successfully integrate many new members into its communications and governance systems. Only if it can do these well can it organically evolve to the state of family grace called "flourishing."

Each of Freeman's and Hausner's chapters poses one of the issues a family seeking to become a "Legacy Family" must comprehend and then offers the practices from many different disciplines that have proven helpful to its resolution. Such great practitioners as Freeman and Hausner never undervalue us as readers by downplaying the complexity of this work and especially of the perseverance needed for its accomplishment. They remind us that in the universal cultural proverb "shirtsleeves to shirtsleeves in three generations" lies the entropic reality of most families' failed efforts. They ask families seeking to be "Legacy Families," to be families who flourish, to accept that the work of growing such a family is extremely hard work with results that take 100 years to achieve. I hope that the great gifts of their professional lifetimes, which they share here so freely and abundantly, will help your family become a "Legacy Family."

Often those of us who have given our lives to the service of families and to the belief that families can flourish are guided by the wise words of the Iroquois elder when he or she convenes the tribe to make its most important decisions those about its continued life: "Let us hope that our members, seven generations from now, will honor the care, diligence, and wisdom we will bring to our decision making today, as we honor those seven generations ago who made it possible for us to be here today."

It is seventh-generation thinking that keeps a tribe, The Iroquois, which is always and only an extended family as Hiawatha taught, alive and flourishing for now nearly 500 years. May your family be graced to do seventh-generation thinking and to flourish.

Thanks Doug and Lee for your legacy of service and now for the gift of what you have learned.

A very deep bow!!!

JAMES {JAY} E. HUGHES, JR.

ACKNOWLEDGMENT

One cannot prepare a book of this nature without acknowledging the contribution of so many people whose wisdom, insight, and values helped to shape our perceptions and, indeed, our experiences. This book is dedicated to Lynn, my loving spouse, whose 42 years with me have provided the bedrock upon which I have built my life; to Darren and Brett, my incredibly talented children, who have blessed me with their own success and with such joy at their strength of character and compassion; and to my grandchildren for whom I hope the lessons taught here will benefit. Lest anyone doubt it, none of this would have been possible without my parents, Elaine and Jack, who instilled in me all that I am and hope to become, and to my fantastic brothers, who kept my feet on the ground and my eyes focused ahead. And to my partner, Lee, I thank you for the years of collaboration and inspiration. Writing this book with you was the capstone of my most interesting career.

Douglas K. Freeman
July 2009

This book represents a culmination of the work that I have been privileged to do with so many wonderful families as well as the intellectual stimulation I have been so fortunate to have received from my many colleagues in this field, particularly my partner in this exciting endeavor, Doug. Freeman. I recognize how blessed I have been to have received the love, wisdom, and guidance from my parents Ernestine and Leon that has provided the core values upon which I have always operated. I am very .grateful for the loving support that I have always received from my husband, Murray and my two children, Bryan and Carrie. They have been the experimental laboratory for many of my ideas and it is with great pride that I have watched them achieve their own personal success and have chosen the type of partners in Stacie and Matt who now contribute to the growth of our legacy family with the addition of my grandchildren Cayla, Zach, Ava, Haley, and Eli.

It is my hope that this book will give you the support and guidance to be able to experience the fulfillment and joy that comes from creating your own legacy family.

Lee Hausner
July 2009

PROLOGUE

Much has been written about the failures in families. The tabloids are full of stories of celebrities whose dysfunctional lives or the chaos of their families provides comic relief for others. Although it may be true that we learn from failure, ours or those of others, it's far more productive to study the lives of the successful. None of us raise our children with the goal of creating heartache, stress, or failure. We all want them to be successful and happy.

How do financially successful families perpetuate their success three or four generations past the wealth creator? How is it that some families remain productive, contributive, and connected long after the initial wealth creator has passed away, whereas others descend into intra-family litigation, financial abyss, criminal convictions, or alcohol and substance abuse? Why do some families build on the success of prior generations while others fall victim to the "shirtsleeve to shirtsleeve in three generations" cliché?

Over more than three decades, we have studied financially successful families, learning from those that have succeeded, as well as those that have failed. We call the multigenerational successful families *Legacy Families*. One outstanding characteristic of these families is that they understand that the true wealth of the family is not reflected in a numerical balance sheet. This understanding becomes particularly pertinent in a time of financial turmoil when, in fact, the actual financial balance sheet has significantly decreased. However distressing, this scenario provides greater impetus to concentrate on building human, intellectual, and social capital while increasing financial competency in order to preserve what remains of financial capital.

We hope, through the models we present and with the help of our observations and reflections, your family may become one of those *Legacy Families*.

A few overriding observations to you as you begin this quest:

- Every family, regardless of financial condition, has the ability to be a *Legacy Family*.
- Your chances of succeeding are directly proportional to your planning, preparation, and faithful execution.

- You will not be remembered for the size of your balance sheet, but for the value of your life and the legacy you leave for others.
- We have been privileged to know many great families, some of who are described in this book. If we enlighten you on your potential, your gratitude is owed to those families that have inspired us and so many others. To each of our wonderful family clients, we profoundly thank you.

INTRODUCTION

The Legacy Family

In the five generations since the death of John D. Rockefeller in 1937, the Rockefellers have produced business leaders and bankers, industrialists and oil barons, senators and governors, a vice president, educators, artists, writers, and, of course, philanthropists. It is a family known not only for its inherited wealth but also for its creation of new wealth. It's estimated that nearly 40 nonprofits, including public and private foundations, were started with the resources and leadership of the Rockefellers, from the University of Chicago to the Rockefeller University, and from the Rockefeller Foundation to the Rockefeller Family Fund. The Rockefeller philanthropy has extended from fostering health worldwide to the preservation and collection of the world's greatest art, and from preserving our historical treasures, such as Williamsburg, to our natural resources and national parks. Today, there are over 150 living blood relatives of John D. Rockefeller. If there is such a phenomenon as a Legacy Family, the Rockefellers would certainly be one.

Successful families, like everyone else, hope that each of today's members of the family and all those generations to follow will be successful, healthy, and content.

Some families have been able to perpetuate their success for many generations. Their progeny become new titans in business or assume leadership in public service, nonprofit institutions, the arts, and science. Their extended families enjoy each other. Each new generation seems to build on the shoulders of those who preceded them.

There's a name for these special families. We call them *Legacy Families*. In these families, members recognize the importance of contributions to the financial, human, intellectual, and social capital of their family and community. They are connected to their heritage, maintain positive family relations, communicate effectively, and promote generational governance structures that assure the success of those to follow.

What is it that characterizes a *Legacy Family*? Is it power? Fame? Fortune? Good works? While every family is different, we have been in a unique position to study hundreds of such families and have identified four core characteristics of a *Legacy Family*. These families demonstrate:

- *Capacity.* Members of a *Legacy Family* contribute regularly to the financial, human, intellectual, and social capital of their family and community.
- *Connection.* Members of a *Legacy Family* are connected to their ancestors and their extended families and are concerned about their descendants. They work hard to maintain positive family relations, effective communication, and effective generational governance structures.
- *Compassion.* Members of a *Legacy Family* recognize their good fortune, empower each family member to become the best he or she can be, and willingly embrace their responsibility to give back.
- *Competency.* Members of a *Legacy Family* develop the competencies to handle the responsibilities of wealth, effectively utilize the opportunities that have been provided to them, and become productive members of their communities.

These qualities do not occur by accident or mandate. They are the consequence of thought and effort by each generation, a reflection of a strategic decision by the early wealth creators that the members of this family will do more than live off the earnings or achievements of others.

These *Legacy Families* are all in the "business of the family." In other words, they apply best business practices, to the "business of the family." These include family meetings, a Family "Constitution," mission statements, assessment, checks and balances, and a host of other valuable tools that we will explore throughout this book.

Meet a *Legacy Family*

Let us tell you a story of one real *Legacy Family*. It won't be your story. It's not for replication. They didn't start out perfectly and not everyone in the family is perfect. But at an early point in the multigenerational lifespan of this *Family*, which we'll call the Anderson Family, the leadership "got it." They figured out that if they didn't get organized, all that had been built since the initial wealth creator, our "Generation One Wealth Founder," began the path to financial prosperity would be lost. It would be the traditional "shirtsleeves to shirtsleeves in three generations" and the only stories that would have been told were likely to be about the business failures, intra-family lawsuits, and personal tragedies. The names and some of the underlying facts of our *Legacy Family* have been changed for obvious reasons. But the story is one that will give you a glimpse of the threats and opportunities, risks and rewards, ahead.

The story begins with Homer Anderson. Born in 1867 in the town of Springfield, Kentucky, Homer was not the picture of a future baron. His father was an itinerant farmer; his mother a part-time seamstress. At 18, Homer left home and moved, on his own, to Oregon. He worked on a small farm in the Willamette Valley. At 20, the owner of the farm died and his widow willingly sold it to Homer for $100. In 1892, Homer met and married Louisa Parks. The Andersons had three children. Homer was a good farmer and he saw opportunity in the rich Oregon land. He began to buy other parcels and he began to envision a family that would stay together, work together, and protect each other. He loved to preach to his young children "always remember to put family first." He was a good church-going man, but his success both financially and personally was based on his focus, hard work, consistency, and his sense of family.

Homer's oldest child, Horace, took over management of the farm upon Homer's death. He quickly modernized and improved its production. Horace's sister, Grace, was uninterested in the farm, but her husband eagerly joined the business. It was his vision to expand beyond farming, so he convinced Horace to use the family resources to buy timberland and boats to help transport the timber down the river. The youngest sibling, Victoria, wanted nothing to do with business. She became a school teacher and moved to Portland. Generation Two (G2) was on its way. Business was good. It had successfully survived the succession of leadership and expanded to take advantage of related, but independent, business lines.

The real challenge came in Generation Three (G3). These were the children of Horace and his sister Grace. Victoria never married and never had children, though she was, from all the stories, the wonderful aunt who could tell stories by the hour of Grandpa Homer and Grandma Louisa. Those stories linger today, magnified no doubt with a bit of exaggerated (or even fabricated) drama and humor to keep the younger generations amused. Victoria would enjoy knowing that today's generation has as many stories of her as they have of Homer and Louisa.

Horace had three children. Joshua took over the timber production and expanded into coal and natural gas. Carl ran the farms and shipping. Francis, the daughter of Horace and his second wife, Pauline, became a physician. She was the most respected of her siblings because she had taken her education beyond anything others in their family had ever done. Her husband left his own business in retail and joined the family in the real estate division as a salesman. Grace's son, Peter, had taken some of the underperforming farms and aggressively expanded the company into commercial real estate development. Within ten years of G3's ascension to power, the family company had reorganized under four divisions—farming; shipping; natural resources, and real estate development. Business was good. The family had weathered a divorce and remarriage. But the problems were just beginning.

How was this conglomerate to be governed? How were resources to be allocated? What was the rule about family members who wanted to join the company, but had no experience or demonstrated skill? Cracks in the relationships began to appear. Family meetings became triggers for family fights. The family formed a foundation, which was intended to provide a platform to work together in a noncompetitive environment, but the rivalries and dissensions were merely carried over to the foundation governance and grant making. At one point, Grace's wing of the family, represented by Peter and his family, demanded that the company be split up and the control of each division be allocated amongst the four leaders of G3.

It was at this critical juncture that the family realized it was now or never to build a generational Strategic Plan. Much of what we will talk about in this book reflects the tools utilized by the Andersons' extended family.

Today, G4 is running the businesses and governing the foundation. The seven bloodline members of this Generation, who are the great grandchildren of the original wealth creators, Homer and Louisa, are living with and working through the Anderson Family Strategic Plan. They function under a set of rules agreed to by G3 and G4 and are governed by a Family Council, consisting of a representative from each of four branches.

Some of the G4 members are in one or more divisions of the company. Some are more engaged in the foundation. Still others are shareholders but not employees or managers of the family company. Instead, they have their own personal businesses and professions. All have some role in the foundation. Most are involved in family-generated deals and partnerships outside the business. Some family members are investors in the companies started by other family members.

Generation Five (G5) is starting their climb. The oldest is 31 and the youngest is 10. No doubt, the real test of the Strategic Plan will be whether it gives the same freedom and opportunity, voice and input, to G5 as it has for G3 and G4.

Throughout the 120 years of this family's wealth creation, family controlled businesses, and extended family philanthropy, there were all the expected challenges—divorce, life-terminating illnesses, wartime deaths, uneven scholastic performance, personal conflicts and rivalries, personal financial crises and bankruptcy scares, learning disabilities, and substance abuse. Their unity was sustained through their organizational structure that implemented the vision passed down from Generation One family first. From this simple concept they developed a plan that enabled diversity to flourish, talent to rise, voices to be heard, and conflicts to be resolved.

A 100-Year Plan

As the Anderson Family learned early, the Strategic Plan is not a short-term, quick-fix family plan, but one intended to span generations; a business plan to last a time frame of which any family could be proud. We like to think of it as a 100-year arc, long enough away to be out of reach of today's senior generation, but within sight of the youngest generation.

The Strategic Plan is based on values, not on wealth. The challenge is not easier because of the wealth. In fact, it often becomes more difficult. The wealth of the family often gives its members the financial resources to permanently distance themselves from each other. Unless connected by shared assets, such as a family business, family members that don't like each other have little reason or motivation to stay connected. Warring factions and wings of an extended family are well known and often publicized. It's unlikely that Sumner Redstone, the mogul chairman of Viacom and CBS, and owner of Paramount Pictures and DreamWorks, spends long relaxing weekends with his children these days. Their lawyers might not permit it.

A Family Constitution

For the Andersons, the solution began with regular, structured, and facilitated family meetings. The family had to learn to listen, respect boundaries by not interrupting or being insultingly dismissive, hear divergent opinions without taking it personally, and develop a model of conflict resolution which can be used to the satisfaction of all members of the ownership team.

A very common step used by many *Legacy Families* is the creation of a Family Constitution, which formally sets the rules for the family's governance, power sharing, communication, and problem solving. Just as every corporation has its set of bylaws, *Legacy Families* have their Constitutions.

A Family Constitution can set rules on how many years of work experience in nonfamily businesses is required before being allowed to work in the family business; how compensation and benefits will be determined for family members in the business; how profits will be distributed to family members in the business; how profits will be distributed to family shareholders; and how family members who choose to exit the business may do so without creating financial problems for the business.

In Chapter Two, we'll explore in greater detail how a Family Constitution is constructed and operated.

Financial and Life Skill Training

Legacy Families recognize that the best wealth transfer plan will fail if left to incompetent, indifferent, and ungrateful heirs. Clearly all adults, but especially young adults, need to acquire financial competence, which includes how to build, manage, preserve, and transfer wealth. Competent adults must also demonstrate critical life skills, including listening, leadership, team building, negotiating and conflict resolution. *Legacy Families* set out the expectations and requirements that family members must meet to work within the family businesses, receive funding for their individual enterprises, or access the vast network of relationships that open doors and leverage opportunities.

We talked about this issue with one very wealthy elderly couple, who readily acknowledged that their children, now in their mid-50s, depended even today on financial bailouts from their parents. The children compete and often fight amongst themselves. But this couple had hopes that their grandchildren, all of whom were then in their early 20s to early 30s, could learn the financial and life skills that were so useful to them as the wealth creators. This underscores an important principle. The road to a *Legacy Family* is neither straight nor smooth. There will be gaps and breakdowns within and between generations, but, with enough determination by family members and consistency through the years, these bumps in the road can be overcome.

Meeting some resistance from their parents, the grandchildren learned the critical skills required to become independent, self-sufficient, and productive, and, just as important, have learned to like each other, notwithstanding the tensions in their parents' generation.

Family Philanthropy

One of the most common public indicators of a *Legacy Family* is the expression of generosity and philanthropy. It's not just the message of the initial wealth creator. Each generation has its own philanthropic initiative, whether through new foundations or structured initiatives.

One need only look to the Rockefeller family to understand the importance of philanthropy to a *Legacy Family*. Today there are nearly 40 separate foundations, donor-advised funds, and philanthropic organizations founded by the five generations of Rockefellers, starting with John D. Rockefeller in 1890.

From this founder of the classic *Legacy Family* we move to you and your family. Where are you right now in your quest for a *Legacy Family*? Remember, this has nothing to do with your financial statements or net worth. Our definition of success does not focus on spread sheets and ledgers but on families and generations.

In other words, does your family have the tools and determination it needs to remain productive, contributive, and connected for the next 100 years?

The Four Capitals of the *Legacy Family*

We understand the challenges, responsibility and opportunities of raising strong families, dealing appropriately with financial success, passing important values down to children and grandchildren, responding to differences in talents and attitudes within and between generations and contending with social pressures and the expectations of others. However, most individuals will judge wealth by a number on the financial statement.

A *Legacy Family* realizes that if you regard wealth in terms of numbers only, you will be doomed to failure as you will not have directed sufficient energy into building the three other critical capital accounts, those of Intellectual Capital, Human Capital, and Social Capital (this is where the philanthropy piece fits in).

It is the combination of the four capital accounts—Human, Intellectual, Financial, and Social—that determines the true wealth of the family, and when we plan wealth transfer strategies, we need to keep in mind how we create structures to transfer all the capital accounts (thus again the use of a family foundation).

When we speak about Human Capital, we're talking about the following:

- Effective parenting and grand parenting
- Communication
- Consensus building
- Team building
- Conflict resolution
- Leadership training
- Values, morals, ethics
- Spirituality, and
- Goal Setting.

When we work to increase the Intellectual Capital accounts we are focused on:

- Education
- Career choices
- Coaching and mentoring
- Governance
- Rights and roles of trustees and beneficiaries.

When we work to increase the Financial Capital account, we are concerned about:

- Creating wealth
- Managing/investing wealth
- Effective transfer strategies
- Financial parenting (preparing the next generation to be responsible stewards of wealth)
- Family business issues, and
- Understanding the psychology of money.

When we seek to add to the Social Capital, we are working on

- All the philanthropic activities of the family, from check writing to family foundations and donor advised funds, and volunteer time to full-time public service.

Like any successful business, there is more than one active account; *The Legacy Family* addresses all four of these critical accounts in useful ways that are real and actionable in daily life. So what are you waiting for?

The guide to the next 100 years starts on the very next page...

★　★　★

"Every family has a story. Only a few have a legacy."

~Carrie L. Huntley

CHAPTER ONE

Roadmap to a Legacy Family

While sitting at his office desk, surrounded by pithy statements like "By failing to prepare, you are preparing to fail"—Benjamin Franklin, Jack seemed unusually perplexed. "I run a $150 million dollar a year business with 350 employees and worldwide sales. Why can't I jumpstart my own kids?" Jack's three young adult children were educated, grew up in a loving home with solid parents, seemed to like each other, and had all the opportunities that money could buy. But none of the children were working at a steady job. Only one of the three children, now 32, had moved out of the home. One child, then 27, was doing part-time work at Jack's company, but only because he was told to work or get out of the house. The youngest child, who had just turned 25, was in the fifth year of college, which had been interrupted by 18 months of living abroad during a period of "soul searching" and "personal discovery."

Jack was one of the entrepreneurs in business who read Peter Drucker's books every night before going to sleep. He prided himself on being a strategic planner. Everyone in his business, even at the lowest ranks, participated in building the great plan for the company. And it worked. The business was very profitable and Jack had turned down a cash offer of several hundred million dollars. But, when it came to his family, it never occurred to him that you needed to plan for anything more than your vacation or your kid's college choice.

Like Jack, if you were going to build a great and enduring business, you'd start with a plan that would define your company's mission, a statement of its core values, a focus on what you would like to accomplish, and a strategy to accomplish your goals.

You'd strive to understand the economic implications, and you'd assess the skills and talents you and others have now and will need in the future to be successful. You'd create a process to communicate with your team, benchmarks to measure your progress, and a system to review, evaluate, and adjust the plan as needed.

Planning for a family is a bit different. You can't fire your kids and replace them with others you like better. You can't order them to have talent or intelligence. You might influence their choices in life, but the more you tend to dictate their choices, the less likely you'll succeed and the more likely you'll have active and passive rebellion.

But *Legacy Families* do plan. They visualize the type of relationship they want with each other. They think about the core values that are most important and that define their individual and collective character. You may be quite surprised to realize the detail of the planning that such families conduct. These families decided that its members will do more than live off either the economics or achievements of others. Their plan is not short term, but is intended to span the generations. The most effective plans we have seen span a 100-year arc, long enough away to be out of reach of today's senior generation but within sight of the youngest generation. The secret is how the plan is formulated. It engages the family. The *Legacy Family* understands the adage *if you build it, you'll own it*. It focuses on process and doesn't try to anticipate changes in lifestyle, business, and personalities. It adjusts structure over time but its principles remain timeless.

This may be a great challenge for some wealth creators. The stereotype personality of a wealth creator is a Type A powerful personality, not always right but never in doubt—on a good day, a benevolent dictator. Consensus to this personality is everyone agreeing with his or her predetermined idea. Asking the powerful wealth creator to agree to engage others to help formulate The Plan may be more difficult than teaching him/her ballet at the age of 65. But it is exactly this type of personality that needs more than most to engage his or her spouse, children, and grandchildren if the success of the family is ever going to be replicated. The Plan is not something that can be imposed from above. It will need the consensus of successive generations and thus their input is vital.

Ask the Right Questions

No plan can be developed unless you ask the right questions. If you approach this step properly, you will find yourself asking very tough questions, and ones that will take much thought and discussion. You might as well start with the most difficult.

> *"How would I describe the legacy I seek? What would success look like in my eyes and the eyes of my family members 100 years from now?"*

This is the start of the vision for your family. It may sound lofty and unattainable, but it's the flag at the peak of the mountain. Others have attained those heights. Why not you?

The Lawrence family defined their vision in the following way:

Our family is connected through its heritage and shared values. We make it a priority to take time to
- Love, care, and respect each other;
- Communicate openly and honestly with an expectation for personal accountability;
- Encourage the pursuit of excellence and the achievement of personal goals; and
- Generously share our time and resources to positively impact the lives of others.

It's not easy to arrive at these shared values. We've seen the dialogue, sometimes heated, sometimes laughingly, take hours, change over the days, and evolve through the years. Each word carries symbolic meaning and brings with it both positive experiences and failed hopes. Sometimes the vision reflects what might have been, not what was. But, to paraphrase Walt Disney, if you can dream it, you can do it.

Each word is loaded. What is the behavior that would tell us we are a loving family? Maybe it's as simple as remembering each other on important personal occasions—birthdays and anniversaries and the like. Or maybe it's being with each other in times of disappointment, failure, and personal tragedy.

What does it mean to "respect each other"? What if my lifestyle is different from yours? My choice of a spouse doesn't meet with your expectations? I use my talents to teach rather than to make a large fortune?

Communication is one of the most common issues described in a family vision statement. We'll address this again in much greater depth later, but what do you mean by "communicate openly?" Speak your mind, even if it hurts others? Use language that offends others? Say only that which is safe, rather than that which is honest?

You will find that articulating the vision and defining what you mean is among the most challenging tasks you will ever experience in your quest to build your *Legacy Family*.

Here are some other questions you may want to ask.

Who is my "family" today, tomorrow, and over time?

This may sound like a simple question, but it's actually very complicated. Does "family" mean a blood descendant only? What about adopted children? And if you included adopted children, should there be any age limit or requirement that the adopted child has lived in the family member's home for some period of time?

Will a spouse be considered "family?" What would the consequences be if a spouse is excluded from participating in family activities? Remember, the spouse of your child could well be the parent of your grandchild and certainly one of the most important individuals in the life of your child. What about a same-sex marriage or civil union partnership? Will children born through in vitro fertilization or surrogate parents be considered your issue?

If you don't address this question of who is my family today, tomorrow, and over time?, then the very notion of planning for the future of your family will become difficult, if not impossible, to implement.

> *What business, social, cultural, civic, or philanthropic impact*
> *might our family have achieved over those ten decades?*

In business, we define our success by quantitative benchmarks—stock price, earnings before taxes, sales, profit margins—and by other measurable milestones—breakthrough technology, website hits, and extent of global outlets. In *Legacy Families*, success is often measured by qualitative achievements—love and respect by family, peers, and the community; achievement in the arts, philanthropic initiatives, and so on.

The process of asking what success looks like will often start with specific achievements—ownership of a company in the Forbes 500; election to a high political office; the winning of the Nobel Prize. But it will eventually have to evolve into more thematic concepts, because it would be fruitless to try to define specific achievements that grandchildren and great-grandchildren will accomplish. After all, even our prototype wealth creator will have a hard time anticipating, much less dictating, what those future generations will be doing and how their success will be defined.

The Edwards family framed their response to these questions by including, in their vision statement:

> Demonstrating a strong work ethic and a desire to live life to its fullest, the members of our family achieve notable personal and financial success through educated decisions and smart choices. Understanding that money alone does not buy happiness, our family places a priority on our faith, family, friends and a desire to share our good fortune with those who have not been as blessed.

> *What are the resources—financial, human, intellectual, and*
> *social—our family will need to achieve these lofty goals?*

This may be the easiest question of all the tough ones we can frame. If you know what success looks like, you can more easily determine the financial resources, as well as the tools, skills, knowledge, and talents that would be necessary or even just helpful. Surprisingly, the economics are often the least challenging. For many affluent families, there is often a surplus of financial wealth available to meet or exceed the needs of future generations. Remember for *Legacy Families*, financial success, whether in business or through investments, achieved over the generations is likely to be self-generated, not inherited. The resources provided by earlier generations start with solid parenting, good education, exposure to opportunities that are pursued to advantage, an embedded work ethic, strong values, and *just enough* capital to enable the aspiring wealth creator to take advantage of the opportunities.

This question was resolved by the Carmack family, which derived its wealth from three generations of oil and gas, ranching, and real estate development. The Carmacks established a family council that oversaw the entire extended family of 32 individuals, 20 of whom were adults, plus another 15 spouses (and even an ex-spouse favored and loved by all, it seemed, except her former husband!). The family council is one of the governance structures we'll discuss later in the book, but in the Carmack family, each 25-year-old member or older was eligible to present a life plan, consisting of personal and family goals for the next ten years. This plan, like any good business plan, had one or more defined goals, a game plan toward achieving those goals, and a description of the resources necessary to enable the applicant to best meet or exceed the self-described goals. It would be wrong to assume that this is all about financial support. It was important, to be sure, and actually the easiest to explain. But, if the goals required learning a profession or skill, mentoring or networking, internships or partnerships, the family council had the authority and the resources to make it happen. This is how families support the dreams and aspirations of their members. They empower; they don't guarantee.

In the Appendix, we'll provide you a checklist of other questions you may want to ask during this most important first step in your journey to a *Legacy Family*.

Engage the Family

It may now seem obvious that the inquiry stage is all about engagement of the family. Engagement is more than sitting everyone down to hear your decisions. It means listening. Really listening. Sometimes it means hearing about differences in personal goals and dreams, values, expectations, irritations, and disappointments.

Not surprisingly, it's often very difficult to engage the family in constructive dialogue. This may be because open and honest discussion was never practiced in the family before, or because the matriarch or patriarch is too focused and determined to hear other's views, perceptions, hopes, and fears. Sometimes siblings are harder on each other than parents. But it is fair to say that without broad engagement and dialogue about the vision of the family, it will be much harder to build consensus and broad participation.

We'll spend more time on this later in the book, but suffice it to say that this step is the most important step of all.

Build the Plan

The vision of the *Legacy Family* is incorporated within a long-range strategic plan that asks the question "how can we attain this vision today, tomorrow, and through the generations?" It's not enough to wish for success. It requires a thoughtful plan of action.

The Strategic Plan of the *Legacy Family* is based on values, not on wealth, power, or tax. It engages rather than imposes. It focuses on process and is designed to take full advantage of the *Legacy Family's* human, intellectual, financial, and social capital, to empower and challenge each generation, and to set milestones and benchmarks for the future. This plan must be relevant, realistic, flexible, and measurable.

It must have the capacity to change with the times and with the generations. It should, however, be capable of adhering to its core principles and goals, which is to perpetuate a caring, connected, and competent family through the generations. Each Plan will be customized, but most will have several common features:

- *Family vision.* This is where the vision of the family is expressed. It drives everything else.
- *Statement of mission.* The mission statement focuses the family on what it must do to realize its vision. Like every successful business, the *Legacy Family* knows where it wants to go and what success will look like long into the future. Success to a family, of course, will look quite different than success to a business enterprise. It will be measured by other factors besides net earnings or market share, and it will focus on the success of the combined family group as well as each member of the family. They say that a chain is only as strong as its weakest link. We know that parents are only as happy as their least happy child. *Legacy Families* are fulfilled only as much as their least contented member.
- *Statement of values.* The Strategic Plan contains a clear expression of the *Family's* core values. These values bind the *Family* to each other, and often include respect, trust, integrity, dignity, compassion, curiosity, ethics, and morality, to mention but a few. They may not all think alike, vote alike, or prefer the same music, art, or poetry but these core values are passed down from parent to child to grandchild. They are more than statements posted on the refrigerator. They guide the *Family* in its individual and collective attitudes and behavior.
- *Definition of family.* For all the reasons mentioned earlier, identifying who is considered a family member is essential.
- *Allocation of capital.* The Strategic Plan establishes priorities in the effective utilization of the individual and combined resources of its members. Financial capital is intended to empower and create opportunity for future generations. The structure is designed to discourage indolence and dependence, and to reward hard work, initiative, and self reliance. The *Legacy Family's* intellectual capital is marshaled to

encourage the pursuit of knowledge, through formal education, personal mentoring, and training of the younger generations. The human capital is directed to effective parenting, open communication, and resolving the *Family's* inevitable challenges within and among the generations. The social capital is set aside to support and promote the collective and individual philanthropy of the *Family*, and to perpetuate many of its most precious values, including compassion, generosity, and gratitude. This may be manifested by a single family foundation or multiple foundations, as well as donor advised funds, direct family philanthropy programs, and public service.

- *Governance and leadership.* As in any effective plan, the *Legacy Family's* Strategic Plan defines its governance system, leadership criteria and opportunity, and succession. It grants authority with appropriate responsibility, and assures accountability and communication. It sets reasonable expectations for those charged with the task of guiding the extended Family as well as for those who may benefit from the combined resources of the Family. There are a variety of favored structures for this purpose, which might include a family council, advisory board, board of directors, a family office, or family executive committee. But the choice of structure is not nearly as important as identifying a process for resolving the challenges of the Family through the years and giving all family members a vehicle for expression.

Implement the Plan

Once you have produced a comprehensive written plan that incorporates the decisions reached, it will become the blueprint for you and the family, as well as for your team of professional advisors, including a family office, accountants, and investment managers. The plan documents the mission, vision, and goals of the family, as well as its structure and process. You will need to create a monitoring process, to be sure that the implementation is consistent with the plan.

Every parent dreams of a successful lineage of well-adjusted, caring, and competent descendants. The challenges are great, but the rewards for executing a thoughtful strategic plan are clearly worth the effort.

Financially successful families, like all concerned families, hope that each of today's members of the family and all those generations to follow will be successful, healthy, and content. Wealth should help to make this possible. After all, the members of a wealthy family have all the advantages money can buy—the best education, the best health care, and the best connections.

Unfortunately, yesterday's wealth is no guarantee of tomorrow's success. The adage "shirtsleeves to shirtsleeves in three generations" is not without its basis in fact. Yet, contrary to common belief and experience, some families have been able to perpetuate their success for many generations.

Their progeny have become new titans in business or assumed leadership in public service, nonprofit institutions, the arts, and science. Their extended families enjoy each other. Each new generation seems to build on the shoulders of those who preceded them. There's a name for these special families. These are *Legacy Families*.

★　★　★

"Would you tell me, please, which way I ought to go from here?"
"That depends a good deal on where you want to get to," said the Cat.
"I don't much care where-" said Alice.
"Then it doesn't matter which way you go," said the Cat.
              ~Lewis Carroll, *Alice's Adventures in Wonderland*

CHAPTER TWO

Family Constitution

If the Strategic Plan is the virtual roadmap for the family, then the Family Constitution creates the guard rails alongside the road that keeps you from veering off track or crashing into a tree as your family, and legacy, evolves. Every country has its constitution; every corporation has its bylaws. Most families just have mom and dad. They make the rules as they go, change those rules to fit the circumstances, and rarely feel bound by them.

A Strategic Plan is only a plan, after all; action is the glue that binds planning and purpose together to create measurable results. Your Strategic Plan must be implemented through a series of practical and often measurable steps. One such step is the creation of a "Family Constitution," which formally sets the rules under which the family's governance, power sharing, communication, and problem-solving systems are established.

If the Strategic Plan is the broad expression of intent, the Family Constitution is the tactical expression of the agreed rules. Some Strategic Plans incorporate the provisions that would otherwise be contained in the Family Constitution, while others merely define how the Constitution will be developed, followed, reviewed, and modified. Much like a corporation has its set of bylaws under which it conducts its business, so too do *Legacy Families* have a set of rules—both formal and informal—by which its members agree to function together.

When it comes to drafting a Family Constitution, timing is important. When the family is still relatively small, that is Mom, Dad and their immediate children, it is easier to operate without the formality of a documented plan. However, as the family grows, the founding parents are no longer living and later generations pick up the reins with new spouses added to the mix, things become more complicated and the necessity for a more formal governing structure becomes more urgent; priorities shift, younger generations are less connected to the values, discipline, and heritage of their hard-working elders and it becomes easy to lose the focus and connectedness that *Legacy Families* demonstrate. Every time we read about another young heir arrested for substance abuse or involved in another tabloid scandal, every time we read about family members suing each other or once-great businesses torn apart by petty family infighting, we realize how challenging it is for families to remain connected, positively productive, and contributive over multiple generations.

As we have observed in so many families we see, it is likely that these families did not understand the necessity of taking the time and energy to document guidelines for the continuation of the "business" of the family—or even know how to begin this important task. The creation of a Family Constitution becomes an important priority as the family business grows along with the expanding family. In fact, the more complicated the family becomes, the greater the need for the articulated principles, guidelines, and rules, which are contained in a Family Constitution.

This is the time that the family needs a set of rules that they have helped to shape and that they have accepted. To avoid seeing the values of the original family enterprise dissipated, such a Constitution creates guidelines that later generations can use to keep the legacy alive.

What is found in a Family Constitution? Here's a typical outline of the key topics and issues.

What do we mean?

Words have meaning, but what, how much, and to whom? Misunderstandings occur when we use words that mean one thing to some people and another thing to others. This becomes an even more significant issue as one generation speaks to—or *tries* to speak to—another generation. How many times have you puzzled over the words, phrases, or slang of your children or grandchildren that either meant absolutely nothing to you or something so different that you thought they were speaking in code? This is hardly the basis for cooperative communication and, as you can see, the disconnect between words and their meaning creates a scenario that is ripe for miscommunication and, even worse, misunderstanding. A Constitution can create a "dictionary" of sorts where words have definite meaning to avoid confusion.

For example, just who is a member of the "family" as defined in your Family Constitution? Does it include the spouses of your descendants? These are your in-laws, and generally the parent of your grandchildren or great-grandchildren. How about ex-spouses who still remain in the parental role of your descendants? Will you include civil union partners of your descendants or same-sex, legally married spouses of your descendants? How about common law spouses or just the long-term life-partner? Are adopted children part of the family? While you might agree quickly on this one, consider the real case of a 27-year-old grandson who adopted his 28-year-old girlfriend, in order to put her in the lineage for inheritance? Bizarre or just imaginative? Such real-life anecdotal evidence supports the need for defining words such as "family"—very specifically in your Constitution.

How will we govern ourselves?

How will your family be governed today, while you're here, tomorrow when you're gone, and 25 years from now, when your children may be ready to transition leadership to the next generation? Leadership is critical in every business and the quality and style of that leadership can either enhance the goals of the *Legacy Family* or make achieving those goals difficult.

There are many forms of family leadership. During the lifetime of the wealth creator, it's not unusual to experience the benevolent dictator or the compassionate oligarch. Children often remain deferential to the wishes of the parent, so the decision-making process in this family structure is simplified. The family discusses; the parent decides.

The leadership styles of a single powerful parent do not smoothly transfer to the next generation. Siblings may respect each other, but won't accept the unilateral decision making of any one sibling, as the interest of the family and its legacy may take a backseat to self-interest. Children may be willing to follow even autocratic dictates of parents, but they won't accept the same authority from a brother or sister. However, in many families, the primary model the children have experienced is that of a strong parent making all major decisions. Therefore, when this parent is no longer in a position to do so, the result may be anarchy amongst the children, as one sibling tries to impose this same type of authority over the other siblings A new leadership model needs to be developed and the ability to build consensus becomes the critical leadership skill.

Effective family leadership and an organized decision-making process can have significant impact on a variety of issues. Various talented family members may assume different leadership responsibilities like organizing the collective family meetings, overseeing the management of its shared assets, assisting each family member with fulfilling his or her own personal dreams and aspirations, as well as achieving the extended family's mission and vision.

These issues can raise thorny problems. How will assets owned by the children be managed? How will the profits of the shared assets be distributed and to whom? Who decides on how the family-owned cabin will be used? Who decides on whether to sell the apartment building, convert it to a condominium, borrow on the equity, or let all the adult, unemployed family members live rent-free in the available units? Such questions and concerns can quickly spiral out of control. Without a structure and process, the varying agendas and concerns of the family members will likely create conflict, inefficiency, and frustration. We'll explore some of the most effective leadership structures in Chapter Five.

How will we manage our shared assets?

In most affluent families, it is almost inevitable that some assets will be gifted to family members during the lifetime or at the death of the wealth creator. The asset in question might be the family business, investment real estate, the family farm, or even an airplane, vacation property, or other personal-use assets. We'll explore the specifics in Chapter Eight, but the decisions about how such Family Shared Assets will be managed and maintained for the benefit of the family need to be discussed and considered, and documented, preferably in writing in the Family Constitution. Additionally, you might want to have a separate shared asset agreement amongst the family members. Joint ownership is challenging and, without clarity, can create the type of disagreements that can tear the family apart.

How will we communicate with each other?

Families that are successful in staying together through the generations have mastered the challenge of effective communication. The best-laid plans for the future will fail if the family can't talk to each other in a respectful, constructive, and honest way.

How will the managers of the shared family assets inform and educate their owners, so that everyone can understand and appreciate the gravity of the situation? Not everyone learns the same way. Some prefer numbers and graphs, ratios and returns. Those classic "left-brainers" expect and appreciate the constant flow of numbers. Then there are those who think in concepts, pictures, and colors. Numbers put this group in a daze. You can present reams of financial statements, cash-flow projections, and budgets, but you won't successfully communicate in a way that these family members can appreciate. The Family Constitution should set the basic rule that "each member of our family will be entitled to receive the relevant information that affects the assets we share together *in a format that is understandable to that member.*" This will require taking some time to determine how to assure that communication is meaningful and useful. When family members feel uninformed, they have a tendency to become frustrated, suspicious, and maybe even hostile.

Because it is important to have a regular format for communication in place, *Legacy Families* schedule organized family meetings and family retreats. Not everyone will likely attend every meeting, but just making it open and informative, as well as fun and engaging, will help keep the lines of communication open and reduce the chance of bottled up frustration or anger that might result in the absence of such regularly planned family gatherings. There are many ways to facilitate a family meeting or retreat, and these will be explored in greater depth in the next chapter.

The Family Constitution establishes the requirements for these meetings and may even set the parameters and guidelines for how, and how often, they are conducted. But, in this area, as in so many others, the implementation of these guidelines is best left to the imagination and input of the family members. It's another example of how important good leadership within the extended family will be to the long-term emotional and financial health and well-being of the family, and all the more reason why assisting that leadership with a formal Constitution is so vital to the family's continuing success.

Communicating within the family raises the question about how personal and confidential information shared and disclosed through these meetings and documents will be protected from outsiders. What is the family's expectation of privacy? What would the consequences be if confidential financial or business information were disclosed to competitors, family friends, or even the press? Dealing with sensitive family information is no less important than it would be if you were on a business or not-for-profit board of directors. In a sense, you hold a fiduciary responsibility to honor the rule of privacy and confidentiality that the family imposes on itself.

What behavior do we expect from each other?

It's not unusual to find a code of conduct within successful businesses. In some cases, it's mandatory. Ask any human resources officer how many rules of conduct exist in the business—rules that prohibit sexual harassment, age or gender discrimination, or access for employees to complain or make suggestions—and you're more likely to hear an answer in the double-rather than single-digits. Our schools have rules of conduct for students and faculty. Many not-for-profit organizations, from the Boy Scouts or Girl Scouts to the board rooms of the university or hospital, have their own rules of conduct. Less common, unfortunately, are written rules of conduct for family members.

During the parenting years, mom and dad set the conduct rules. They may or may not be accepted by the children but, regardless, the rules have specific consequences if broken. As children grow up and move away, the rules often disappear. So, how are family members and new spouses expected to conduct themselves with each other if there is not clarity regarding behavioral expectations As siblings grow up, they acquire behavioral "tics" or styles that each has learned to expect or tolerate from the others. Sarcasm, loud voices, slang language, teasing, silent treatment, or even mild physical abuse may be tolerated amongst the siblings, but may not be received well by other members of the extended family, including in-laws, nieces, and nephews.

Therefore, it is important for the members of your extended family to articulate what is acceptable behavior and what is not. Furthermore, knowing the rules isn't quite enough; there must be repercussions and ramifications as well. Specifically, what are the consequences of unacceptable behavior? Again, timing grows more critical as the family grows and divides. Unless the members of the family arrive at a consensus at early stages of the family's evolution, this challenge will be harder to deal with through the years.

How will we resolve conflicts amongst us?

Regardless of the closeness of any family, conflict will inevitably arise over the years and through the generations. Conflict is not the problem. In fact, conflict ensures that different views are aired and considered. When family members feel free to raise their voices and air concerns, priorities are challenged and leaders are forced to explain and defend potential decisions—often to the betterment of the entire family. This tends to improve the final action and it certainly respects the voice and concerns of the stakeholders.

However, unresolved conflict is a problem. It festers within those who feel ignored or dismissed. It can erode the confidence that family members have in their leaders and each other, and it can magnify into open warfare if allowed to continue. In one of the oldest and most respected families in Southern California, a five-generation business was forced into a sale because of the hard feelings created through litigation amongst members of the second generation. Though those early members were long gone, some of their descendants continued to stoke the hurt feelings, distrust, and resentment left behind after they passed, proving that there is no statute of limitations or expiration date on unresolved conflict.

Techniques for effective conflict resolution will be expanded in Chapter Twelve, but what is fundamental to the generational success of every *Legacy Family* is that there is a functioning, proactive, and adaptable process for dealing with conflicts that can't be resolved by the parties themselves. That process should be fully explored and mapped out in the Constitution.

How do we keep the Family Constitution
fresh, relevant, and practical?

If this document is to help implement the 100-year Strategic Plan and form the framework for how the family will function over time, then it must have a process in place designed specifically to help it remain current. As problematic as it is not to have any goals or direction, it's even worse to have gone through the considerable effort to articulate a vision and create a plan but then fail to follow the plan because it has already grown stale, unrealistic, or dated. It must adapt over time as the family decides, and it must benchmark its progress in order to evaluate its performance. A Family Constitution may be a critical component of the success of the Strategic Plan, but it must adjust with the realities of the family dynamics, the changes in economic conditions, and the unanticipated changes in the lives of the family members if it is to stay relevant. Families should not rush to change a structure that was created through extensive family discussions and sensitive compromises. But it must be possible when the need for change arises.

The Family Constitution must be flexible and responsive to the needs of the extended family, but it should, to the extent that it is possible and practical, remain consistent with the family's stated vision, mission, and values, as those are specifically expressed in the document. It should be reviewed periodically, especially as each generation transitions leadership, and updated as the need arises. There should be realistic metrics with which to monitor and measure the success of the extended family's expressed goals, be they financial, professional, or simply personal. These benchmarks and milestones should always be a stretch, to encourage the family to grow and improve, but not so ambitious that the very effort would appear fruitless and unattainable.

How is this goal achieved? Some families establish a Governance Committee to focus solely on the Constitution and the Strategic Plan. Other families actually invite outside experts to visit the family and to offer their assessment and recommendations. Whatever process is selected, it needs to be used to assist the family to objectively focus on itself.

Once a change seems appropriate, this should become a priority agenda item of an extended family meeting. To change critical items of the Constitution, such as the family vision and mission, may require not only a majority agreement on the part of the adult family members, but perhaps even a "super-majority" of those members. It's not irrelevant that both state and federal constitutions require more than just a simple majority to change the fundamentals of these entities. Unanimity may seem a good threshold, but it could give the minority too much power. Conversely, a decision of the majority is usually appropriate, but it should not disregard the most important interests and concerns of the minority. Like any good democracy, all family members are equal and should be made to feel as such.

We've given you a sample Family Constitution as a guideline. However, your family is not the Model Family portrayed in this document. Each family has its own special and unique considerations and this needs to be reflected in any document you create. To build a structure that doesn't fit your family circumstances today or over time will not serve you very well!

★ ★ ★

"The strength of the Constitution lies in the will of the people to defend it."
~Thomas Edison

CHAPTER THREE

Family Communications

A well-groomed woman entered the offices of a divorce attorney and assertively announced that she was there to begin divorce proceedings immediately. In an attempt to begin to understand the facts of this particular situation, the attorney reached for his yellow legal pad and began a series of questions. "Madam, do you have any grounds?" he initially inquired. "Of course" was her immediate retort. "We live on a two-acre estate in the Bel Air hills." Somewhat taken aback, he tried another approach. "Madam, do you have a grudge?" Again she snapped back a response. "With that acreage, of course we have a garage. In fact, we can park four cars in it." Undaunted, the attorney tried again. "Madam, does your husband beat you up?" At this point the client replied with great annoyance "I will have you know that I have been up before him every single day of our 20-year marriage." At this point the frustrated attorney queried, "Madam, I am afraid I don't understand why you are here. What seems to be the problem?" to which she replied, "My husband says that we just don't communicate."

The art of effective communication is at the core of all successful interpersonal relationships, and it is the ability to communicate across multiple generations that is one of the outstanding hallmarks of *Legacy Families.* Unfortunately, communication is a skill we learn too early and only realize we haven't mastered until it's too late.

We grow up in families where we learn to talk, so we make the false assumption that we can successfully communicate. But merely talking is not the same as the type of skillful communication that builds personal connections, particularly between family members. Regardless of how soon you learn your ABCs, communication is not a skill with which you are naturally born and the degree of this type of communication success is the result of genetic factors, life experiences in your family of origin, and skill training.

The dictionary defines communication as the "act of giving and receiving information." It's such a simple explanation for a complex act serving as the basis for the success of our interpersonal relationships. Enter any bookstore and you will find numerous titles addressing various aspects of the art of successful communication. So, with all this intrinsic and extrinsic information on how to communicate successfully, why is it we so often fail in this task? If your family is going to succeed through the generations, it has to learn how to communicate effectively. What do we need to know to improve this critical life skill?

We often communicate without saying a word

Communication is not only the result of what we say. Sometimes it's what we don't say that actually speaks the loudest. Sometimes it's just our look. Nonverbal communication can be just as powerful as our words. Do you remember the first time your spouse gave you "that look?" No words needed to pass to convey his or her meaning. How about the time you gave your kids one of your "looks?" Weren't you trying to communicate a clear message to them? No doubt, they read it loud and clear.

When a speaker is standing in front of an audience, he or she may be in charge of the microphone but every member of that audience is giving continual feedback. If they are in agreement with what is being said, the speaker will notice nonverbal signals such as smiles or slight positive nodding of the head, which indicate approval. However, if the speaker should say something controversial with which the audience is in disagreement, smiles suddenly change to frowns, the forehead becomes furrowed and arms may suddenly become folded across the chest in glaring disapproval. Not a word was said, and yet volumes were expressed.

Suppose you have just had a heated argument with a brother-in-law or a sister-in-law and, upon entering a social gathering, you see this individual across the room. At the moment your eye makes contact, this individual suddenly turns his or her back to you and quickly walks away. Not a word has been spoken, but the nonverbal communication is powerful. Clearly there is a problem. But how do you handle it? If this behavior is ignored you cannot assume that the negativity being silently expressed will just go away. This situation calls for a follow-up meeting with the angered individual with the following type of dialogue.

"John, I am aware that there is some unresolved feeling following our recent argument. Can we get together and see if there are some points about which we can agree and if not just respectively agree to disagree? Our personal relationship is too important to me to let this argument cause hard feelings." If this individual was not a family member and someone with whom you could easily avoid additional contact, it would not be so important to get some resolution. But when it is a member of the family, unresolved conflict is like a psychological cancer cell. It will spread, involve other members of the family, disrupt family activities, and create the type of negative headsets that will be discussed later in this chapter.

Remember hearing it said, "Don't say one thing and do another?" It is important that our verbal and nonverbal language is in sync. If this is not the case, pay attention to the nonverbal cues you are giving out when you speak. This can be challenging, as oftentimes nonverbal communication is done almost unconsciously. The grating of our teeth when a "certain someone" walks in the room or the eye-roll we give during a family meeting when sister's talkative husband begins pontificating sends very definite messages. Words do not always convey genuine emotions, as people can develop the skill of masking true feelings with socially acceptable language. But it is hard to fake body language and it is exactly this nonverbal language to which others will respond.

When listening to the conversation of others, our
understanding and subsequent responses are influenced
by the "headset" through which the communication passes

What is a "headset?" It is a type of psychological filter that affects how we interpret verbal and nonverbal communication. This headset, in turn, influences our response to the stimulus we are receiving. We don't even realize how our perceptions of people or events are affected by these hidden filters.

For example, let's assume that Fran Smith is the speaker at a luncheon to which you have been invited. When Fran arrives, she energetically enters the room with a wide smile and states, "I am so happy to be here today with you. I have heard so much about your interest in my research and it is always exciting to be able to share my passion with an interested audience. I was a little nervous that I might be late as the traffic on our freeways is becoming so unpredictable and I never can judge exactly how long it might take me to get where I am going." Would you have found anything offensive about her introduction or opening remarks? Probably not. You might even feel a positive connection with her, because you probably have also experienced the challenges of fighting freeway traffic and the particular anxiety that comes from being late through no fault of your own.

Now assume that, prior to Fran arriving, the host of the luncheon announces to the audience, "We are very fortunate to have our esteemed presenter with us today, but I have heard that she can be very critical. So, I hope that everyone will pay close attention. Please no distraction on your Blackberry because we want to leave a good impression." Fran then arrives and, with the same display of enthusiasm as in our first scenario, delivers the same introduction and comment about freeway traffic. Now, instead of feeling sympathetic or at least neutral to the comment about freeway traffic, you and others may now be saying, "Wow, she's been here for less than a minute and she's already complaining!" What you heard was affected by the filter in your headset and although the basic message—the actual words spoken—did not change, thanks to this filter, your interpretation of the words certainly has.

"Stop being so bossy and controlling all the time," Jane explodes at a bewildered Philip.

"I was just trying to be helpful and supportive," is his surprised response.

If, in this scenario, Jane was raised in a household with a domineering father figure, even though Philip may be nothing like her father. she may have a headset that tells her that men will *always* try to dominate and control her and therefore *anything* that Philip might do or say could be misinterpreted through that headset filter that Jane developed growing up in her family.

This filter has very real and, if not addressed, permanent ramifications for Jane and Phillip's relationship. Words will cease to have accurate meaning because Jane's headset is always on and communication will eventually break down completely.

During a lunch break at a recent family meeting one of the attendees was worried as she felt the patriarch was "angry" with the comments she had made during the meeting. We had been carefully observing this individual throughout the meeting, as he had been somewhat hesitant to participate in the process. We were pleased to see how positively engaged he was and, in fact, as he was leaving the room, he had commented on how well he felt the morning had gone. When we shared our objective observations of her father with her, she seemed pleased and relieved. She suddenly realized that she was experiencing a faulty headset by interpreting his quiet demeanor as disapproving, as that is what she had experienced growing up. By changing how she labeled his behavior she could feel far more comfortable in his presence.

Have you ever been in a social situation where someone does or says something to you and a friend? You became incensed with the remark while your friend seemed very indifferent to it. "How can you tolerate that type of comment?" you angrily question. Your friend regards you in a quizzical manner. "What's the big deal?" she asks. Obviously, you both heard the same comment but because her headset was different from yours, she responded favorably—or at least innocuously—while you overreacted. You both heard the same thing and reacted completely differently. Here again we see the power of a headset at work.

In any family, each family member will be influenced by their individual headsets. Filters are affected by our personalities (some of us are the "glass is half-full" type, and others are the "glass half-empty" type). They are also affected by our circumstances and experiences. Consider how different the headset forming experiences will be for siblings growing up in the same household but with a 15-year span between the oldest and youngest child. This may result in responses so different to similar situations that it is hard to believe that these individual came from the same household.

Growing up in a family, each sibling has a defined role and will develop headsets resulting from both the treatment received from his or her other siblings, as well as remembering all the foibles the individuals experienced in growing up. The irresponsible, heavy partying older brother will always be pegged with that image in spite of adulthood and maturity. These headsets are carried into adulthood and determine how much consideration will be given to his comments or leadership attempts. Sisters who have fought competitively while growing up will continue this disruptive family behavior unless they learn a new manner of listening and dealing with each other in a calmer, more positive manner. Often this learning process needs to be facilitated by a supportive spouse, a family council, or trusted family advisor who can help the warring sisters interpret behavior that habitually causes inappropriate emotional responses between them in a more detached, objective manner.

So, when you puzzle at the reaction that your spouse, children, siblings, or in-laws have to your actions or comments, it's probably because of their different filters. Understanding this phenomenon will make your efforts at clear communication less frustrating and more effective. When the words being spoken are consistently being misinterpreted, it is time to explore what headset might be interfering with the objective flow of information.

How we communicate with others is shaped
by how we process information

When we are communicating with an individual from a foreign country, we are sensitive to the fact that understanding might be compromised, because English is not his or her primary language. As a result, we will take the time to speak more slowly and repeat important information. What we may not realize, however, is that many people who speak the same language may also need us to talk more slowly and repeat more often. In other words, each of us process information differently, regardless of whether or not we are both speaking the same language.

When we are communicating, it is important to understand two important parts of the language processing cycle. The first is the ability to hear what is being said. It's called the "receptive" area of language. Individuals who have difficulties at this level may be either deaf or have some type of hearing loss. This is more easily recognizable since the listener clearly demonstrates the difficulty in understanding by requesting repetitions or utilizing the assistance of listening devices such as hearing aids.

The second part deals with how language is transmitted to the brain. This neurological function is where understanding occurs and is called the *associative* area of learning. The ability to process at this level is not at all related to intelligence, but is instead related to the neurological organization of each individual. Some people can immediately understand what is being said. Say it once and they get it. Teachers love these learners, because they seem to be paying attention. Many others need to hear it again, maybe three or four times, before actual understanding occurs! The advertising world is well aware of this phenomenon. That is why those annoying ads repeat the name of the product five, six, or seven times.

Additionally, family members who have been diagnosed with attention deficit disorder (ADD) will absolutely require multiple repetitions in order for all the information to be organized in the brain. They suffer from a neurological condition that causes them to be easily distracted. When attempting to listen, they may only hear bits and pieces of the conversation at any one time because their ability to sustain concentration the first time information is presented is compromised. When it is important to obtain a thoughtful response from these family members, the presentation must be concise, repeated multiple times, and ideally backed up with visuals.

Weakness at this level of processing is not as recognizable as it is at the receptive level. Even the individuals who are experiencing this type of challenge in processing might not understand what is happening. They know that they have always experienced frustration with instructions and directions given verbally and school has been a challenge. They lack the confidence to ask for multiple repetitions for fear that they may look stupid because that is how they have felt throughout their school experiences as they were not given another explanation for their difficulty. And if they are in-laws, they are entering the family as adults, having now mastered the art of "cover up" so that their new family would not be aware of their limitations. Therefore they are often a source of frustration and irritation when they are given responsibilities and do not carry out the task as expected. In most cases this is not a lack of intellectual ability. It is an issue of recognizing this often unidentified language processing disability and taking the time and effort to make sure that what is being asked of that family member is thoroughly understood. Since this is an auditory processing disability, following up verbal information with a written summary is very helpful. Although written memos are more often associated with the business community, using this same process when dealing with family members, particularly when engaged in some type of group project, will eliminate a great deal of tension and frustration.

In order to make sure that what you are trying to communicate is being understood in the manner in which you are anticipating, it is important to ask for feedback. For example, if you ask your children to do something specific, follow up with the question "What is your understanding of what I am asking you to do?" This will quickly determine whether your message was heard in the manner you wanted it to be understood. Don't be surprised if you have to repeat or even if you have to describe the task with different language. And remember, you may be a one-repeat person, but your spouse, children, employees, and friends may be multirepeaters. They may be just as smart as you, but they process differently. Ignoring the necessity for multiple repetitions will only result in poor communication and often unnecessary disappointment and frustration.

Some of us learn by what we hear, others by what
we see, and the rest of us by what we do

If you find that your words are not being communicated effectively enough, try demonstrating what you mean or drawing a picture of what you're asking the listener to do. Where you can use all your forms of communication, just to be sure and to reinforce both understanding and retention. We know from both formal research and our own life experiences that we often hear what others say, understand what we read, but remember what we do.

Men (really) are from Mars and women (really) are from Venus
Gender differences in the manner in which men and women communicate have been well-documented by researchers, most notably in the works of Deborah Tannen, author of *That's Not What I Meant* and *You Just Don't Understand Me.*

As a result of different socialization experiences, girls tend to

- seek connection through conversation;
- prefer interdependence and cooperation;
- seek approval from peers;
- share problems;
- focus on feelings;
- ask for help and support; and
- strive to understand problems.

Boys, on the other hand, tend to be socialized in a manner that reinforces them to

- seek status and view other males as rivals;
- prefer autonomy and seek space;
- keep problems private, even from family;
- give advice and feel responsible to solve problems;
- avoid asking for help or advice, as it is perceived as diminishing status; and
- focus on facts rather than feelings.

As a result of these observable characteristics, men and women use language in a very different manner. Men tend to use language to solve problems while women use language as a means of connection. Or stated in another manner, men often use language to *report* while women tend to use language to *relate.*

You can spot these differences among the kids at recess time in school. The boys are generally playing competitive games, using minimal language.

"Give me the ball!"

"Nice shot."

"Out of my way!"

The girls, on the other hand, are wandering the grounds, arms interlocked, giggling, and talking continually. They use their words to not only relate, but they verbalize their process of problem solving. Young girls can spend the entire day with their best friend, only to immediately call the same individual on the phone upon her return home and then talk for hours more. This type of socializing experience will define behavior and needs to be clearly understood in order for families to be aware of these differences in all their interactions. What this means to family relationships is that women need to understand that the men in the family do not always want to talk about their problems until they have already figured out solutions. So, pressuring her husband, father, or son to verbally share challenges they may be experiencing may be met with resistance and withdrawal. If the woman's headset interprets this behavior as "rejection" instead of merely the "need for privacy," the response may be quite different.

Women, on the other hand, often verbalize their issues in the process of problem solving. This does not mean that they need or even want someone to tell them what to do. In fact, they are usually just looking for the type of sympathetic ear they receive from their female confidants. So, when Mary comes home from work and complains to Russ, "I can't get anything done, because we have meetings all day," Russ is likely to have a quick solution at hand, even if he has little information upon which to make his suggestion. If there's a problem, he'll fix it; just as he's "wired" to do. And he may have little patience with Mary, who pushes back on his obvious solution of "just don't go to all the meetings." When Mary ignores or rejects his suggestion, Russ feels confused, maybe even hurt. "Why did you ask me for help when you're not interested in my answer?" In reality, Mary never asked him for help. She was just verbalizing her feelings and thinking out loud. Once again, their different understanding of the use of language resulted in unsatisfactory, responses from both parties.

Around the dining room table, Martha and Julie may eagerly chat away about their day at school, while John sits silently eating his dinner. This does not mean that John does not want to engage with the family. He will just prefer to interact in a more physical, nonverbal manner.

These differences may often be observed during family meetings. The men in the family will begin to lose patience with the women who appear to verbally over evaluate a situation in seeking answers. When the men quickly supply a solution they are met with resistance and rejection of their opinions. What is missing in this interaction is the understanding of the females' need to problem solving verbally. They are not looking for the answers to be supplied by the men. They are enjoying the camaraderie of the dialogue with the other attending females. In applying our understanding of this difference in the way we communicate with each other, it may be helpful to follow a simple rule: adults do not fix the problems of other adults unless they hear four magic words, "What should I do?" or "Will you help me?" Without the magic words, just listen attentively. With that specific invitation, you can fix away!

God created man with two ears and one mouth

In other words, biologically speaking as well as emotionally, listening is twice as important as talking. Effective listening is one of the most important communication skills. Mastering this skill will enable you to build relationships that will be everlasting. Visualize someone with whom you choose to spend your personal time. These individuals are generally good listeners with whom you can share intimate details of your life knowing that there will not be judgment or criticism and you will leave feeling supported. That is why you will want to remain connected.

Now think of people who don't invite your conversation, or do so under false or misleading circumstances. Unfortunately, many such individuals are pseudo-listeners, characterized by listening only for a break in the conversation so they can insert their thoughts, an anecdote, or opinion, or merely listening for a weakness in one's point of view so that they can offer the "correction." These individuals half-listen only so that you will have to listen to them, or half-listen because they don't know how to terminate the conversation without offending the speaker but their body language reveals their lack of interest. How much time will you want to spend with this type of person?

True listeners listen to understand what's being said, to enjoy the interaction, to learn new things or to give support and comfort to the speaker. They understand that genuine listening involves maintaining eye contact and not being distracted. You'll notice these individuals through their posture and body language. They tend to listen with their bodies in a slightly forward position with their eyes focused on the speaker. They may be nodding in agreement or frowning in disagreement, but they're actively listening in either position. You've likely experienced talking to individuals who are lounging on their backs, eyes closed, unresponsive to your comments. They might as well have their iPod headphones on as far as being engaged listeners to your conversation.

Mark and Cynthia were equal partners in several real estate ventures that they inherited from their parents. Mark was a hard-charging, bottom-line entrepreneur who prided himself on his quick grasp of business challenges and his rapid problem-solving skills. Cynthia, on the other hand, was more of an artistic, creative, thoughtful decision maker. When they found themselves required to manage their assets collaboratively, Cynthia became increasingly irritated by that she experienced as Mark's inattentive, dismissive attitude when she was trying to fully verbalize her concerns. Mark was convinced that Cynthia was purposefully trying to annoy him with what he considered to her long-winded discussion of ideas and laborious decision-making process. Fortunately Mark and Cynthia sought professional assistance to help them with their communication challenges before their relationship had totally fallen apart. Mark learned how to listen in a more supportive manner instead of trying to cut the conversation short and when Cynthia felt she was really being heard by her brother, she was able to practice conversing in a more concise manner. Additionally, instead of interpreting Cynthia's more deliberate decision-making style as passive/aggressive, he learned the value of considering a greater variety of options. Cynthia on her part was able to agree to a course of action in a more timely fashion. The end result is a now successful sibling partnership.

Effective listeners have mastered the art of acknowledging not only the content of what is being said, but most importantly the feelings behind these statements. This is how the other party feels heard. Understanding these emotions is the landmark of what is often described as *reflective listening*. This type of listening is particularly important when individuals are communicating issues that are challenging.

"I am at my wits' end trying to deal with my teenage daughter," your friend confides to you breathlessly. This is not an invitation to offer suggestions since, at this point, you don't even know exactly what the problem is nor have you heard the four magic words. ("What should I do?" or "Will you help me?") However, this does call for a listening response, which communicates to your friend that you really want to offer support. When you listen in a reflective manner, you initially reflect upon what the speaker may be feeling. You are not focusing on the content quite yet (since there is still more to flesh out in that department), but on the underlying emotions that led to the statement in the first place. And you then communicate it in a suggestive manner since you cannot be sure precisely what the exact feeling might be. In this specific situation you could respond, "It *sounds* like you are feeling frustrated."

Or, another way to word this response might be, "It *seems* like you are feeling frustrated." That simple statement is all that is initially needed. Now maybe your friend is not frustrated but is, in fact, irritated. He or she will make the correction, "I'm not so much frustrated as I am just annoyed and irritated," but you will still get the credit for being a reflective listener, a person with whom it is safe to share feelings. Your friend may then proceed to volunteer more details but without the four magic words, "What should I do?" You don't have to be a fixer at this point, just an active listener. As your friend shares more details you can offer, "Is there any way I can be of help?" But often the speaker will dismiss the offer but thank you for just listening to them blow off some steam.

The reason that this type of listening is so powerful is that everyone would like to have feelings acknowledged. After all, emotions are the essence of our being and so, when one feels this type of support, the connection is powerful. In essence, the simple act of unburdening oneself and being acknowledged sincerely is often remedy enough for the speaker; and simple enough for the listener. But the acknowledgment of feelings is not easy for individuals who have not been accustomed to speaking in this manner. And if a child has grown up in a household where it was not safe to express feelings because of negative repercussions, the ability to respond in this manner will take practice. It certainly does not come naturally.

You may need to practice this skill. Try this exercise. For one week, just listen to what people are saying around you. On a pad of paper write down the feelings that you think are being expressed. Try to identify at least five feelings per day. A suggested list of feelings will be found in the Appendix of this book. When you become more comfortable in identifying the emotions, you will become increasingly skillful in verbally responding in a reflective manner.

For parents, the challenge with your adult children is to hold back from "fixing" the problem. The key is to hear and verbally acknowledge the emotion behind the comment, to be concerned and supportive without rushing in with your parental instincts when they are not warranted (yet). It may be tempting to do otherwise, but offer your solution ONLY when—and if—you're invited to do so.

What in the world do you mean?

Even in the best of circumstances, the same word can mean different things to different people. This is certainly true when one generation is speaking to another. It may also be true within the same generation. When we don't understand the meaning behind our words, our communication will be vague at best and, perhaps, incomprehensible at worst.

> "I need you to be more thoughtful and considerate," Martha complains to Michael.
>
> Exactly what is Michael expected to do? Was Martha asking Michael to:
>
> "Call me during the day;"
> " Plan a special night out;"
> "Give me compliments on my looks;" or
> "Spend more time with me?"

Obviously, Martha has a very clear idea of the specific behavior she considers thoughtful and considerate. Michael also has his picture of what behavior he considers to be thoughtful and considerate. Martha might be expecting to receive a call from Michael during the day. Michael feels that because he plans a special date night from time to time, however infrequently that might be, he is being very thoughtful. If Martha does not speak openly and honestly with Michael, in words he can understand—and vice versa—they will always be two trains running on parallel tracks, destined never to meet in the middle because the communication gulf is too wide. Without communicating clear behavioral expectation, neither party will have their needs met.

This also becomes very important when communicating to children. "I want you to be good in school today" is a rather meaningless statement from a parent unless it is followed with the specific behaviors that make up the vague communication of "good" in a way the child can clearly comprehend. For some children, merely showing up at school can be considered "good" behavior while, for others, getting straight-As is their only possible interpretation of "good." Clear communication would sound more like this: "Today I want you to go to school and not talk in class without raising your hand and being acknowledged by the teacher, play on the yard without hitting any other student, and give your homework to your teacher as soon as you arrive in class." Now we have clearly expressed our behavioral expectations and the child can understand what "good" means—and how to deliver it.

If you have something to say, then say it to me

One of the most irritating forms of communication is when you try to deliver a message through another individual, rather than directly to the person you want to receive it. We call this "triangling." When Betty wants to communicate information to her father but, instead of dealing directly with him, she enlists mom to deliver the message, she is "triangling." What Betty is really doing, of course, is hoping that mom will take the initial blow if dad erupts. Or perhaps mom will add her own spin in support of Betty's request. But, it's this very use of the intermediary in the first place that creates the risk of miscommunication. As children, we played the game of "telephone," passing a message through one or several individuals. By the time the message was received by the last person, it usually bore no relationship to its original content or tone. This demonstrates how even the simplest message becomes distorted when passed through numerous headsets.

Healthy families learn how to say what needs to be said directly, clearly, and in a manner that will be received in the most positive approach by the listener. Families that fail to communicate directly are unlikely to be able to remain closely bonded, reach compromises on competing agendas, or resolve conflicts inevitable in every family.

Cultural differences can determine what count as acceptable and unacceptable forms of communication

As our families expand and introduce in-laws from different cultures and backgrounds, the innocuous language, customs and slang we take for granted, and the activities that we have traditionally practiced, may be misunderstood or even create hurt feelings among these new additions. Diplomats assigned to a foreign post typically undergo intensive multicultural training so that they will not create tension and animosity from ignorance of local customs. Your family may need its own "short course" in the features of the culture of your new in-law, so that this new family member does not accidentally feel disenfranchised from the larger family unit. The ability to increase the effectiveness of communication is one of the critical life skills. Every day you interact with significant people in your lives and the degree to which you seek out new information on this topic and continually practice the fine art of communication will directly relate to the positive quality of your life.

★   ★   ★

"I've learned that people will forget what you said, people will forget what you did, but people will never forget how you made them feel."

~Maya Angelou

CHAPTER FOUR

The Family Meeting

Mark and Jenny were co-owners of a successful clothing manufacturing company. Each Monday all divisional heads gathered for their weekly meeting and then dispersed to their respective divisions with a coordinated, documented weekly plan that would be reviewed at the following weekly meeting. Mark and Jenny felt proud of the effectiveness of their management program and the success they had been able to create for their company.

What a different scene occurred at home. Things were chaotic. Their two children, Robbie and Marci, seemed to always be arguing and fighting. Parental requests were ignored until Mark or Jenny found themselves yelling and threatening. Fortunately, their local P.T.A. began offering a series of parenting programs and it was there, one evening, that Mark and Jenny heard the instructor describe the importance of family meetings. Suddenly the light went on. They immediately recognized that meetings were a critical part of their business operations and, through the process of joint problem solving, participants felt empowered and committed to action plans in which they had ownership.

They wondered, why couldn't this be equally as effective with the family? They decided it could be. Mark and Jenny eagerly instituted this practice in dealing with the challenges of the "business of the family." Weekly meetings were scheduled and all family members were encouraged to submit topics for discussion. At first Robbie and Marci viewed this new activity with suspicion and resistance but now, several years and numerous meetings later, these gatherings are acknowledged by all as an integral part of the successful operation of their family.

The creation of a successful family is one of the most important endeavors parents undertake during their lifetime. However, crossed fingers and wishful thinking that everything will turn out favorably often substitutes for the type of disciplined strategic planning outlined in Chapters One and Two. Just as successful companies schedule regular meetings to facilitate communication among employees in order to advance the strategic plan of the business, family meetings provide the communication platform necessary for dealing with the equally important "business of the family."

Ideally, parents should begin family meetings when their children are young and thus there will be a structure and process in place for a family that grows with the addition of in-laws, grandchildren, and so on. However, if you are just beginning this process with a multigenerational expanded family, there is no time like the present to get started. Family meetings provide the venue for creating and implementing all the strategies that will support the development of *Legacy Families*.

The factor most likely responsible for whether we have a happy and satisfying family life is how well we communicate with each other. Do we feel we are heard and understood by our spouse, children, parents, or extended family members? Is the whole family involved in problem solving and decision making together? Do we tell each other what's (*really*) on our mind? Do we listen when others tell us the same? All the individual skills that interpersonal relationships require, as we discussed in the preceding chapter, are magnified many times over in the context of a family, especially as it grows in size and complexity.

One of the best methods for promoting positive family communication is to institute a program of regular family meetings. You may think you're already doing this, so let's get specific. A family meeting is a structured discussion time that typically involves all members of a family. They differ from the day-to-day conversation that may occur during meal times or on the run in both their structure and focus.

Modern day family life has become very complicated, with each member involved in so many varied activities that it is a rare event when families can sit calmly for a specific length of time and actually communicate in a meaningful manner about a specific topic or even agenda of topics. School, extracurricular activities, demanding work schedules, and social and community responsibilities are all vying for quality time with the family. If we're not careful about scheduling such meetings, the good intentions of meeting as a family are overlooked and allowed to fall by the wayside. Thus, regularly scheduled family meetings create a priority for getting the family together and signals to the younger members of the family that their input and participation are important.

This is more than just an opportunity to air grievances. These meetings open the lines of communication and help family members, especially children, learn to work and solve problems within a group. Additionally, family meetings encourage everyone's participation. Children feel respected and heard, which strongly contributes to increased self-esteem. As this forum is a vehicle for problem solving, they learn to take responsibility for their behavior as well as contributing to solutions. When family meetings begin with school-aged children, adolescence is more easily endured by both teenagers and parents since the lines of communication have already been so well established.

Ideally, family meetings should begin within the primary family unit and include all family members eight years old and above. Having said that, if meetings are being held in a family that is composed of a 9-year-old, 12-year-old, 14-year-old, and a 6-year-old, the younger child in the family might want to participate as well. If this is the case, permit him or her to attend for as long as the child can concentrate and not become disruptive—with the option to leave at any time without suffering any adverse consequences.

Parents introduce the concept of the family meeting by sharing with their children their desire to always work to make the family the best it can be for everyone. They continue by stating that, because they feel that the family is so important to them, they want to have a regular time to sit down and listen to each other with no distractions or interruptions (cell phones and Blackberries are not permitted) and talk about what is working well in the family and what might need to be improved.

This is also a time to make family weekend plans, delegate household responsibilities, plan a family vacation, or discuss family philanthropy or other projects. The meeting might deal with daily decisions, such as who will drive the kids to sports practice, who will be handling carpooling for school, or more serious issues such as a possible change in the finances of the family due to a career change or the possibility of moving to a new city.

There are some important principles that facilitate the process and help to make the family meeting productive.

Establish a specific regular meeting time/place and keep this appointment
as you would any other important scheduled activity
This regularity reinforces the message that parents regard family as a priority. No one will take family meetings seriously if they are frequently canceled or forgotten, if they are rushed or overlooked or if, when meeting, four out of five participants are distracted by vibrating cell phones or the TV in the other room.

Remember that scheduling the meeting is not enough; participation is required. Having regular meetings that aren't productive, taken seriously, or attended by one and all are just as bad as having irregular meetings or no meetings at all.

If parents do not treat the meetings as serious, their children most certainly will not. This should be a time that will be convenient for everyone and should have a clear time for beginning and ending so that participants will be able to arrange their personal activities around this designated family time.

Develop operating ground rules
Some examples are given below:

- *Focus on one topic at a time and try to develop action plans to deal with that specific issue.* If you don't, you will just end up having the same discussion about the same (unresolved) issues at every family meeting. If it is necessary to get additional information or resources, then the issue can be postponed until a further meeting. Just make sure that it does not get forgotten.

- *Take turns speaking so that everyone gets a chance to voice an opinion.* If the family is large or the meetings frequently take on the appearance of a shouting match, have an object or certificate that entitles the recipient—and only the recipient—to talk while in possession of it (see below for clarification).

- *Do not interrupt when others are talking.* Highly verbal families often find this a hard rule to follow and, if this is the case in your family, you might want to develop the custom of using a talking stick. The idea is that the holder of the stick (or maybe a sea conch, as used in the novel *Lord of the Flies*) is the only one who can speak and when he or she is finished with their thought, the stick is handed to the next speaker.

- *Dads, avoid being directive.* Let your family members express their own opinions.

- *Moms, avoid deferring to Dad.* Express your opinion, even if it differs from your spouse.

- *Prohibit yelling, swearing, fighting or excessive emotional outbursts.* Lead by example and expect others to follow your lead. One of the important outcomes of successful family meetings is to demonstrate to the younger members of the family the power of rational conversation and trust in the freedom to exchange independent ideas. If you do one thing and say another, younger family members will take the cue and think it's okay to yell, swear, and be excessively emotional as well.

- *Avoid discounting of opinions, put-downs, or sarcasm.* One quick way to silence participants in a family meeting is for them to feel that if they express themselves honestly it might be met with a personal attack, ridicule, or punishment. During a family meeting there are no "stupid" questions or answers.

- *Establish consequences for breaking the family meeting rules.* Good intentions for family meetings can quickly run afoul if everyone knows your threats have no merit and/or your rules have no consequences. Be firm in minding the rules and certain in addressing those who break them. For younger children, consider restricting video game or TV time. For older family members, you can try restricting computer or cell phone time. The idea is not punishment, of course, but to maintain order and seriousness at the family meeting.

Develop written agendas

When it comes to the "business" of family meetings, take this business seriously by developing a written agenda to follow during the meeting. Some families have created a "suggestion box" into which any family member can put any item he or she would like to have on the agenda for the next family meeting. It is important to speak about what is working well in the family as well as the challenges. The family meeting should not become the weekly gripe session or a chance for several family members to gang up on one unsuspecting victim; agendas help keep things on track. Each meeting should begin with everyone sharing one positive thing that has occurred in the family since the last meeting.

Challenges should also be presented as a general topic and not as a personal attack on an individual family member. For example, "there has been too much fighting and arguing among brothers and sisters" or "homework time is becoming very stressful because too much work is being done at the last minute. How are we going to solve this problem?"

Any topic should be open for discussion. If one family member has a concern, regardless of the feelings by other family members that this is too trivial a matter to take up time at a family meeting, that concern must be respected. After all, who is to decide what's trivial and what isn't? To the person experiencing the problem, it is very real. Discounting a feeling— any feeling—is a psychological affront to the individual who is expressing the concern and will send a message that it will not be safe to share personal issues during a family meeting, undermining the very purpose of the meeting.

Try to stick to the agenda; it's a good way to get meetings back on track when things go astray. If you don't get to every item on the agenda, circle those you missed and put them at the top of next week's agenda. If you find yourself consistently not getting to the last three or four items, even though your meetings are productive, consider having fewer items per agenda.

What kind of items should be on your agenda? Typical topics range from family issues to financial matters and from broad policy questions to specific implementation rules. For your convenience, we've listed a host of ideas and a sample agenda in the Appendix. Remember, all work and no play makes the meeting dull and too much like your job at the office. Make the experience fun, educational, engaging, along with short and productive.

Rotate leadership each meeting

The purpose of the family meeting is not to have domination by strong verbal adults. By permitting each family member to take a turn in the role of chairperson, a clear message is sent that each participant is equally important. Consider the feeling of empowerment that is created when an 8-year-old is given this type of responsibility and what a tremendous training ground for the future leadership, which is so important in *Legacy Families*.

However, just because the leadership of the meeting is rotated, and all family members are encouraged to express an opinion, it does not mean that parents do not have the final say on important parental decisions for their young children.

Knowing when to step in—and when to stay out—is of paramount importance to the success of each meeting. Beforehand, parenting partners should decide what are the "A" issues for the family over which they will exercise final control. Sometimes staying out of the fray can teach us as much as wading in. After all, on the issues of less critical importance, when parents can honestly let their children share in the decision-making process, they strengthen their children's confidence in their own judgment. This security will serve them well during those turbulent adolescence years, when the ability to resist peer pressure in favor of maintaining personal values is critical.

When the meeting includes your mature adult children, decision making must seem fair and reasonable. Keep in mind that your words aren't the only variable with meaning; actions count for a lot, too. If the discussion is robust, differences of opinion are invited and shared, and then mom or dad proceed to impose their decision without much regard to the overwhelming views of others, the process may seem cosmetic only. The comment "I'll mail in my vote, since it will be ignored anyway" is an often unstated but strongly felt disclaimer by family members.

Continually work on applying the effective communication skills outlined in Chapter Three

Be alert to ongoing education in the field of communication so that the family can incorporate new techniques into the family meetings. Stay abreast of the latest techniques by subscribing to parenting or psychology magazines or visiting respected blogs or forums where such information is frequently updated. The basics will serve you well, but there is always room for improvement. Remember the rules:

- Listen well. Remember…one mouth—two ears.
- Communicate in the language and methods that enable everyone to understand. Some of your family members like to see numbers and charts; others want to see pictures and colors. Some members will crave facts; others want to hear the feelings. Sometimes an anecdote or parable will work where statistics won't. Say it once for the meeting minutes, but say it several times if you want everyone to remember.
- Respect the views of others, even if you disagree.
- Define your terms and describe the behavior or results that you expect or anticipate.
- Listen well, listen well, listen well.

Utilize a decision-making process to teach problem-solving skills

Solve every problem according to a specific issue, but use the same five-step process to arrive at a solution. Ask yourself:

1. What do we have? "The garage has become so cluttered with disorganized 'stuff' that it is impossible to garage both cars."
2. What do we want? "Organized space so that the intent of a garage (to park two cars) can be utilized."

3. How can we get there? "Everyone has to commit to donating four hours to a 'garage cleaning party.'"
4. By when? "A date will be selected within the next two weeks when everyone is available."
5. How will we evaluate our success? "We will take before and after pictures and evaluate our success at the following family meeting."

Although, in this example, this problem-solving methodology has been reduced to the simple task of cleaning the garage, it is the same process that large organizations use to solve complex issues. By teaching family members how to effectively utilize this approach, you are educating them in a very valuable life skill that they can apply to the varied challenges they will meet in their lifetime.

Keep notes in a record book and document decisions and who will be involved for future reference and accountability

Business meetings have minutes. What do family meetings have? A record book. Without some type of written reminder, it is easy to forget what the agreed upon action plan is and which individuals within the family have the responsibility for the outcome.

The record book serves as a reference source at future meetings. The job as Family Recorder is an important one and it is often a good opportunity for younger members of the family to be involved. With their computer skills, they are often the best prepared for this task. It also requires the family meeting leader to ensure that the decisions were clearly described, so that even the younger members can understand.

When time permits, plan a fun activity following the family meeting such as a special dinner, favorite dish, afternoon at the park, or a good movie

Positive reinforcement typically works no matter how sophisticated the audience. By pairing a family meeting with pizza and a movie night or putt-putt afterward, you subconsciously help "wire" the meeting and fun together. If this is an event where the family grows together and plays together, they are more likely to stay together. And be sure to thank everyone for their participation and contributions. Sharing their day with the family should not be taken for granted.

As you have been reading this chapter, you may begin to feel somewhat overwhelmed. Don't be deterred. At this stage of your life, you may have grown children, each married with several grandchildren in each family. Should you still begin to organize and plan regular family meetings at this advanced stage? Absolutely! You are now developing a *Legacy Family* and, in order for your 100-year plan to be successful, you have serious business to which you must attend. When you do, you will likely get strong encouragement and support from other members of the family. Share the responsibility with them. There's an old adage that applies to the strategic planning of a family, much as it applies to many facets of life: *If you build it, you'll own it.* So, the more others help you to build the plan and program, the more they will have a stake in its success.

The benefits of regular and well-attended family meetings are well worth the effort and can serve as a reference point for a family full of very different people to come together for one common cause. Think how different your children are today, even though they might have grown up in the same household with the same set of parents. Now add spouses to the mix, who likewise come into your family system with a unique set of values and principles developed from their own family backgrounds.

If you have several married children you have just added several completely different family systems to the mix and, eventually, your many grandchildren will add their own partners to the mix. Suddenly your home has become more like "corporate headquarters" and this "business of the family" has suddenly become very complicated and family meetings all the more important if you do not want "in-laws" to become "outlaws."

It is through this process that they begin to truly understand the ethics, values, and the heritage of the family and can begin to understand what role they can play in building positive family relationships. This is even more critical when there is a major shared asset such as a family business that will require collaboration in the decision-making process.

The process works! We received a letter from Margaret, a 50-year-old member of a large family that was enjoying three and going on four generations of a family business. The challenges were not insignificant but, as you can see, the optimism pervades at least this one stakeholder:

I wanted to jot a quick note to you before I left for our family meeting. I've been going to these meetings as long as I can remember. It's become our annual ritual and I wouldn't miss it for the world. I think Ben and our two kids (both finished college this year...hooray!) seem to enjoy it as much as I do. Three days with grandma, Aunt Carol, Uncle Fred, and my 8 cousins and 11 nieces and nephews, would scare most people, but we just love catching up with each other, telling our stories for the last year, and learning more about the company and our family properties.

It's especially important since Carol and her family live in the Northwest, Fred and lots of the cousins and their kids still live in the Philly area where the company offices are located. We escaped the cold and rain and found paradise in Phoenix, but we still love the beauty of Seattle and the dining delicacy of a Philly cheese steak. This year we're meeting at our lake house outside Philadelphia, so it's going to be a cheese steak weekend.

I've been thinking about how much we have learned from these meetings through the years. We have all benefited immensely from the family business, but without these meetings most of us wouldn't have a clue what the business actually does or how it has survived all the challenges over the last sixty years or so. We'd never appreciate what grandpa had to overcome to enable the company to survive the Depression, take advantage of the war to grow the business, give dad a chance to expand and diversify, and then be sure that Louis and my cousins were ready to take over leadership. Imagine if he hadn't prepared for this by the time that he got sick. And when mom died shortly thereafter, Louie and I were really lost. Fortunately my brother was so smart, because I couldn't have helped very much.

Now the challenge is how to prepare Generation Four. Some of the kids assume they will be given jobs at the company. Some of them are pushing to sell the company and divvy up the cash. College was a party for a couple of my nephews. My kids are figuring out their own lives. They better get their act together or they may experience the pain of hunger!

So this year's meeting is about expectations—theirs and ours. We have our job cut out for us. But Louie and I, along with my cousins, are committed to keeping our family vision and mission in focus. I'll let you know if G3 can turn G4 around. I remember dad and Uncle Fred saying the same thing about us! And, oh yes, we're going to a Flyers hockey game. Some things never change!

Best,

Maggie

You can introduce the process of an extended family meeting in the same manner as you would the meetings with your immediate family. If your children, siblings, or parents share your desire to build a *Legacy Family*, you'll need everyone's participation to make it work.

Your initial meetings may be to express your shared goals, understand the concerns of all the individual family groups and their members, determine how the family can help each member achieve his or her dreams and build positive interpersonal relationships. At this early stage, you may need to articulate the family vision and mission, and to craft the outlines of your long-range Strategic Plan and Family Constitution.

If you are just beginning the process of family meetings at this stage of development, you might want to consider utilizing a professional who specializes in facilitating family meetings to start the extended family on the right track. This individual will generally want to interview all the adult participants so that he or she has a good understanding of the family dynamics, individual agendas, key issues, and any underlying emotions or conflicts so that surprises can be minimized and/or dealt with productively. Since the facilitator is not a party to any family politics, he or she can handle emotional issues with neutrality and will not be viewed as being on one "side" or the other. Additionally, families tend to behave with less negative emotionality when there is a stranger in the midst than they do with individuals with whom they have long-standing familiarity.

Running an effective extended family meeting requires preparation and planning. Do not be discouraged if some members are skeptical or resistant. Depending upon personal family history as well as what interpersonal challenges may have already transpired in the new family complex, they may view this process with suspicion—and even fear. Family members who have had difficult relationships with siblings, cousins, and parents may also be hesitant to participate. If individuals absolutely refuse to participate, do not let this stop the process. Hold the meetings anyway and, when the resisters hear of positive outcomes from these sessions and are warmly *invited* (not forced or shamed) to participate, they will generally come around. (For once, the family grapevine can really pay off!)

Coordination of extended family meetings involves complicated logistics
Like our success story about Maggie, successful families begin the process of meeting regularly by selecting a venue that is workable and appealing to all participants and will provide an opportunity for both learning and "playing" together (witness the salivary glands working in overdrive in anticipation of local treats like the famous Philly cheese steak).

In order to build friendships that last, family members need to interact in a variety of situations...in a "classroom" learning environment, sharing dining experiences, and involving themselves in sporting or cultural experiences. The goal of a successful family meeting is creating an informative educational experience combined with fun and laughter and the eager anticipation of the next family gathering. Then:

- Create family committees to handle various tasks such as venue, food, extracurricular activities, and programs so that many individuals feel a part of the process.
- If a multiday retreat is involved and young children will be in attendance, provide acceptable child care so that adults can attend all meetings with minimal distractions.
- Schedule the dates and times well in advance so that these meetings will be a priority for all family members.
- Begin meetings with a quick personal update from each participant. Extended family members are living in various locales and are often unaware of what other family members have been doing or have accomplished. This personal sharing time becomes an important method for bonding and supporting each other. This process has led many families to create a family web site (a type of family Facebook) upon which all members can post updates on their activities. If this concept is foreign to the senior members of the family, enlist the assistance of the younger family members who so expertly know how to create social networks. Let them become the instructors of the technology neophytes and you'll be pleasantly surprised by how quickly the older set catches on—and become equally addicted.
- If there are shared business interests (i.e., family business, vacation property, the family ranch, family office, or family foundation) the agenda

should include both business issues (i.e., Financial Capital) as well as agenda items that build Human, Intellectual, and Social Capital.

- Determine the appropriate individuals and ages for attendance. If there are family businesses to be managed by future generations, involving the teenage population in the business portion of the meetings provides them with a better understanding of career options, as well as an understanding of the qualifications necessary to enter the family business and/or becoming responsible stewards of the wealth. This can positively influence the educational choices they make in the future.
- Establish rules of conduct that assure that participants will feel safe to express opinions, feelings, and concerns in an accepting, non-judgmental manner. This is especially true for welcoming members of your extended family to participate fully.

Establishing a tradition of attendance at extended family meetings is critical to the process of creating Legacy Families

Families can discover and build upon common ground by developing a vision and mission for the family that encompasses all points of view. In so doing, an environment is created that facilitates the transfer of values, family history, and culture. Through this process all family members develop a basis of communicating and upholding common values and goals which, in turn, builds healthy long-term relationships.

Think about those individuals with whom you choose to associate. Generally speaking, they will be the people with whom you hold similar basic values and principles. How wonderful it is when these individuals are members of your own family.

Through the process of family meetings, education and mentoring occurs frequently. As families determine what it is that they need to learn in order to continue to build their Human, Intellectual, Financial, and Social Capital accounts, families can seek out educational resources to become part of the agenda at future family meetings. Thus everyone is exposed to this information at the same time and can support each other in integrating it into their daily lives.

Participants feel empowered by the ability to express their feelings, ideas, opinions, and concerns without feeling judged. One of the causes of fractures in family relationships is the inability of individuals to be able to express themselves without being ignored, criticized, or humiliated. This can be as silent as individuals rolling their eyes and sighing when certain members are expressing their thoughts to direct verbal confrontation such as out and out vocal histrionics. Therefore, it becomes very important to remind family members before each meeting of the agreed upon rules of behavior that require each participant to be treated in a respectful manner. Many families keep these family meeting rules posted in an easily visible place throughout the meeting as a constant reminder.

Through facilitated family meetings, families can learn that conflict is not something to be avoided at any cost. In fact, conflict often opens up other options for consideration and the resulting compromise may result in a more productive action plan. However, unresolved conflict will erode relationships as surely as running water or the sands of time erode national landmarks. Learning the most effective conflict resolution skills is one of the educational agendas items that should be included on a regular basis.

Family meetings create an opportunity for the appreciation of the diverse talents of varied family members. This is enhanced when families develop specific collaborative projects that utilize the varied talents of family members. The philanthropic interest of the family is one initiative that easily lends itself to these types of projects and provides new leadership opportunities. The ongoing development of leadership talent at each generational level enables the family to maintain its productivity when the senior generation is no longer around to provide direction and guidance.

Legacy Families understand the importance of developing a governance structure at each generation and the necessity for a different style of leadership when assets are passed from the original wealth creator to the successor generation.

Who will be empowered to make decisions affecting the group, how will these individuals be held accountable and what roles will be played by other siblings and/or cousins? The original wealth creator is most often a sole entrepreneur and therefore only accountable to him- or herself. Decisions are made independently with little need for explanations or compromise.

However, in successor generations, leadership is given to those individuals who are most skilled at developing cooperation and consensus. While children may tolerate domination or intrusion into their lives by parents, they will emphatically resist a similar leadership style from a sibling or a cousin. Ongoing—and regular—family meetings provide the opportunity for the individual members of each generation to develop the levels of trust and comfort with their peers that will lead to a comfortable governance structure for decision making.

Though the task of beginning this process might seem daunting at first, the end results will be well worth the effort as the positive power of families will blossom.

★   ★   ★

"There is more than a verbal tie between the words common, community and communication. Try the experiment of communicating with fullness and accuracy, some experience to another, especially if it is somewhat complicated and you will find your own attitude toward your experience changing."
~John Dewey

CHAPTER FIVE

Family Governance

Governance was easy when dad was alive. He decided. We followed. After dad's death, my older brother, Ron, assumed the mantel of authority. Only problem was that mom thought it was her turn and our oldest sibling, Sara, who used to help Ronnie tie his shoes, didn't really like being told what to do by her younger brother. Mom kept the lid on until she became feeble. Then, we started to argue. We have lots of assets we inherited and own together, a family foundation on which we all serve, and family gatherings that we all attend. I don't mind input by my siblings, but I'm 48 years old and don't really want to be told what to do by my siblings.

~Rick, Los Angeles, CA

Like any good business, a family needs strong, capable, and assertive leadership. Leadership sets agendas, calls meetings, holds people accountable, and enforces the rules, customs, and protocols that are as common in family units as they are in business. Unlike a business, however, the common objective for families is not necessarily to increase the financial bottom line for investors and shareholders. Instead, the leaders of the *Legacy Family* seek to help each family unit and individual members increase the four capitals of family wealth—human, intellectual, financial, and social.

It's a bit more complicated in a family than in most businesses. The family leaders can't simply "fire" a family member for some misgiving, either real or perceived. Once you're in the family, you're there to stay. But like any good leader you can impose consequences that the family acknowledges are reasonable and appropriate. Troublemakers and irresponsible members don't have to be invited to gatherings, nor do they have to be included in shared investment opportunities or be elected to serve on the foundation's board of directors.

So leaders have a tougher challenge. They must mobilize resources, gain consensus, reconcile differences, push the agenda, and drive the family to the next level of growth and achievement. All this is in a consensual relationship built on bonds of love, respect, trust, and integrity that derives its strength from both a genetic and legal connection that forms the basis of our society.

We're a close family. Why do we need a leader?

The larger the family group and the more complicated the family assets, the more obvious and necessary becomes the need for leadership, structure, and process. With a single child or heir, the role of leadership falls naturally on that individual. The decisions by the "benevolent dictator" are unlikely to be challenged. Of course, neither is the burden of the work shared. But with each passing generation, as the family grows in size, the simple governance structure will dissolve and, if another structure is not put into place to replace it, chaos will rule instead.

Just think of the many areas in which our decisions affect others. Rick's family, which we'll call the "Kline family," is a perfect example of just how intertwined families and their financial affairs can get. Rick's parents, Larry and Frances, lived a long and prosperous life. They have three children, each of whom is married (and one married twice), and there are seven grandkids, now in their teens and early twenties. When both mom and dad were living and active, the family got along great. They enjoyed each other's company. All of them are productive and intelligent. We'd describe them as a very good, loving, and functional family. They enjoy holidays and birthdays together, even though family members had scattered around the county.

The estate has been well planned for tax purposes by their professional advisors. There is a family business, which runs a series of mini-markets in five states. Its value is substantial and it generates considerable cash flow. Ownership was transferred years earlier to a family limited partnership, originally led by Larry. Frances was named the backup general partner, but, since Larry's death, has since become the managing partner. There are two other family limited partnerships, each of which own investment real estate. These, too, were once led by Larry, and are now under the control of Frances.

With the passing of the life or active management of the wealth creators have come real management challenges. Frances was never really involved in either running the family business or the real estate investments. Larry did all that. The third born child, Sara, joined the company nearly 14 years ago, and has run the finance office ever since. But her two siblings have had little involvement since their school days. As for the real estate, the oldest son, Ron, is quite capable of handling this work, though he lives in Philadelphia, which is not particularly close to the properties in Chicago. Rick has his own thriving business, which sells time for advertising on national and local television. Frances is neither comfortable, nor, in the last few years, physically capable of handling these matters. The partnership agreements provide that the limited partners, each of the kids, can name a successor general partner, but there's a strong disagreement about who should be designated for each of these three entities.

Other complications persist; there's the Aspen vacation house, the Florida second home, and all of Frances' personal financial matters. At this point in her life, Frances is just not able to make decisions—big or little—and has asked her daughter, Sara, to do that for her. Her two brothers are delighted someone else is doing the work. But they would like to decide together before any money is spent. So, Sara has the unenviable job of having all the responsibility but none of the authority.

In those families with several children or heirs, it would be wonderful if each had the time, talent, and interest to split up the work, take on the responsibilities, and work harmoniously with the others to ensure competent, effective, and unbiased decision making. Sometimes the wheel of good fortune spins in favor of the family. But to assume this result is to gamble on the long-term success of the family. A risky gamble, at best.

As challenging as this all sounds, however, for the Kline family, the problems have just begun. Increased years have brought increased sophistication when it comes to securing all those transparent assets. Subsequently, there's a brewing battle over who should be running the business, the real estate, *and* mom's personal affairs. When all Sara had was responsibility for Frances, her siblings were more than happy to let her do the caretaking work. Now that financial reward is in the mix, they are none too happy about the potential of being "shut out." This skirmish will likely spill over to the family foundation.

Currently, the warring factions are at a stalemate. Family holidays are on hold. No one is organizing the events and mom is not able to call the group together—and keep the peace—as she had always done. At least she is still living, so the need and desire to visit on her birthday and hold the traditional Thanksgiving dinner still draws everyone home. But, what will happen upon her death? How will these issues get resolved? What we leave to fate, gravity often decides instead; the path of least resistance is often the road to ruin. Without a structure and an agreed process, the cracks in the relationship are likely to widen, perhaps irreversibly and a wonderful family will lose its way.

Clearly, these are large and multifaceted issues. We'll talk about some strategies for managing shared assets in Chapter Eight. But here we need to talk about a structure for the oversight of the extended family issues. Some of these issues are economic, like many of those facing the Kline family. Other issues are more about the relationships and the emotional, intellectual, and social aspects of the family.

So, how should we organize ourselves?

Despite growing tensions, the Kline family still has a very good chance to create a *Legacy Family*. They start with all the right ingredients. They like each other. They are educated and motivated and self-sufficient. Even the former in-laws are not considered outlaws. There's plenty of wealth, but no one is waiting to inherit in order to provide for themselves. Their values are strong and have been so impressed upon the kids by Larry and

Frances that it is likely the third generation will accept them as well. The danger ahead is the leadership vacuum and who, if anyone, is qualified to fill it.

The *Legacy Family* acknowledges the need for strong, effective leadership that is capable, qualified, and committed to fostering the shared principles and values of the family. The *Legacy Family* will accept the leadership offered because it enhances the common good and furthers the goals of the Strategic Plan. This compact is essential if the family is to move forward productively. If it dissolves into feuds, misunderstanding, and irreconcilable differences, the likelihood is slim that this family will remain a *Legacy Family* for another generation.

In the *Legacy Family's* Strategic Plan, family leadership is defined and the structure is explained. The Family Constitution may set out, in greater detail, the criteria for potential leaders of the family, how leadership will be selected, what responsibility and authority such leaders may have in each of the areas that affect the extended family, to whom the leaders will report or be held accountable, how long they may stay in that position before being reelected or replaced, and how and by whom they will be compensated, if at all.

There are many variations of family leadership. Let's look at just three: the "Family Executive," the "Family Council," and the "Family Office." You will hear and read about many formats. Friends will share their experiences, good and bad. Some structures have stood the test of time; while others may have been created so recently that they have not been "seasoned" yet.

Just remember, how your family will be led, by whom, in what areas and with what expectations, will vary from other families because of the personality and talents of your members, the nature of your circumstances and a host of other factors that make your family different from theirs. Always be on the lookout for new information, resources, and successful techniques to help guide your *Legacy Family*, but likewise view them skeptically and see how they might be applied to your family, in particular.

Some families actually elect a leader, who is responsible to the family and replaceable by the adult members

This structure relies on the decision making of a single person. The obvious advantage to this style of leadership is that it is often the most familiar to Generation Two, each of whom likely grew up under a similar leadership of the single wealth creator.

Expediency isn't an issue with this form of family leadership. It's certainly easier to make a decision if you don't have to rely on a committee. Unlike the wealth creator, however, this elected leader (let's call this person the "Family Executive") will be accountable to the extended family. As a result, the Family Executive can't impose arbitrary decisions on the family that fail to meet the needs and concerns of the majority. Otherwise, the tenure of this leader will likely be short.

To make this style work, there must be clear criteria that define the characteristics and clear rules that define the job. The Family Constitution will articulate the election process. Just who is eligible to participate in the election? Will it be all the adults in the extended family? For argument's sake, is an 18-year-old experienced and wise enough to be considered an "adult" for this particular purpose? Should such a young adult be given this power before experiencing the complexity of the family? Will the young adult population of the family outvote, by sheer number of members, the older generation of the family, perhaps wreaking personal and financial havoc on the family due to simple inexperience, overemotionality, or naïveté?

Some families organize themselves like the federal system of American government. We all learned in grade school that, to avoid the pitfalls of mob mentality or the American popularity contest, each state elects representatives (or "electors") that choose the president of the United States. Should large wings of the family have more "electors" or votes than smaller wings? Will this give unfair advantage within the extended family to the larger groups?

Maintaining balance amongst the family groups is often an important factor in motivating compromise and collaboration. One method that ensures such balance provides that each family group (so, in the Kline family, each of the three siblings would constitute a separate family group) votes within its group for the Family Executive. A majority (two of the three family groups in the Kline family's case) select the individual to serve. If there's a tie, some families rely on a nonfamily representative to vote. Others insist on either reaching a majority decision on the existing candidates or finding another candidate that would receive such a vote.

Some family groups choose to rely on the "senior generation," namely the oldest living generation, to vote on behalf of the family group, while others allow adults defined by them (which could be all the members of the extended family above a minimum age, like 25) to vote within the family group and their collective decision then determines the family group's vote for the candidate.

It can sound complicated at first but once the process is determined, it becomes familiar and routine, thus relatively easy to implement. But this style is not without its problems and detractors. Relying on a single person to serve in the role of Family Executive restricts access to leadership and can generate a sense of loss of voice and influence on the decision-making process. The politics of a family are no less thorny than the politics of any other group entity, including a community, state, or nation. But thorny or not, leadership is required and the challenges must be faced and resolved. In some families, the single Family Executive can be the answer to those pressing issues.

Some families prefer a committee or "Family Council"
to make decisions that affect the larger group

The Family Council often is created during the lifetime of the wealth creators and is designed to include them as well as a member from each of the children's family groups. This gives everyone a chance to participate and become familiar with the structure. It gives the wealth creators a chance to start delegating responsibilities and authority to various members in the Council, which is helpful for preparation of these new leaders and also for testing their commitment and talent.

Even if the Family Council is formed after the passing of the leadership of Generation One, it is often an effective way to ensure that each family group has a voice in the leadership and decision making. The burdens of leadership are easier to share in a collective structure, and the various talents, time, and interests of the extended family are sometimes more available.

Even with a Family Council, someone has to organize, call, and chair the meetings. City government may be led by a city council, but there's usually a mayor or other official that takes greater responsibilities than the others. To avoid lapsing into a Family Executive role, this "first among equals" position can rotate periodically or can be the person selected by all the family groups from amongst each family's representative. Again, there's no one "right" answer, only a solution that works best within your extended family.

The criteria for membership on the Family Council, process for election, duration of the appointment, responsibilities and authority, compensation and expectations, must be defined and outlined within the Family Constitution. Before committing such ideas to the family record, consider: What are the qualities of leadership that your family wants today and over time? What temperament, commitment, education, life experience, integrity, and experience does the family want for its leaders? Be careful what you wish for. You may get it.

If the family groups participated in designing and approving the Constitution, they will more likely accept the results of their actions. Of course, this structure can change, much like everything else in the family, but this too must be defined in the Constitution. Rules cast in concrete will crumble over time, but those which require thoughtful deliberation, collective decisions and constant assessment have the greatest chance of surviving and adapting through the generations.

Perhaps a combination of both types examined so far can work best for you. In fact, one interesting variation in structure is a combination of the Family Executive, elected by all the family groups, and the Family Council, in which each representative is elected by a separate family group. The Family Executive reports to the Family Council, which serves more as a policy maker than as an administrator. Unlike the more utilitarian nature of the first description, in this case the Family Executive merely implements the policies approved by the Family Council, within a budget that is set by the Council. Accountability is an important quality in any leadership structure. Unlike the world of the wealth creators, who were only responsible to themselves, those who serve the interests of subsequent generations have responsibility to many stakeholders.

In this case, the Klines might prefer a Family Council. Since Rick has made it clear he doesn't like his brother directing him, a Council in which each sibling has an equal voice, which can then give direction and approval to Ron, if he's the point person to carry out the decision, might make all three siblings happier. But, when a family is geographically dispersed, and the assets are varied and complicated, it's often impractical to govern by committee. Perhaps the combination of a senior executive (which could be one of the siblings or it could be a nonfamily member) and a governing body like the Family Council, would provide the best balance.

There's nothing in the rule book that says you must have only one executive for all the various intertwined financial and personal matters of the extended family. It might be that Sara would serve as the executive in the business, while Ron focuses on the real estate. Maybe Rick would enjoy the role of supervising the foundation, though it might be any member of the extended family that is best suited and has the time and interest in doing so.

Remember, if there *is* a governing body, like the Family Council, no one family member can run amok. The scope of authority and the exercise of discretion, especially those decisions that have a financial impact, are all subject to the approved strategy, budget, and oversight of the Family Council. Since each of the key stakeholders has an equal voice, the sources of much of the conflict, such as lack of communication, can be avoided.

*Some families delegate the responsibilities of
leadership to a Family Office*

Family offices have become increasingly popular over the last few decades. Some family offices serve only one family (as in the case of a "single family office" or SFO) and some serve many families ("multifamily office" or MFO). Some family offices are run or staffed by members of the extended family, by nonfamily members, and others by a combination of family and nonfamily members. Some financial institutions, accounting firms, and law firms have set up their own "virtual" family office, to provide the administrative services and investment management of the extended family. Some will take responsibility for the qualitative issues of the family— communications, financial and life skill education, conflict resolution, and the like. The family foundation can be administered by the family office or it can, and often is, outsourced to specialists in that field.

Whether an internal or external staff can perform all these issues efficiently, effectively, and with the necessary people skills required will depend on the talents and resources of the family office, and the clarity of its responsibilities and authority. Good decisions are not limited to those within the family. In fact, built-in biases, generated by their personal history with siblings, cousins and other members of the extended family, can sometimes impede and sometimes enhance their decision-making abilities.

Supervising a family office can at times be less emotional than running a family by Executive or Committee. At the same time, nonfamily members can be recruited with the specific technical and personal skills needed by the family, held accountable and easily discharged. It can be hard to fire your sibling, even if it's clearly warranted. But, few nonfamily members will have the same level of commitment and concern for the family as those who are members of that family. There's a reason why family businesses are generally more profitable than nonfamily–owned businesses!

In nearly all cases, however, the extended family, which could be represented by the Family Executive or a Family Council, chooses the head of the family office and oversees its performance. In the absence of this oversight, family offices have been known to "run amok," creating disillusionment and disaffection within the family, and generating the very conflict that the office was intended to avoid.

An important reminder

The best form of governance depends on the nature of the specific enterprise. An operating business doesn't work well under governance by committee. Though even the CEO of a company should report and be accountable to a board of directors, the management duties and authority must be delegated if the enterprise is to be successful. A family foundation, on the other hand, works best under the leadership of a board, even though administrative tasks that have limited authority should probably be delegated to an executive director or other senior staff member or even outsourced. Investment assets, often held in a partnership or limited liability structure, must be specifically tailored to fit the nature of the activities and responsibilities, even though the manager in charge must still be held accountable by the stakeholders.

Much of the difference between the three entities above lies in the degree of autonomy and authority granted to the operating officer. So, as you design the governance of your family, be sure you have a good understanding of the needs of each enterprise affected and the attributes and characteristics of the most appropriate structure for each such enterprise.

★   ★   ★

"The life of a family is dynamic; the governance system it develops must be just as dynamic."

~James (Jay) E. Hughes

CHAPTER SIX

Family Wealth Planning

I'm a 58-year-old entrepreneur, who, together with my wife of 28 years, built and sold three businesses. We took one company public and changed the way our industry did business. My three kids are young adults, well educated, world traveled, perfectly normal, and completely clueless. I gave each a small interest in my businesses. I just did a bit better than I figured and now each of them have a personal net worth of over $25.0 million. They are each receiving annual cash flow over $1,000,000 a year. None is employed. None has ambition. None has the least desire to use the education or opportunity provided. They have lived off me all their lives and I doubt that will ever change. So, why am I spending thousands of dollars a year on life insurance to provide them an even bigger estate? Why am I paying thousands of dollars in legal fees to create estate plans I can't understand? What's it all for? Just how much is enough for these kids? What have I done?

~Carl, Chicago, IL

It's clear, from what we have already covered so far, that legacy can neither be mandated nor guaranteed. It is often thoughtfully designed, carefully implemented, and perpetually nourished. It is also quickly lost and easily broken. Not all those for whom the legacy was created accept or appreciate their gift. For many, it is not even a gift, but perhaps an unwanted burden that robs them of their ambition or individuality.

There are many manifestations of legacy, but most certainly one is wealth. How wealth is transferred and how future generations are treated, prepared, and measured are among the most discussed issues in any analysis. Because of the obvious economic implications for professional advisors and financial service companies, this area—which is often lumped into the discussion of estate planning—receives the most attention and is often the area of greatest abuse.

From the perspective of family wealth advisors, legacy planning often means multigenerational estate planning. In other words, how can today's wealth be protected and preserved for future generations? In recent years, because of the combination of lifetime and deathbed income and transfer taxes, any discussion of estate planning for affluent families will inevitably include tax avoidance, protection from real or imagined creditors, protection against real or imagined future divorces, and even protection against the real or imagined financial incompetence of younger and future generations.

Driven by concerns over tax, litigation, and unprepared beneficiaries, many advisors have developed a host of sophisticated, complicated, expensive, and sometimes untested tools and techniques. The term "legacy" has come to mean, to some, a tax-driven arrangement in which wealth will be protected against attacks from all sources. But Carl's thought-provoking questions of "how much is enough" and "why do I want my wealth to pass to my descendants" is often not asked, much less answered.

It is our contention—and this book's as well—that real legacy is, of course, far more than the preservation of wealth. When a *Legacy Family* designs its wealth transfer plan, it focuses on impact, not tax, and flexibility, not perpetuity. The wealth transfer plan is guided and shaped by several fundamental principles.

Lifetime gifts should create opportunity but not remove the challenge

It's fun to give and even more fun to receive. A gift that is enabling, and that creates choice and opportunity, can open the imagination and stimulate the possible for both the giver and the recipient. But the wrong gift, or the wrong amount, at the wrong time and for the wrong reason, can do just the opposite. It can create dependency, expectancy, and even family jealousy. It can encourage indolence and divert otherwise capable individuals from their education or career choices.

A *Legacy Family* shares its good fortune with each family member, but only to make it possible to succeed, not to guarantee success. Parents are often tempted to make life "easier" for the child, but sometimes forget that it is life's challenges that forge character, discipline and courage. If this is not quite enabling them, it's certainly not empowering them, either. The better goal is to create more opportunity for your child to achieve, not to facilitate your child's retirement before success is even possible.

What's really at stake here is the family's work ethic, which is, after all, what built the wealth in the first place. A *Legacy Family* focuses on the process of building wealth, not the balance sheet or even the products that created the wealth. An estate plan that encourages financial competency, personal effort, willingness to accept appropriate risk, strong ethics, and best practices, is one which will develop new wealth, using the financial, human and intellectual capital provided by prior generations.

When Carl referred to his kids, he said *"None is employed. None has ambition. None has the least desire to use the education or opportunity provided."* Carl may have accomplished the wealth transfer goal, but it would be hard to conclude that he feels good about the result. Spreadsheets notwithstanding, saving the tax and losing the child is *not* a good plan. When asked what he really wanted for his kids, he said what many of us would have said:

> I want them to be successful in their own names. I don't want them to see me as an ATM machine or their own private social security system. No one made it easy for me. I thought I was doing the right thing for them to make their lives easier than I had it. If they take these funds for granted, what will it mean for my grandkids? Will they even have a chance?

Carl has stated that he wanted to make life easier for the kids than he had endured during his wealth building years; in that he is in good company. We all want our kids to thrive and be secure. Sometimes we mistake security and opportunity with ease and comfort. Security cannot be given to you. Ironically, some of the most insecure people we've ever met are the heirs of the Fortune 500 families. For many of these privileged individuals, life depends on how others manage and deal with their wealth. Never having created wealth (nor attained the skills required to do so), the possibility of losing it can be literally terrifying. (Witness the sudden rash of suicides appearing in headlines as the downturn in the economy affected those heavily invested in the volatile stock market and real estate futures.)

Instead of security, Carl should have focused on providing opportunity, fostering financial and life skills, and managing expectations. Instead of guaranteeing comfort and ease, he should ensure that each would be given the chance for personal success to create their own sense of comfort and ease—on their own terms. But remember one reality—you cannot achieve success without the risk of failure. In fact, the degree that one can fail in an effort actually defines the reach of your potential success. You can go bust in business, but you can reach the Fortune 500 list of the most successful businesses as well.

Ironically, Carl's proudest accomplishments were building a business that led an industry, gaining the respect of his peers and competitors, earning a visit to the White House, and sharing his good fortune with his alma mater and more Boys and Girls Clubs than he could visit in a month. Despite their considerable "riches," his kids will never have that joy, nor will they appreciate the opportunities given to them.

Gifts at death should reward effort, achievement, moral standards and strong values

With good parenting and a lot of luck, each of your children will aspire to personal achievement and productivity, and will live a life that reflects those core values with which you raised them. They won't be exact clones and will have their own variations of those values. But you hope that they will be compassionate and caring, thoughtful and appreciative, respectful and trustworthy, ethical and moral. Few families grow up in the serene image of a Norman Rockwell painting, but you certainly hope to raise children that won't sue you because you have failed to give them the wealth to which they think they are entitled!

In one of the most infamous cases, a 50-year-old son sued his 73-year-old father *and* his own 24-year-old son because of the fear that grandfather would leave more wealth to his grandson than to the son. Truth is stranger than fiction.

An inheritance is a gift, not an entitlement. When this message is lost, the meaning of the wealth is likewise lost. To reward a beneficiary at the time of one's death for life-long behavior that was considered inappropriate, excessive, counterproductive, or perhaps in direct conflict with the family's core values, is to encourage the continuation of the very behavior that was offensive in the first place. This does not mean that children, who choose a different lifestyle, career path, or religious framework, should be deprived or punished. Indeed, *Legacy Families* celebrate their diversity. But the family's core values are unlikely to survive when those who promote contrary values are rewarded. Additionally, this sends a very poor message to successor generations. Remember the family grapevine; when the prodigal son or daughter acts reprehensibly and still makes out like a bandit, what then is the motivation for anyone else to act otherwise?

Ruling from the grave is a good way to assure a
revolt from those who remain

When the wealth creator attempts to dictate the future career path, life-style, marriage criteria, or other expressions of individuality of future generations, the results are not surprising. Very often the same qualities that enabled the success of the wealth creator, including intelligence and imagination, stubbornness and drive, insight and creativity, focused achievement, and confident decision making oftentimes carry future generations in entirely different directions. As has been said by so many others, it's not the score that counts, but playing the game.

Your wealth has given your children something you may not have had—choices. What a privilege it is to be able to follow your own dreams and passions, knowing that there are resources available to enable you to be productive and contributive and be able to create a life of meaning for yourself without financial concerns or limitations. That is, after all, one of the great benefits of being your descendant.

One of our favorite *Legacy Families*, the Rockefellers, has produced industrial and business giants, civic leaders and philanthropists, artists and writers, loving parents and grandparents. Who amongst the generations of this family has contributed the most to their community? Each of those members who has fulfilled a personal dream, added to the composite of the family's history and legacy, raised another generation of educated and motivated young adults, and shared their time, talent, and treasure with their community, has fulfilled the vision of the founder of this extra-ordinary family.

Good planning anticipates and adapts

In case it was not obvious, the law as we know it today will be different next year, and every other year. The economic conditions, for individuals and for nations, will constantly change. The unexpected must be expected. What makes good business sense today may seem foolish tomorrow. Skills appreciated today may become extinct in the future. Long-range planning that does not contemplate such change and that can't be adapted to new realities will soon become oppressive and costly.

Unfortunately, much of today's estate planning is often designed to avoid the possibility of change. How will future generations feel if assets are forever locked away, under the control of others, when the estate tax is repealed, the marriage is solid, and creditors nowhere to be seen? Will the dragons of today become the house kittens of tomorrow?

Family businesses will evolve and maybe end, but
the family work ethic can endure

So much of current estate planning is focused on transferring and perpetuating the family business, despite all the statistics that demonstrate the improbability of retaining the majority of businesses past the second generation. Some may point to the onerous tax burdens that make the family business so difficult to retain. But this vastly miscalculates the importance that differences in individual lifestyle, skill, and interests of future generations plays in the decision to retain or dispose of the business. The greatest family wars have been fought over the business and rarely has the tax law been the real culprit.

There are many reasons why only about 40% of family businesses pass successfully from Generation One to Generation Two and less than half that again—or a paltry 12%—will ever survive in Generation Three. Sometimes it's because there's no passion for the business in the next generation; sometimes it's because family members lack sufficient competency to run the business. In some families, the goal is to take advantage of the financial wealth that can be generated from the sale of the business, so that each of the stakeholders can find their own careers and opportunities. In other cases, there's so much jealousy and competition amongst the inheritors that the financial consequences of selling are less onerous than the emotional consequences of keeping it together.

An estate plan that encourages financial competency, personal effort, willingness to accept appropriate risk, strong ethics, and best practices, is one which will develop new wealth, using the financial, human, and intellectual capital developed by prior generations.

Few people may remember how Generation One created the wealth. Was it oil? Was it steel or automobiles? Was it the railroad? (And what's a railroad, anyway?) But most everyone in the family will know how the wealth was left and what family fights or family achievements were generated along with it.

The moral of this story is that how you leave your wealth is much more important than how you earned it.

Effective wealth transfer is value driven, not tax driven

Perhaps the most challenging aspect of effective estate planning for *Legacy Families* is how to identify, nurture, and perpetuate the core values of this family. Beware of "parenting by spreadsheet." Wills, trusts, and other gifting arrangements that avoid the tax but lose the child are failures at best and tragedies for most.

Perhaps this is why philanthropy has become so important to *Legacy Families*. It has become a platform to teach responsibility, communication, compassion, collaborative decision making, life skills, and financial competency. It creates a message for future generations and it raises the level of family conversation from "what's in it for me" to "how can we make a difference to ourselves, our family, and our community?"

How much is enough and when is it too much?

How much of your financial wealth do you want your children to receive after you are gone? In reaching this conclusion, you may naturally choose to leave *everything* to them. But, before deciding, ask yourself...

How much will help them? How much will hurt them? And what lies in the balance? At what point will any gift to them be excessive or counterproductive, that is, undermine their own willingness or need to earn and become financially independent? Will the amount of wealth distract them from their chosen businesses or careers? Will it encourage them to retire on the date of your death, thus short-circuiting them of any personal legacy they may have been on the way to achieving themselves? Remember, too much, too soon, can be very harmful to motivation, drive, and work ethics.

Do they need your additional wealth, or have they achieved financial success on their own, or through your prior gifts? Will equality determine the size of your gift or are there differences in talent or opportunities amongst your children, so that you would like to help one more than the other? In making this decision, try to avoid enabling the underachiever who has the ability, but chooses not to utilize his or her talent, at the expense of the child who has achieved much through hard work, sacrifice, and talent. In other words, don't penalize those who have earned their success to reward the prodigal son(s) or daughter(s).

That being said, if a family member follows his or her passion into a career that does not provide great financial rewards, many *Legacy Families* provide some type of matching funds so that economics do not limit career choices. They recognize that one of the benefits of wealth is that it enables members to productively follow their passion without having to choose life work solely on the basis of financial returns. Likewise, if certain members of the family do not have the intellectual or emotional resources to be as successful as others, but have the attitude and effort, additional funding can be considered.

Have you built up expectations about your estate and your heirs' perception of their "rights" to it? This doesn't mean ignoring their concerns. In fact, we encourage discussion about your plans and hearing about their interests and goals. But you don't want to create the impression that their sole business in life is to preserve your estate for *themselves*. Look at each family member as an individual and answer the above questions as it may apply to him or her. Remember, anything you leave to the family is a gift, not an entitlement. Ignoring these questions can do more harm than good.

Some parents choose to leave assets to their children based on how much can pass tax free; others focus on how much will be left *after* taxes are considered, and yet others consider how much is appropriate. Remember the tax rules are changing, mercurial and are constantly evolving. The amount that may pass to your heirs tax free is now $3.5 million. What the tax rate will be through the coming years is anyone's guess. So, to set the gift amount to your children based on what the law then permits to pass tax free may result in too much or too little, depending on the tax year of the gift. It's unlikely that basing the size of the gift on the amount of the tax exemption will be just the right amount to meet their needs and your goals.

In deciding on the distribution plan for your children, prioritize your goals. Leave enough to enable the children to grow up comfortably and securely, and to complete their education and begin their careers. Believe it or not, owing to the habitual nature of human beings, leaving too much could actually impede this process. Avoid blanket gifts without plateaus or addendums. Instead, leave additional assets in such a manner as to reward hard work, initiative, and self-sufficiency. In other words, be aware of the danger that can occur when you provide an "allowance" or steady income to young adult children, when they should, at that point in their lives, become independent of your resources and actually "earn" such a privilege.

The estate plan is really just a continuation of the way you would have provided for your children and other heirs if you were still living, had all the resources you needed for yourself, and would be making decisions on a case-by-case situation for additional funding. Disregard taxes in this stage of your thinking. Instead, focus on how you would want your wealth to be used by others to increase self-sufficiency and decrease dependence. Finally, remember that how you leave your wealth, and the message it delivers to your children and future generations, will definitely affect how they live the rest of their lives.

Warren Buffett is famous for his response to the question "how much is enough." He was quoted in *Fortune* magazine, in 1986, to have said that he wanted to leave his children "... enough money so that they would feel they could do anything, but not so much that they could do nothing." In other words, how would you feel if the date of your death starts the beginning of your children's retirement, regardless of their age, stature, or degree of success and/or fulfillment? Do you really want them to start where you left off, without ever having learned from their own journey or reached for anything themselves?

In trying to answer this question, many parents choose to leave everything to their children. The results are not often what was expected or hoped. However, it is impossible to know how much the "right" amount is. Some parents choose to err on the side of leaving less, rather than more, in order to avoid the potential harm that is often caused.

The hard but essential task is to identify and explain the purposes for which you want to leave these funds. Here are some of the ideas that have been used by thoughtful families as they tried to answer the question "how much." Each of these goals represents different phases of your children's (or grandchildren's) lives and different objectives that you may have for them:

- *If your children are young and still in school, you'll want to ensure that there are sufficient funds to provide for their support, health, and education.* Some families describe this as their "Support Fund." It's not intended to provide a comfortable, easy lifestyle for mature adults, but it is intended to fund the cost of raising, educating, and launching the minor children into productive adulthood. This fund may provide additional resources for those individuals who will be the physical guardians of these minor children in the event of the untimely loss of parents. Sometimes the fund continues for several years after college age, as the child transitions from school to employment. But, by age 25 or so, this fund is usually exhausted.
- *After the children reach adulthood, you may want to ensure the resources to provide for their continued education.* Don't just think about college and graduate school for the 18–25-year-olds. Education is a lifelong process. Careers change. Some of our descendants will defer their formal education until long after their own children have grown and left the nest. They may choose to change careers in midlife or require personal or business coaching. These are all worthy objectives and often appropriate uses of family wealth.
- *For the entrepreneurs in the family, one of the greatest impediments to success is lack of capital.* With adequate capital, either to launch a business or to take it to the next level, opportunities expand dramatically. In an affluent family, capital or access to capital is more available. Some families call this their "Family Bank;" others describe it as the "Family Venture Fund" or "Opportunity Fund." Whatever the name, it's a source of capital that enables the beneficiary to combine education, life experience, personal drive, and ambition, with a solid and thoughtful

business plan to launch or enhance a new business and create new wealth.

- *Good health is a priority in every family.* But the cost of care often exceeds the resources of individual family members. You can set aside funds that will always be available to ensure the best quality health care for your family. But, be sure to carefully articulate exactly what "health" means to you. Does it include emotional and psychological health? Counseling and therapy? Drug and alcohol rehabilitation? In-home nursing? Prescriptive drugs? How about funding health insurance premiums or covering the deductible portion? Remember, for some heirs, a vacation in Hawaii for six months is *very* therapeutic!

- *Another concept that has appealed to families is a fund, sometimes called the "Legacy Fund," designed to cover the costs of your children and future generations creating or continuing annual family reunions and retreats.* Families that play together, learn together, and share experiences together have a much better chance of staying connected. While some family groups can well afford to pay the costs of these important gatherings, other family groups may not have the resources. By your allocation of assets for this specific purpose, the likelihood that these activities will continue is significantly greater.

- *Parents want to be sure that their children have the ability to own their home. It's a challenge today for young adults, especially as they get married and start their families, to afford the down payment on that first home.* You can help by allocating funds for the down payment. Be careful, however, about offering too big a residence. Not only might it seem inappropriate for the young adult to start with the "big house on the hill," it may be too expensive for him or her to maintain and will result in resentment for being placed in a situation where they are "house poor." One of the best models for this process is to offer to provide a down-payment up to a specific fraction of the purchase price (maybe 25% or 30%), subject to the condition that the child have sufficient *earned* income to service the debt on the rest. This tends to keep the size and cost of the home more in keeping with the age and circumstances of the child.

- *In some families, the next generation will produce teachers and writers, civic leaders and philanthropists.* It may not be easy for these individuals, who have had the privilege of following their passion and talents, but who may not have created significant wealth from their careers, to retire in comfort and security. You can ensure that there will be sufficient resources for them to do so. These assets are not expected to provide lifestyle support during their working years, but to protect each of them in the event that they may be unable to create the wealth they need at the time of retirement.

- *There could be many other reasons that you feel appropriate to leave wealth to your children and future generations.* As you define and describe these reasons, remember that someone, perhaps a trustee, will be asked to use his or her or even its interpretation of your goals. The more you have clearly articulated those goals, the easier it will be for those responsible in making allocations and distributions to carry out your wishes.

- *At some point, you may find that your accumulated wealth exceeds the amount necessary to provide for your heirs.* Even after the estate tax is covered, and taking into consideration some cushion you may want to leave on top of the other funding options, there may be excess. These additional resources could create the social capital that will play an important role in reinforcing the core values of the family as well as affording additional leadership opportunities for your extended family. Your philanthropic initiative may take the form of a family foundation that you create, either during your lifetime or upon your death, perhaps a donor advised fund at a community foundation, or directly to charities that you select. What the amount may be will vary depending upon the timing of your death and the size of your estate. You may prefer to allocate your estate in percentages or in flat dollar amounts to the various pools, some outright and unrestricted. The choice of how much to each, and for what purpose, is yours to make.

> *Conflict within wealth planning should be anticipated, not ignored*

Fighting over the wealth or over the management of the wealth is so commonplace that it sometimes seems like it's the norm rather than the exception. Some of the fights, especially within prominent families, have become the source of Hollywood movies and television shows. The weekly soap opera entitled *Dirty Sexy Money* is but one of the more recent iterations of this sad dilemma. When Liesl Pritzker, at the age of 18, filed a multibillion dollar lawsuit against her father, Robert, and 11 older cousins, accusing them of looting her trust funds and those of her brother, Matthew, 21, this action shattered the entire extended family as well as the wealth generator's dream of leaving a *Legacy Family*. However, with thoughtful planning you can avoid this type of heartache. Don't let your good intentions become either the cause of the conflict or the excuse for it.

Often conflicts are generated because of the dynamics of relationships within the family. These dynamics are the backdrop to conflict often triggered by otherwise logical wealth planning strategies and, as such, must be accounted for. Burying your head in the sand or thinking that "once they get the money they'll be satisfied" will only contribute to further strife down the line.

Among siblings, there may be varying levels of rivalry, sometimes leading to incompatibility and distrust. Some children may feel, and sometimes are treated, as the "favored" one. Jealousy and resentment by the remaining siblings are often the result. Therefore, the selection of one family member over another to receive certain assets or to be given certain power or authority over others may be the flashpoint that leads to open conflict and, in some cases, outright (legal) warfare. Such conflict may have simmered for years under the surface but, once the patriarch or matriarch is no longer here to control the situation, old "sandbox rivalries" may emerge.

Every family has its array of talents and skills, challenges and problems. There are likely many different levels of leadership, experience, intelligence, drive, and passion within each family. Each may have a different sense of entitlement and expectation. As a result of the wide range of qualities and characteristics within the family, the perceptions of and reactions to the planning strategies will likely be very different. Some reactions may be quite positive, while others can be benign or even poisonous to family harmony. We would all like that proverbial Rockwell painting family, but in its absence understanding the realistic environment and landscape of each family is essential to weaving a plan that is thoughtful and efficient, appreciated and appropriate.

Perhaps the most frequent source of conflict in the Family Wealth Plan is the shared ownership and management of the family business, financial and other investment assets, as well as personal-use assets, such as vacation property or the private plane. Each such shared asset has the potential for disrupting the family, reopening old wounds or highlighting the differences amongst the inheritors. The issues are varied and complex, but so common that Chapter Eight is entirely devoted to it.

An obvious source of tension is the allocation and distribution of the estate assets. Though usually well-intended by the wealth creator, with logical justification based on history and behavior, the perception of the inheritors (or their spouses, issue, or advisors) can be quite different and quite hostile. The list below details some of the issues *Legacy Families* need to resolve:

- *Equal vs. unequal allocations.* Some wealth creators wish to benefit the hard working and successful heir, rewarding achievement with a greater allocation. Others choose to help the heir who failed to accomplish similar economic results but who may need the extra resources to bridge the gap. Will rewarding the successful family member while punishing the failure in the family create conflict and hostility between them? Will the reverse plan send the appropriate message to the successful family member? How best to reward industriousness without punishing lack of vision?
- *Cumulative lifetime gifts vs. estate gifts.* Some parents wish to equalize gifts made amongst their children over their lifetime. For example, an unequal lifetime gift may have come in the form of a larger gift of a down payment on a home for one child than that provided to another child. A makeup provision often occurs at the death of the surviving parent. How will the makeup gifts be determined? Should the values be based on the same amount given during lifetime to others,

even though those recipients may have had years of use, income, and appreciation? Should the values be based on actual economic value or the discounted value that may have been used at the time of the gift? Will the different beneficiaries respect and accept the decision of the wealth creator or estate fiduciary?

- *Selection of assets.* Sometimes, in anticipation of the potential conflict created by shared assets, wealth creators allocate specific assets to different individuals. But will those assets have equivalent value? Is a business that must be worked daily and has significant downside risk as well as upside potential the equivalent of a passive investment that may have less upside but less personal effort and risk? Will the recipients of each perceive the economic equivalent or will they resent the selection made for their benefit?
- *Timing and amounts.* How much should be distributed to heirs and will such distribution incentivize and encourage hard work and financial independence, or will it generate dependency and indolence? How much should be distributed during career-building years and will it have a positive or negative impact on work ethic and lifestyle? How much should the wealth creator control from the grave? Should the wealth creator strive to ensure that future beneficiaries start where the wealth creator left off or should the wealth creator focus on providing the resources to allow the inheritors the opportunity to create his or her own success?

Sometimes the problems are created from lack of preparation or training:

- *Should wealth be left outright to those who are ill-prepared for its responsibilities?* Has the wealth creator prepared the inheritors for these responsibilities? Can and should beneficiaries be required to undergo financial skill training, including budgeting, credit management, and wealth creation, before distributions are made? If so, will the reward be incremental, that is dependent on how many classes/courses taken and will those who opt out of such further education be penalized?
- *Will shared assets left to heirs create financial exposure to each other because of the actions or inactions of one or more?* Will siblings find themselves in partnership with an ex-in-law, creditor, substance abuser, or trustee in bankruptcy?
- *Will handouts beget more handouts?* Heirs who have blown through their inheritance can become the family mooch, leaving siblings and cousins the distasteful task of either repeatedly bailing them out or providing continuous support out of pressure—or guilt.

Wealth creators and their advisors often turn to both professional and nonprofessional trustees to administer the wealth plan for the immediate and future generations of inheritors. Those professional trustees who are experienced in the field know how difficult and contentious this role can be. The explosion of fiduciary litigation between trustees and beneficiaries is an obvious indicator, and often the result of the following issues:

- *Selection and qualifications.* As careful as the planning may be, leaving the implementation and management to those individuals or organizations unqualified, poorly prepared or inadequately supervised can create antagonism, dysfunction, resentment and litigation. Who should be selected? Who should have the power to remove? If these fiduciaries are to function over time and perhaps for generations, how will future fiduciaries be selected and by whom?
- *Authority and responsibility vs. experience and expertise.* Perhaps private fiduciaries, whether family members or friends, will have the appropriate sensitivities to the family values to serve, but will they have the fiduciary experience and financial skills required? Will the selected fiduciaries have the impartiality needed to differentiate amongst beneficiaries and act as the wealth creator would have wished or anticipated? Should more than one fiduciary be appointed to act together? Can and should responsibilities be allocated between them?
- *Compensation of family trustees.* How will such fiduciaries be compensated and to what standards should they be held? Will they perform the same services at the same level of experience and training as the professional fiduciaries? If not, should they receive the same level of compensation?
- *Communication responsibilities.* Should fiduciaries be required to communicate clearly and regularly with beneficiaries? If each inheritor has a different learning style and perspective, should fiduciaries be required to communicate in a manner understood by each inheritor? Should the fiduciary have the educational responsibility to prepare the inheritors for the income and wealth being distributed?
- *Conflicts of interest of fiduciaries.* If fiduciaries are compensated based on the size of the assets under management, is there a conflict of interest that might discourage the fiduciary from making significant distributions to the beneficiaries?

Developing a comprehensive wealth plan requires the input and advice of a range of professional advisors, which may include financial experts, legal counsel, tax advisors, and professional fiduciaries. The team may also include a professional who has special training in family dynamics and qualitative issues. The challenge is to blend the skills and perspectives of the advisors with the goals, needs, and dynamics of the family. This is more challenging than it might appear, in part because of the different agendas of each participant, which may include any or all of the following:

- *Tax planning vs. value-based planning.* If the wealth creator is motivated to shift wealth to accomplish specific goals and perpetuate core values, then advisors who are primarily driven to minimize tax and maximize the amount of wealth transfer could be at odds with the intent of the wealth creator.

- *Mutual economic dependency.* Differences in goals and strategies amongst the advisors is not as much a risk to developing the appropriate strategies as the absence of independent judgment and perspective, sometimes caused by economic interdependence and cross referrals among the advisory team.
- *Personality vs. planning.* A desire to be the one in control of the client relationship can lead to power struggles among highly competent professionals.

How do you proceed through these landmines without losing credibility or injuring the feelings of others along the way? First, think about how your plan will function in real time and over time. Will it be practical and effective? Does it take the very real factor of human nature into account?

Second, communicate and dialogue with your adult children. Planning "for" them instead of "with" them is a risky business and far less appreciated. Never underestimate the value of "ownership" and trust that the more they know about your sincere and thoughtful reasoning behind an issue, the more they'll respect you for it and participate in facilitating it *with* you. Managing expectations is very important for setting the stage for a conflict-free transition of assets. Also, if they help you build it, they will likely own it.

Third, since we know that disagreements are inevitable, always create a process for resolving conflict that the parties recognize is both fair and equitable. This won't eradicate disputes altogether, but it will create a process for dealing with them effectively. Finally, surround yourself with advisors who focus on what's in your best interest, not theirs. In Chapter Twelve we'll explore how to build your own brain trust. Don't fly blind into areas that you have not experienced before; let a team of experts show you the way.

Every wealth creator and those that follow must ultimately ask the question...what will my legacy be? Will it be the size of my balance sheet or the values that shaped my life and upon which I have relied to shape the lives of others?

★   ★   ★

"Money brings some happiness. But after a certain point, it just brings more money."

~Neil Simon

CHAPTER SEVEN

The Family Bank

Dad, you know that I've always been intrigued with the world of business. Though nearly everyone tried to dissuade me, I majored in business and entrepreneurial studies at college and did well. For the last five years, I've worked at McElroy and Company and provided consulting services to growing mid-market companies. My focus was developing international markets for U.S. domestic enterprises. I've been successful and have been promoted steadily, but I still want to create a business of my own, much like you and grandpa did. But, to start my business, I need capital. I have to rent an office, buy equipment, and hire an assistant. I'm 27 and, if I start this business, I won't have any income for a while or hard assets to pledge to get a loan from our bank. I've got a good business plan; I know my field. I think I can be very successful, but not unless I can get started. Tony may feel that it's unfair that I get help from you when he has not received anything. But he's 30 and probably will want to stay in teaching. I don't want him to be upset with me, but I could really use your help.

~Katherine, San Francisco, CA

The source of much of the wealth that exists today was created by entrepreneurs through a combination of focus, drive, and great personal and professional risk. Many entrepreneurs struggled in the early years and even long into the process of wealth creation; for many of them, the greatest challenge was lack of capital.

Every entrepreneur has experienced the dilemma of seeking credit from financial institutions in order to fund start-up and expansion expenses. Not surprisingly, most lenders are reluctant to provide credit unless there is a proven track record, adequate security, and a steady source of repayment. So, how does an aspiring young entrepreneur get the resources necessary to even borrow funds to begin? In other words, if you're successful, everyone is there to help. When you're new and struggling, you're often all alone.

Legacy Families have an enormous advantage over *many* families because they have already created and accumulated wealth. Many wealth creators choose to leave their wealth to their children on the chance and hope that the heirs will use the funds to build their own successful businesses. Unfortunately, what often happens is that instead of being used responsibly, the funds are used to enhance an extravagant lifestyle and support a habit of unbridled consumption. This is not the path to a *Legacy Family*, but the pattern of "shirtsleeves to shirtsleeves" that, unfortunately, we see far too often.

Your Family's Private Equity Bank

The "Family Bank," which some call their "Opportunity Fund" or "Family Venture Fund," is designed to provide the seed business capital for the family's children and later generations. The goal is to provide resources for each generation to become independent and self-sufficient. But, unlike the typical trust fund for heirs, this arrangement is created to support their entrepreneurial inclination and passions. It becomes the family's internal venture capital resource, helping the heirs acquire, start, expand, or maintain their own business or career.

As one might imagine, this can be a significant motivator to individuals like Katherine who, even though they've proven themselves outside the family business, can borrow more successfully from the Family Bank than from commercial banks, thus securing funding for her carefully planned new business venture.

Investing in any new business, whether initiated by a family member or not, involves a high risk of failure and potentially modest financial returns. For precisely this reason, traditional commercial lenders are reluctant to provide funds and private equity firms are unlikely to back the venture of an untested, even if talented and ambitious, young entrepreneur.

Your "Family Bank" is designed to accept this risk for your descendants, whether you are here to make that decision or not. The risk of the new venture can be reduced by setting appropriate criteria for the investment in this type of business. To put this concept into perspective, think of this scenario. While you are living and have the resources to help one of your children get started in business, would you do so? If the answer is "yes," then we are only talking about how. The Family Bank ensures that this goal remains available long after you're no longer here to make those decisions yourself.

You don't need the formality of a Family Bank to implement this program during your lifetime. You can make these decisions on a case-by-case basis. Creating a program, whether formally through a trust or other structure, or informally, by just developing the rules and guidelines and making all the decisions when the opportunities arise, will give you a chance to test the criteria and adapt to realities that you discover along the way.

But without a more formalized structure, who will provide this specific type of funding after you're gone? If it is not clear to your children that you're willing to help seed their opportunities even though you may no longer be physically present, many of them will never allow themselves to dream the possibilities in the first place or, they will feel that they have to settle for less favorable and more limited options. The allocation of funding for a Family Bank assures family members that they are not just another number in the traditional banking system.

Keep in mind that the Family Bank is not intended to provide ongoing income for the daily needs of successor generations. Heirs should not look at the Family Bank as a source of their lifestyle income. It is only to be utilized as an opportunity to launch or expand the business venture that will later produce that income. They should clearly understand that these resources are to be used to capitalize their business, not replace it.

How Should You Design Your Family Bank?

There are a variety of ways to design a Family Bank. Usually it's formed as an irrevocable trust, either during the wealth creator's lifetime or at his or her death. It could be created as part of a larger trust fund that can be used for the beneficiary's education, health, and other traditional purposes, as well as seeding a new business opportunity.

This arrangement enables the fund to be used wherever it may be required. Its flexibility is helpful and keeps the resources available to meet a wide range of possible needs. But it can also create some tension. Whoever the decision maker may be, usually a trustee, he or she must decide whether to "risk" the capital on a new business for the beneficiary or to hold back most of the funds because of other possible needs, such as education or health.

The problem is magnified exponentially if there are multiple beneficiaries. Naturally, the needs or interests of one beneficiary can often conflict with the expectations and requirements of another. The more beneficiaries that are involved, the more challenges are likely to ensue in deciding how to allocate limited financial resources. If the funds are used disproportionately for one beneficiary compared to the remaining beneficiaries, there can be resentment and jealousy. This is certainly likely if one beneficiary is an adventurous entrepreneur, while another beneficiary is a risk-averse school teacher or public servant who might never qualify for this type of funding.

In the prologue of this chapter, we heard from a young 27-year-old burgeoning entrepreneur who felt herself ready to take that first step. Her story is a good example of the challenges involved. At first glance, Katherine makes a very appealing request. She's had the schooling and training, has created a reasonable business plan, and certainly has the ambition and drive. What would hold you back?

In this family, it was Katherine's father who was forced to wrestle with this problem. His son, Tony, is bright and a wonderful primary school teacher. His career path seems clear, at least for now. But the children were always competitive and, though close as adults, might react differently to Dad providing funds for Katherine without mention—or even stipulation—of future, equal funds for Tony. How might Tony feel if his younger sister received these dollars, when he would not have the required business purpose to qualify for the same?

Other questions plagued Dad as well. What if Katherine's business venture failed? How would this affect the remaining funds in the estate and how much should Katherine then receive as an inheritance? Should this be a gift? A loan? An investment? We'll revisit more of the these questions in a moment, but the first question parents should consider is whether to set aside some funds for those in the family, today and through the generations, specifically devoted to capitalizing business opportunities.

Dad also had to decide whether to create one large fund that can be utilized by both children, even though he knows that it's likely only one of them will take advantage of it, or to create separate funds for this purpose for each of the children and their future branches. In this case, Dad chose to split the assets into separate funds, primarily because of the existing competitiveness between Katherine and Tony, but also because he didn't want the success or failure of either child to affect the resources available to the other. In other words, he didn't want Katherine's use of the resources to deprive Tony or his future children of an equal financial opportunity.

Once you decide to create the trust structure for a Family Bank, you will need a trustee or cotrustees for its administration. The choice of this individual or group of individuals, commercial trust company, or some combination of these alternatives, will determine its immediate and long-term success. Trustees must understand your intent and the specific criteria for heirs to access these funds, be willing to devote the time and attention that will be required to do the job correctly, and be prepared to make hard decisions. Trustees need to consider your priorities and expectations, as well as the family dynamics (like the competitiveness between Katherine and Tony). The process will operate much more successfully if your current family members as well as future potential beneficiaries realize what's expected of them and what they might expect in return. Because this trust is often designed to remain for several generations, the clarity of purpose and criteria will be critical for all those affected by the decisions.

The process of selecting, removing, and compensating trustees should also be very clear and practical. Each person or organization serving in this role will expect to be protected from possible verbal and legal attacks from disgruntled or rejected beneficiaries. So, be sure to indemnify these fiduciaries with respect to their management and discretionary decisions, provided that they have acted in good faith, and not with intentional or reckless disregard for their duties.

Be Clear About Your Goals

The Family Bank is usually created to continue for many generations. Therefore decision making in the future will not be done by the
individual(s) who created the Family Bank. What would you want that
individual or trustee to understand about your motivations for creating
this fund? How would you allocate funds for this purpose? Who are your
primary beneficiaries and what are their strengths and weaknesses?

When you create the Family Bank, document your goals as if you were
in the room talking directly to your descendants Let them understand
the many reasons why you feel so strongly about this fund, who are its
intended beneficiaries and what are your expectations. This exercise is
important for those making the decisions on your behalf as well for those
who seek your help.

Encouraging entrepreneurship is one obvious reason for creating a
Family Bank, but there can be important educational goals as well. You
may want to encourage family members to learn business principles, how
to read and understand financial statements, credit, budgeting, negotiating, and investing. Fiscal competency is as good a reason for creating
this fund as any. It will be useful for heirs to learn how to manage wealth
and to work with professionals in the fields of finance, business, law, and
accounting. You may feel it appropriate that these funds be used to teach
other critical life skills, such as leadership and collaborative decision making, effective verbal and written communication, and conflict resolution. All these attributes and skills can be appropriate utilization of the
resources in a Family Bank.

The fact that you are setting aside resources to be used through the
generations to help launch the entrepreneurial efforts of your descendants
should not be interpreted by anyone to indicate that you have less respect
or appreciation for other career paths.

In every family tree, within each generation and over many generations,
there will be a wide range of career interests. Some will become teachers
or craftsmen, scientists or physicians, lawyers or accountants. Some family
members may choose to pursue other lifetime dreams far from that of an
entrepreneur including spending their lives raising their children. Some
may devote their time to public service and philanthropy.

The Family Bank is not intended to provide for every career choice
or lifestyle. Its primary focus is to provide the resources to capitalize and
launch the entrepreneurship of those members of the family so inclined.
To provide for the nonbusiness activities of your descendants, resources
may be provided in other trust vehicles if you so desire.

The same can be said of education. A fund for the education of your
descendants is valuable, but only to those who seek to take advantage of
such opportunities. A fund for health will likely be used more by some
than others. But, by setting aside a fund for entrepreneurship, which
accepts a higher level of risk and is willing to support the future business

success of your children and issue, those who aspire to this life's work will know that the resources are available for them.

How Much Should You Allocate to the Family Bank?

The Amount of assets contributed to the Family Bank, whether in one fund or a separate fund for each beneficiary, depends upon a variety of factors that include the time horizon anticipated before the assets or earnings will be needed, your investment style and risk tolerance, and your willingness and capacity to transfer assets.

How much capital do you feel will be needed to provide the resources for your initial beneficiaries? Some parents answer this question by trying to calculate, in today's dollars, what they might be willing to provide each of their young children who want to go into business at some point in the future, assuming that the child is then fully qualified, educated, trained, and mentally prepared to do so.

Using a present value calculation, they then fund at a level which, over time, will likely grow to that dollar equivalent, Of course, inflation and taxes will erode the value, so don't forget to think about those factors when considering the original amount. But, if you have time on your side, you'll be surprised by how little may be necessary to ensure that the funds are there for your children at the time they will need it. It's not much different than funds set aside today for the college education of your children tomorrow, and clearly a small price to pay for capitalizing the entrepreneurial efforts of your descendants.

Other parents start by deciding how much they want to leave their children for all the reasons we talked about in Chapter Six. Let's say you've decided that $5.0 million is enough for each child. You might then allocate those dollars into various purposes, from education, purchasing a home and funding health care needs, to launching new business opportunities.

How much you choose to leave to your children, for what purposes and under what conditions, are amongst the most difficult family wealth issues you are likely to face as you continue your march toward becoming a *Legacy Family*. But, once you have wrestled with this task, you will be able to begin the process of funding the Family Bank, or at least preparing the structure and process for it, so that you will know that, should future members of your family choose to follow a path of entrepreneurship, risk, and wealth creation, the money will be there to help them do so.

What Criteria Do You Want to Impose for a
Beneficiary to Qualify for These Funds?

Determining Who May or May Not benefit from the funds allocated to your Family Bank begins with a series of soul-searching questions that must be asked and answered before deciding who gets what, how much, and under what conditions.

Would you be comfortable if the Family Bank you worked so hard to create funds the business opportunity of one of your children who dropped out of school, had no experience in the business to be created, or shown any talent, much less drive or ambition to go into business? Would you seed a business venture to be started by your son's college roommate, who has offered a partnership to your son, mostly because of your capacity to fund the deal, even though your son has never expressed or demonstrated any interest in that type of business? If the answer to these types of questions is negative, then you are beginning to set the criteria you expect others to follow.

It's just as important to understand what you would refuse to do as it is to understand what would be acceptable to you. Remember, your aspiring child or future descendant should not be expected to follow your footsteps in the business you created, though this might be welcomed. This fund is intended to encourage your family member to dream big, prepare well, and work hard in whatever career path captures his or her passion and drive.

What are some important qualifications for funding that you might identify? Some Family Banks define the criteria in this manner:

- *The beneficiary should be required to demonstrate to the trustee that he or she has the business skills and has created a thoughtful business plan that will help to ensure success.*

  The business skills might include those usually taught in undergraduate departments and graduate business schools, such as finance, marketing, strategic planning, and leadership. Some of the potential beneficiaries may not have gone through these programs at the university. There are postgraduate programs, apprenticeships, and continuing education classes that can supplement the learning. Some beneficiaries may demonstrate their qualification by past business activities in which they have been successfully engaged.

  If the beneficiary needs help in crafting a business plan, a skill that even many MBAs have trouble in mastering, you can permit the trustee to fund the cost of having others help the beneficiary develop and prepare the business plan. The threshold should be high, but not so high that only the "A" students can achieve. Most entrepreneurs were not straight-A students. Were you?

- *The trustee might also require the beneficiary to utilize his own available personal financial resources, to the extent practical.*

  This might be important to be sure that the beneficiary feels engaged and committed to the project. If they have "skin in the game," namely personal funds of their own to contribute or that you perhaps "match," they may pay more attention to each step of the start-up.

- *The beneficiary must have worked in the industry or business for a minimum of several (e.g., three to five) years before being qualified to receive funding for his own business.*

The beneficiary should be ready for the responsibilities ahead and should have the skills necessary to be successful in this new venture. By demonstrating experience and commitment through working in the field, whether through an internship or as a paid employee, both the trustee and beneficiary will feel more comfortable in funding this venture.

- *The beneficiary must commit to working full time in the business as long as the Family Bank has an interest in it.*

    If your goal includes your desire to launch your son or daughter's business career, then a part-time involvement may not be appropriate to meet this goal. This commitment is intended to separate the casual participant or fly-by-night inventor from the truly dedicated business owner.

Remember, these are only some suggestions for appropriate criteria to stimulate your thinking in this area.

If we revisit the background of Katherine, the focus of our case study earlier on in this chapter, you'll recall that she completed her college education, spent five years working in the field of her interest, had a real perspective of where she could make her mark, had demonstrated success in her current career, and has clearly expressed admirable passion and dedication. She's a good bet for success.

The more beneficiaries and potential beneficiaries, the more questions arise. For instance, what if it's not your bloodline heir who needs the capital to start the new business, but it's your heir's spouse and your in-law. Would you still be willing to fund the opportunity? Would your criteria for funding change? If your first inclination is hesitation or even rejection, remember that your son-in-law or daughter-in-law is the parent or future parent of your grandchildren and the most important person in your child's life. By enabling that entrepreneur to build a business, you are enhancing the quality of life for your child and grandchildren. It's perfectly appropriate, however, to be sure that the ownership of that business will be equally shared by both your in-law and child.

How May Your Funds Be Used?

We've already touched on some of the ways these funds can be used, but ultimately it's up to you to define what you feel would be reasonable and appropriate. Many Family Banks permit the use of the funds to complete the family member's business training and preparation, as well as developing the business plan for the new venture. Other typical applications include starting a new business as well as purchasing an existing company. You can permit the family member to buy out the interest of an existing partner in a company already created or expand the family member's existing business so that it can grow to the next level.

If you create the Family Bank during your lifetime and offer these funds to your adult children, you may find your good intentions tested. Not every member of today's younger generation is interested in yesterday's businesses or even today's businesses, for that matter. The "new" economy of high technology and biotechnology, global finance and health care, may not be as interesting to a generation more interested in creating tomorrow's businesses. These ideas may seem odd or foreign, but many of the parents of the giants in our computer-driven, Internet-based, virtual office world thought these ideas were foolish, a waste of their time, and likely to fail. You may find one of your children committed to developing the new form of veggie fuel for automobiles that uses recycled vegetable oil instead of gasoline or diesel and eliminates both waste and emissions. Will you be willing to hear the next generation—or instruct your trustees to do the same—even when their ideas may seem crazy and farfetched, though based on sound and practical logic?

However, some business ventures may seem too "low tech" for many parents. The aspirations of your children and future generations may be much lower than your own. Will you feel comfortable funding even low-tech ideas if they come from your beneficiaries or their loved ones? After all, opening and operating a yoga studio, a poetry café, or a tanning salon may not be at the level that you had expected or dreamed about for your son or daughter, but it may be his or her dream. Acquiring and running a Harley-Davidson retail and repair shop may defy your *Car & Driver* sensibilities, but could feel like a dream come to true to your "hog" fanatic son.

Remember, failure *is* always an option. In fact, it is the very risk of failure that helps to define success in today's entrepreneurial and competitive times. If your young entrepreneur cannot fail, then it's unlikely he or she ever really started. Businesses do fail, sometimes because of poor management, often because of inadequate capital, and sometimes just because the market wasn't there in the first place or shifted suddenly. Those of you who invested in typewriter companies and rotary phone manufacturers, video companies that relied on Beta version tapes and cameras that required Eastman Kodak film, will appreciate how technology and the marketplace can change and, in some cases, replace entire industries. Many entrepreneurs experienced several failures before finding their "home run." Would one failure, notwithstanding the most conscientious effort, eliminate that heir from reapplying for funding for a new venture?

How should the Family Bank disburse its funds to benefit the family member? The answer will depend on a number of factors. There are both business considerations as well as tax issues.

Of course, the Family Bank can just make an outright distribution to the requesting and qualified family member. This is the simplest and most direct method. Assuming that the family member handles the funds appropriately, the results could be exactly what you had intended. However, without clear guidelines such a setup is ripe for abuse.

For instance, the amount of the funds being sought may be considerably more than you may want to distribute outright, especially if there are preconditions and stages of funding that you establish. Once given away the dollars will be gone and, in time, the Family Bank may be depleted. In other words, a distribution to this generation of family members might prevent the next generation from enjoying this resource.

Alternatively, the Family Bank could loan funds to the family member or directly to the business. For start-up and early-stage companies, providing a loan to it or the family member may create more burden than can be supported, either by the individual or the company. A true loan bears interest and a repayment schedule. The Internal Revenue Code publishes a minimum interest rate that must be charged on intra-family loans. This rate, known as the Applicable Federal Rate or "AFR" is reset every month. It will vary depending upon whether the loan is short- (under three years), mid- (three to ten years) or long term (over ten years).

While the AFR is generally less than commercial rates, it's still a financial burden on a new or young company and one that may be impossible or impractical to meet. You can't just say *"we won't ask for repayment"* because a "loan" that is ignored or forgiven could and likely will be recharacterized by the IRS as a gift.

If you've made a gift, failed to report it, and paid the gift tax, you might find yourself (or your Family Bank) subject to interest and tax penalties. The interest you forgave may still be imputed to you, on which you're expected to pay income tax. So, for simply "forgiving a loan" you could be treated as having made a taxable gift, while still having to pay income tax on interest payments you never received. By and large, this doesn't work too well!

In addition, a company with preexisting debt will have a very difficult time securing commercial loans. These lenders expect and often require a priority position. They don't like to be in secondary position to other lenders. In many cases, the very absence of personal capital in the business is enough to preclude a line of credit or other form of commercial financing. As a company grows, such financing can be crucial. If not designed and implemented properly, the Family Bank can actually get in the way of the normal banking and capital markets.

Another option is that the Family Bank can actually take an equity position in the business venture. Sometimes this equity position is in the form of common ownership, such as common stock, and sometimes it's in the form of a limited ownership, such as preferred stock. The advantage of a preferred stock type ownership is that it qualifies as capital, not loans, but has a more limited upside potential. This enables your family member to enjoy a larger piece of the upside of the venture, while still not having to service a debt on the participation of the Family Bank. Preferred stock usually has a dividend feature, but this doesn't mandate payment and won't interfere in the rights and priorities of the commercial lender. Your heir can be given the option to purchase the subordinated equity position held by the Family Bank, once the need for the capital no longer exists.

In other nonstock business structures, similar classes of ownership can be created, so that the Family Bank has the benefit of a share of the business, which will be used to replenish the coffers for the next family member who needs this resource.

Some Important Loose Ends

As in any sophisticated plan that is expected to span generations, make decisions under circumstances that we can only imagine, and deal with personalities that could range from angelic to demonic, there are difficult design and structural challenges with which to contend. The tax law will limit some of your choices and make the design even more complicated than might otherwise be required. A few suggestions if you choose to pursue this strategy:

- Try it out informally first, to get a handle on some of the issues and challenges. Giving some version of the Family Bank a "test run" will help you formulate a more practical program when the final version is implemented at some later point.
- After the structure is formalized, create a process by which future changes can be incorporated into the program. Sometimes trustees are given this authority and sometimes an outside party with special authority to act, perhaps a "trust protector" or "special trustee," is established. Change is certain, but you would like the change to further your objectives, not conflict with them.
- Discuss your hopes and aspirations, expectations and concerns, with your children. Listen to their responses. If they help you build it, they are most likely to buy into it and support it. Their buy-in is important, since the first generation to take advantage of this program will have much to say about its value to future generations.

★   ★   ★

"To hell with circumstances; I create opportunities."

~Bruce Lee

CHAPTER EIGHT

Family Shared Assets

Be careful what you wish for. We all wanted grandfather's ranch. It was 80 acres, a lake, three homes, a barn, and horses for all. He left it to mom and mom left it to my four siblings and me. Mom's lawyer was smart. He figured out how we could inherit without having to sell the property to pay taxes. He forgot; however, to mention what happens after we inherited. I wanted to keep the property for my family to use and enjoy. Summer on the ranch was a way of life for us. My older brother was totally uninterested in using the property. Sell it and give him cash. Others wanted to tear everything down and subdivide. The interstate is less than a mile away. The property was worth multiples of the current value if we rezoned for commercial use. Family meetings always fell apart because our agendas were so different. We have no way to manage this property. Two nephews are living free on the property, making a mess of the big house and using the horses as their personal toys. We can't even get everyone to pay their share of the property taxes and annual upkeep. If it weren't for the leasing of the range to local ranches for feed, we'd have real problems.

~Roy, Cheyenne, Wyoming

If you have an estate that includes virtually anything beyond cash and publicly traded securities, it's likely you're going to leave assets to your heirs that will be shared. Do you own an operating business? Family office? Vacation property? Investment real estate? Farm and ranch land? Personal residences? How about your boat or plane? Is there a family foundation in existence or perhaps in your future?

These family shared assets can be most any asset in which two or more family members (or trusts created for their benefit) own, control, and enjoy economic benefits from the asset. Everyone who has an economic or personal-use interest in the asset has a stake in the outcome. This will certainly include family members, but it could also include your ex-spouse or ex-in-laws. Let's call all the individuals, including nonfamily investors or partners, as interested "Stakeholders."

With all the obvious advantages of inheriting or controlling wealth, there are equally obvious challenges.

- Who has the right to use the asset? Who decides if there are competing requests for the use of the asset? Should rent or other fees be paid by Stakeholders who use the asset?
- How is income shared? Who decides if, when, and to what extent income is distributed?
- Who pays for the operating expenses and the capital improvements? What happens if one or more of the family owners fails to do so?
- Who pays for damages to the asset, especially if a family member was the cause of the damage? What are the consequences to the family member for failure to pay for the repair?
- Who has the power to decide to sell the asset? Encumber the asset? What if there is disagreement among the Stakeholders?
- What if an owner wants to sell his or her share? Is it permitted? Who sets the price and terms? Who has the right to purchase shares? Does the family want or will they accept a nonfamily buyer or transferee?
- What if one or more current owners want to acquire the interest of others? Is that permitted? Who sets the price and terms? How will it be offered?

For these reasons, *Legacy Families* develop a comprehensive agreement amongst all Stakeholders. It may seem unnecessary at this point, since everyone gets along so well. But don't fool yourself. The more Stakeholders, the more agendas. The more agendas, the more possibility for disagreement, leading to arguments, leading to breaks in relationships, sometimes irreparable.

Enter the "Family Shared Asset Ownership Plan"

The Family Shared Asset Ownership Plan focuses on the long-range goals, dreams, needs, and expectations of the family owners and other Stakeholders, including children and in-laws, and perhaps the adult grandchildren, each of whom have an interest in or expectation of equity in, income from, or use, of a Shared Asset. If these voices are not heard, expect anything from internal discord to public fighting and even litigation.

The Plan articulates the collective vision of these Stakeholders, and establishes the process, policies, and procedures to be followed in the operation of the Shared Asset. It sets realistic expectations, defines responsibilities, and assures accountability. It does not, nor can it, assure the continued financial success or economic benefit of the Shared Asset. That achievement is, of course, the common goal of many of the Stakeholders. But it will give those who chose to continue the Shared Asset the best chance to do so, while helping to reinforce the bonds of family and perpetuate the legacy of the wealth creator.

Remember our *Legacy Family* in the Introduction? The Andersons are now in their fourth generation following the wealth creators, Homer and Louisa Anderson. Besides the 20 blood relatives that are living today, there are in-laws and step-children, ex-spouses, and a host of nonfamily members that are involved in their businesses and real estate investments. There's a foundation and a scattering of donor advised funds in various community foundations. The crisis of ownership arose in Generation Three (G3).

The family company is operating under four divisions—farming; shipping; natural resources, and real estate development. There are numerous privately owned investments in which siblings and cousins have either a partnership or a membership interest in a limited liability company. There's a large family foundation on which each of the descendants of the three children of Homer and Louisa are represented. The collective wealth of this family is substantial and the foundation is both large in size and important in its impact in each of the communities in which it serves.

It was at the time of G3, when the business really grew in value, that the threat to the continued success of the Anderson Family became real. There was real dissention over how the business and its divisions were to be governed. Some members thought it was time to sell. Others just wanted more income distributed and less retained for the company's future growth. There were real battles over whether an Anderson descendant was entitled to work for the company, regardless of talent or attitude. The conflict exploded when one of the heirs, fresh from six months of a drug rehabilitation program, and completely without skills or experience, was being wedged by powerful family members into the company in a position that was neither needed nor appropriate for this level of applicant.

The family foundation was not spared from the conflict, which had spilled over into the personal relationships and other nonbusiness activities. Simmering jealousy and competitiveness made working together, even on such constructive and positive tasks as contributing to worthy causes, increasingly difficult.

It could have exploded on both an economic and emotional level. But it didn't. Why not? Because this family had figured out that they were stronger and more prosperous together than they would ever be apart. Over a nearly three-year span of time, G3 and Generation Four (G4) hammered out a long-range plan that defined their collective vision, set the rules under which they would conduct themselves and deal with their overlapping issues, and manage and enjoy their shared assets. They started with their Strategic Plan and Family Constitution. And they incorporated a set of principles in each of their shared assets, including their company's Stockholder Agreement, and each of the partnership agreements and limited liability company operating agreements. In those assets held for their personal use and enjoyment, like the Aspen home that G4 members, Josh and Carl, own together, they crafted a special agreement between their two families.

Here are the key areas that the Andersons and other *Legacy Families* incorporated into their agreements. Depending upon the type of the shared asset and activity, some of these topics would be more relevant and important than others. But, the process of addressing the day-to-day operational challenges of a Shared Asset is the same in every case.

- *Ownership—today, tomorrow and over time.* Who will be allowed to own this Shared Asset? Some families want to ensure that the Shared Asset remains within the family and is not allowed to pass to a non-family member. But just who is a "family member?" This question should have been answered in the Family's Strategic Plan. But, even if it has, such definition is a statement of intent but it won't bind anyone who has signed a partnership agreement or stockholder agreement or other formal legal document of ownership. That definition should be incorporated in each of those ownership and operating agreements.

  In each of those agreements, there must be clarity about how ownership may be transferred and to whom. What happens in the event of divorce or death? What if an owner breaches the agreement and transfers the interest in the asset to someone or something that is not qualified? If the interest was placed in a trust, but the beneficiary of the trust is not a "family member" is this ok and, if not, what are the consequences to the transferor or transferee?

- *Governance—policies and procedures that determine long-term decision making with respect to the Shared Asset.* What rights do the owners of the Shared Asset have to decide on the long-term issues regarding this Asset? Who has the right to determine if the Asset is sold, exchanged, refinanced, redeveloped, or used by family members? If additional capital is needed to maintain or expand the Asset, who has the right to demand those funds and what happens if some of the owners refuse or are unable to comply? Who is providing oversight to those delegated the responsibility of the day-to-day management of the Asset?

  If this were a public company, there would be a Board of Directors that provided the oversight and represented the interests of all the shareholders. In a family like the Andersons, with over 20 descendants and more than 40 Stakeholders, if you count spouses, step-children, and even trustees, it wouldn't be practical to have everyone involved providing such oversight and policy-making decisions.

  Just who chooses those responsible for the governance of the Shared Asset? How long will these individuals continue in that role? What if the Stakeholders wish to replace their representatives, can they do so and what's the process? Will they be compensated for the time spent on this task? If there's a potential for personal liability as a result of governing this Asset, will those who participate be protected by all the Stakeholders through insurance or some form of indemnification?

- *Management—day-to-day operations of the Shared Asset.* No matter how the governance and oversight is designed, someone will have to be responsible for the day-to-day management. If this were an operating business, such management would fall on the shoulders of the CEO or president. In a partnership or limited liability company, it might fall on the general partner or managing member. These legal structures have well-defined leadership and the agreements often detail such manager's authority. But personal-use assets, like the vacation home, family ranch, airplane, or boat, do not always have an obvious or formal manager. Just how much authority do the Stakeholders want to delegate to the manager? Will this decision be left to the governing group (Board of Directors or a family council, if created)?

  One of the common areas of dispute within families is the absence of oversight of the manager. So, for example, in a family business in which one or a few family members are active in the management, the inactive family members have virtually no say, no oversight, no policy-making role. This often leads to a lack of transparency in the operations. Inevitably, when owners don't know what's going on within a business in which they have a substantial stake, some will become suspicious, leading to intrusions and perceived interference in the operations.

  At the same time, a manager who is subject to the direction of multiple owners, each of whom thinks he or she is in charge, will have a difficult time functioning. . It's no easier when the manager is a nonfamily member caught in between the conflicting demands and priorities of family members. In one well-known fourth generation family business on the west coast, it was the inactive fourth generation owners that forced the third generation (their parents, uncles, and aunts) to fire the nonfamily CEO because of perceived biases in the operation of the business and lack of shared goals. Every manager needs clear direction, delegated authority, a policy-making group that has the power and authority to set budgets and approve long-range strategic decisions, and protection against the attempts by individual Stakeholders to exercise management control.

- *Compensation—of those who manage and maintain the Shared Asset.* A constant source of friction among family Stakeholders is whether and how much to compensate another family member for the services rendered in managing or overseeing Shared Assets. Inevitably, those who perform the services on behalf of the family Stakeholders feel underappreciated and under compensated. It's not unusual to hear the complaint "I've made them a fortune, and all I get are complaints and criticisms."

  But the problem often starts with the wealth creator, who rarely differentiates the economic benefit of being the manager of the business or investment from being the owner of that asset. So, besides a reasonable compensation paid for the services as the president of the company, the founder often takes considerably higher salary and bonuses, as well as other taxable and nontaxable benefits, that come from the profits of the enterprise. It's no wonder that when one of the members of the next generation, upon assuming the role of president of the company, continues to draw similar compensation, he or she often earns the disdain of other family Stakeholders.

The solution to this dilemma is relatively straightforward. In the Shared Asset Agreement, whether in the form of a Stockholder's Agreement, Operating Agreement, or Partnership Agreement, the compensation of an employed family member should be based on the marketplace. What would you have to pay a comparably qualified nonfamily member for performing the same job? What economic and noneconomic benefits would you likely have to provide? If bonuses are appropriate, what are the benchmarks and metrics that would justify such a benefit? If stock options or other forms of corporate rights is appropriate for the type of business and level of responsibility, this may be appropriate in your circumstance as well. It's the governing body that sets this compensation, oversees performance, and holds the executive or manager accountable. That is why the creation of such a body (i.e., Board of Directors) is so important but is often neglected in family run enterprises.

- *Profit allocation—economic return to owners.* The owners of a business or investment expect to derive a profit from their interests. But, the expectations of profit and access to those dollars are likely to differ dramatically amongst the Stakeholders. There will be those who need or want little of the profit, perhaps because they are more interested in building wealth, through expanding the business or growing the investment assets, or because they have sufficient earnings from the business or other activities to meet their lifestyle. There could be tax implications as well, since distributions of salary or bonuses, dividends or rents, might be less efficient.

Other Stakeholders may expect and need more income. Sometimes they need these funds to support their lifestyle. Sometimes they are measuring the return on their investment and demanding performance similar to other assets in their portfolio. When those results are different, it may just be because their sibling or other family member is taking too much out in the way of personal compensation. For some, the need or desire to build wealth is not as compelling as it may be to others. Either because of a difference in their risk tolerance or their personal agendas, these individuals can put unrelenting pressure to increase bottom-line profits and distributions, regardless of the potentially adverse impact on the business or its ability to grow or respond to changes in the marketplace.

The most contentious circumstance is when the Shared Asset generates profit, taxable to each owner in proportion to his or her ownership, but the managers decide to withhold all or a meaningful portion of the cash that might be necessary by some to pay the tax on the profit. So, a Sub-Chapter S corporation, or a partnership or limited liability company, may have profit, but the owners who are required to pay the tax may not have the cash to do so. This "phantom income" can lead to insurrection within the family and cannot continue indefinitely without resulting in serious conflict.

Each Shared Asset Agreement should set forth the policy of the Stakeholders with respect to the standards for distributing profits. At a minimum, cash should be distributed to meet the tax obligations of the owners created by the earnings of the Asset. If there is a realistic and appropriate need to maintain reserves, in order to meet the cash requirements of the Asset, including changes in market conditions, capital improvements, regulatory or creditor minimums, then this takes priority over the demands of the Stakeholders. Thereafter, some formula for distributing profits versus expanding the business or investment might be appropriate. How this formula is developed, reviewed, and modified over the years should be defined in the Agreement, and the decision is one that the governing body (Board of Directors, family council, or the like) or a stated percentage of all the Stakeholders would have authority to modify.

• *Communication—to all Stakeholders on information, decisions, and performance.* As we have seen in Chapter Three, communications amongst family members is critically important. Sometimes we take for granted that everyone we speak to uses and understands the same language that we do. Nowhere is this more evident than in the reporting done to the Stakeholders of a family business or investment asset.

In the well-run family business or real estate partnership, the chief financial officer, controller, or accountant is charged with the preparation of detailed financial statements, including profit and loss, change in financial condition, and balance sheet. Financial benchmarks and standards are often included, and ratios and returns are prominently displayed. What more can a Stakeholder request or want beyond regular, periodic, and professionally prepared financial statements? This is a left-brain–thinker's food for the mind.

However, for a substantial percentage of individuals in every family, the very appearance of a formal financial statement is intimidating. They can't read it, much less understand it. The terms are in a foreign language. The numbers are meaningless. For the right-brain–oriented family members, concepts and feelings communicate clearly. But put a column of numbers on a page and it might as well be in ancient Greek. Some individuals learn primarily from what is heard; others depend on what they see; still others must actually do it to understand it. So, how we understand, learn, and communicate will vary within and among generations, family groups, and each nuclear family.

It's essential, then, that the performance and metrics of these Shared Assets be presented in the forms and formats that are more readily understood by the largest number of Stakeholders. Financial statements may have to be accompanied by pie charts and graphs. Written material may need to be augmented in presentations at family meetings. Everyone involved must have command of the language used in these presentations, and if instruction and mentoring is required, then it must be provided.

It's an obvious reality that informed and educated owners and investors will make better decisions, and be able to appreciate the results of the performance and the services of the managers, than those who are uninformed and uneducated. This won't prevent tough questions from the Stakeholders, but it will make the answers to those questions more meaningful. Holding others accountable without understanding what they have really done is unfair and counterproductive.

- *Withdrawals and removals—who stays and who leaves the ownership group.* We've already explored the issues of ownership and change of ownership. But sometimes it becomes necessary to sever the economic ties that bind family members.

  It's an axiom in business that you don't enter into a business relationship without knowing how you can exit that relationship. This is even more important in a family business or other forms of Shared Assets because personal relationships are often as or more important than the economic ones. Passing ownership to the second generation may be the easy step. But how long will that shared ownership continue and at what price to the family harmony? Every generation past the founder must confront the exit strategy issues.

There are, of course, a variety of techniques to exit the business.

Sell the owner's interest to a third party

This is often more difficult than anyone expects. Few buyers want to share ownership with some other unrelated or unfamiliar parties. This is not the case, however, when the investor is a financial buyer, interested in a major share of an ongoing business, with an expectation of going public in the future or flipping the transaction in a few years to realize a return on the investment. It's also not the case when the investor is a strategic buyer, with expectations of acquiring the entire company over time. In either case, it affords those owners who want out to get out of the shared ownership the power to do so, while enabling others to stay in a continuing ownership with new partners. In both of those cases, the objectives of the potential buyer are very clear and documented. In the more typical circumstances, there are a variety of issues that will affect the transaction.

Sale of a minority interest is usually subject to severe discounts

There are additional discounts for interests that are nonmarketable, such as closely held companies or partnership interests in commercial real estate.

In most business arrangements, the remaining party (or the enterprise itself) has retained the right to acquire any interest that an owner wishes to sell based on the terms of any offer actually received. These rights of first refusal can make it even more difficult to generate serious offers from outside third parties.

Death or disability buyout

These contingencies are the most common buy-sell arrangements in closely held businesses. However, as a practical matter, very few death or disability buyout agreements actually go into effect. In most cases, an owner retires or the business is sold or closed long before there is a death or disability. Furthermore, these events are not voluntary. They occur often without warning and are never desirable.

The price established for death and disability is often set by the ability of the company to afford the payment. Life or disability buyout insurance is frequently the source of the payment, so the parties have to agree on the amount of funds they are willing to spend to purchase these products. As owners get older, the costs of such coverage will likely increase or the product may even become unavailable.

Even in these circumstances, consideration should be given for appropriate discounts for lack of marketability and control.

Sell the company

Selling the entire company is an obvious exit strategy. But this is often the hardest decision of all. It ends the business opportunity for all the owners. This may be very difficult emotionally for many members of the family. After all, the business may have been the source of the family's wealth. It's part of the legacy left by the founder and wealth creator. And it's the only job that many of the family members may know. For those active in the business, it's like selling their job from under them.

Even if a sale is feasible, who has the power to decide? What happens if others don't agree? Minority owners of a privately held business, whether shareholders in a corporation, members in a limited liability company, or partners in a partnership, cannot be forced to sell their interests unless they have previously agreed to do so. This gives the minority owners extraordinary power to prevent a transaction or to force the payment of a premium to them to obtain their participation.

The issues here are obvious...How is price determined? Will owners be entitled to a pro rata share of the proceeds, or will some classes or parties be entitled to a disproportionate share because of their controlling position or to obtain their consent?

Sell the assets of the company

Though the emotional affect is the same, the economic and tax consequences can be very different. In some business structures, a majority of
the ownership interests can cause the enterprise to sell its business assets,
regardless of the objection of the minority. The Board of Directors of a
corporation could, as long as they are acting fairly and within their fiduciary
duties, sell off the assets to a third party. This can also be true in a limited
liability company or partnership. Following the sale of the assets, the enterprise liquidates and the proceeds are disbursed to the owners in proportion
to their respective interests. This, of course, does not solve the problem of
succession in most cases, but will end the shared ownership relationship.

Split up the company

Another alternative is to undergo a tax-free reorganization, in which the
original company splits up into several entities, each of which is owned by
one or more of the former owners of the original company. This is more
complicated, but is often more tax efficient. In our story of the Anderson
family, this was seriously contemplated by Generation Three. In their
business, it was actually feasible because of the multiple business lines and
the involvement of different family members in each.

But it's not always so easy. It tends to be effective only if there are capable owners and managers who can continue each of the respective new
entities. For more passive owners who wanted to retain their interests in
the original company, a split-off is not very helpful. In any event, a part of
the story of the founder will forever be changed.

Liquidate the company

In many states, minority shareholders who have a minimum percentage
of ownership may have the power to force the company to liquidate and
distribute the proceeds to the owners. Operating and partnership agreements can give this power to minority owners, or can restrict the power
under any arrangement to which the owners may have agreed upon joining the enterprise.

Forced liquidations are expensive to impose and often result in considerable price discount on the sale. This is a taxable event that causes further
erosion of value. But, it does give minority owners some leverage in negotiating their grievances with majority owners or management.

Put or call the ownership interest

A "put" is the power of a shareholder to force the entity to purchase the
owner's interest in the enterprise. It gives the owner the absolute right
to withdraw from the business and be paid for the ownership interest.
Conversely, a "call" is the power, usually reserved to the company, to
acquire the interest of an owner at any time. This is the company's leverage to remove an owner who has interfered in business operations or has

made demands deemed unreasonable by management. This could be created in any type of Shared Asset, including a real estate partnership.

A put or call arrangement can be triggered from any number of specific events, such as the failure to meet specific economic benchmarks or targets, or at the discretion of the invoking party. This gives each side the power to get out of the relationship if personal, family, or business conditions merit it.

Will the price be based on a formula, book value, agreed value, or appraised value? For a put to be practical, it must be easy and inexpensive to implement. Typically, this means there is no appraisal, but rather is subject to a formula.

Depending upon the size or block of the interest being sold, an unanticipated put could create cash-flow problems for the enterprise or even violate terms and conditions of the enterprise's commercial financing arrangements. Banks and other lenders often impose limits on the amount of funds that can be paid to shareholders and senior management. There could even be state law limitations on the amount of any buyout, based on the financial condition of the enterprise.

Consequently, the provisions of the put must be subordinate to and consistent with existing financing provisions and state law. At the same time, the exercise of the call usually means that the company has the resources to act and has considered these restrictions. So, exercise of a call often requires immediate and full payment, or at least a relatively short-term payout schedule.

Reciprocal option

A reciprocal option is an arrangement in which each owner is given the right to acquire the interests of one or more of the remaining owners. Traditional rights of first refusal do not resolve the problem, because that tool is only valuable if an outsider wishes to purchase the member's fractional interest, a circumstance rare in a family-owned enterprise. However, the remaining partners may conclude that the time has come to remove one of the family owners and force him or her to sell.

The initial party exercising the purchase right is known as the "Optionor," and the party who is required to sell is known as the "Optionee." In the notice of exercise, the Optionor must specify all the details of the purchase, including price, payment terms, and security, if any. Thereafter, the Optionee is given a period of time, perhaps 120 days, in which to either accept the exercise of the option and sell the ownership interest on the specified terms, or to reject the option and purchase the interest of the Optionor under the very same terms and conditions. In other words, the Optionee becomes the buyer and the Optionor is obligated to sell. The exercise of the option to buy the Optionee's interest by the Optionor is, in effect, an offer to sell the Optionor's interest to the Optionee. Hence, this is really a reciprocal option. There is no further negotiation and no right by either party to back out, unless both sides choose to do so.

The purpose of this reciprocal option is to enable any owner to either buyout another or be prepared to be bought out. Because the price and terms set by the Optionor to buyout the Optionee could be used by the Optionee to buy out the Optionor's interest, it tends to make the price and terms fair and reasonable.

The strategy is most effective when the parties involved are relatively equal in their financial capacity and in their ability to operate the company. Neither has an economic advantage over the other. Should there be no such parity, then the more powerful party could take unfair advantage of the other.

- Conflict resolution—*disagreements can be managed*. Even under the best of circumstances and strongest of families, there will be disagreements. In fact, as we'll see in Chapter Eleven, some of the best decisions are made as a result of disagreements, even strong ones. But, if the conflict is created because of the planning or lack of planning, then it's unfortunate and usually avoidable. Be sure that, however the Shared Asset will be managed, there is a process built into the ownership or operating document for resolving conflict, ranging from routine disagreements, misunderstandings, or complaints, to strong differences in goals and strategies. If the conflict resolution procedures fail, then there must be an option to withdraw or expel. At the end of the day, *Legacy Families* will not permit economic differences to splinter the family or permanently disrupt relationships.

★   ★   ★

"Leadership is getting the right people to do the right thing for the right reason in the right way at the right time at the right use of resources."
~Clark Crouch

CHAPTER NINE

The Family Foundation

On our foundation board, my sister and I participate, along with our parents and our spouses. It's the only opportunity I've ever had to meet my dad on an even playing field. None of us know much about how charities function (or dysfunction!) and this experience is new to everyone. My sister and I live 1,500 miles apart, but the foundation always brings us back home. It's the best family business we've ever participated in. What worries me is can we live up to my parents' expectation that we make a real difference with our funds? We're pretty small in the scheme of things (about $10.0 million), but, if we do this well, the folks may add more through their estate plan.

~Anthony, Age 37, Dallas, TX

One of the most common public characteristics of a *Legacy Family* is the family's consistent, pervasive, and effective expression of generosity and philanthropy. It's not just the message of the initial wealth creator being parroted by future generations. Each generation will have its own philanthropic initiatives, whether expressed through a new philanthropic entity or outright giving. These initiatives represent their own unique beliefs and reflect the needs and circumstances affecting that generation.

Grandpa Joe's philanthropic motivation might have been colored by his own era, to include donating to various veteran's administrations or religious organizations throughout his life. Joe Jr., on the other hand, might become passionate about the plight of third world countries over the course of his lifetime, while Joe III might focus his philanthropic energies toward the environmental causes so dear to his heart. Each generation to his own, we say, as long as the *Family's* core values of generosity, gratitude and responsibility are perpetuated.

Philanthropy may be expressed in a variety of forms, such as the *Family's* foundation, donor advised fund, direct gifts to charity or various volunteer efforts. Philanthropy becomes even more present in the *Family's* day-to-day life, when its members devote their careers to public service, or become leaders of universities, hospitals, research facilities, and human service organizations.

One need only look to the Rockefeller family to understand the importance of philanthropy to a *Legacy Family*. As of today, there are nearly
40 separate foundations, donor advised funds and philanthropic organizations founded by the five generations of Rockefellers starting with
John D. Rockefeller. Their philanthropy began with the creation of the
University of Chicago in 1890, then the Rockefeller Institute for Medical
Research in 1901. It continues today at every generation, in nearly every
facet of the economy.

The value of philanthropy for the recipients of a family foundation's
generosity is self-evident and often publicly acknowledged. However, if
the only importance of the family foundation lies in financial contributions, an equally worthy function is not being utilized—the opportunity
to unify and strengthen the family itself.

Legacy Families thrive through the generations because they recognize that the
real wealth of the family is measured by making deposits in each of its Capital
Accounts—Human, Intellectual, Financial and Social

If you examine philanthropy at its roots, it's not coincidental that Social
Capital enhances the building of the other Capital accounts as well as supports the essential elements of the *Legacy Family's* Strategic Plan.

The Human Capital of the *Legacy Family* is enhanced through philanthropy, especially through a family foundation, because it reaffirms the
parents' emphasis on communication and goal setting, consensus building, and leadership. Because the foundation is designed to reinforce and
perpetuate the *Family's* core values, it offers a unique and valuable opportunity for teaching and practicing many of the values, of compassion,
empathy, trust, accountability, education, and experience.

It connects future generations with ancestors, who lived and practiced
these values and thought it important enough to pass such values down to
their descendants through the foundation, formalizing the message that
each family member shares in the responsibility to perpetuate the *Family's*
core values of gratitude and generosity. The family foundation offers a
platform for working together in a noncompetitive environment, drawing
diverse and often distant relatives together for a shared positive experience
and learning how to reach consensus from the diversity of positions represented. It provides access to the *Family's* full range of talents and experiences, philosophies and methodologies and an opportunity for leadership.

As with any family enterprise, a foundation requires strong, intelligent, and thoughtful leadership. The larger and more involved the family
members may be, the more likely there will be differences in priorities
and concerns.

Even when "doing good," human nature is such that we all "do good"
differently, and therein lies the inherent potential for discord. There
will be those who are most concerned with the human condition and
with alleviating pain, hunger, isolation, disease, abuse, intolerance, or
other afflictions and challenges to a full and enriching life experience.

Meanwhile, others in the family will be more interested in the conditions of the planet, and wish to focus on climate and environment, survival of threatened species, or the restoration of natural wonders. It is this diversity of concerns and talents that make the family so interesting, but it also challenges them to work together to focus, collaborate, and compromise so that in the interest of helping others they don't tear themselves apart in the process.

Governance of the family foundation can provide opportunities for leadership from the family that is different from the styles of the wealth creator or from the family members who choose to enter the family business. In this setting, the family will need someone who is both capable of inspiring and engaging others while overseeing a permanent endowment that is expected to withstand the volatility of the capital markets, overcome the erosion of wealth due to inflation and other expenses and maintain the distribution requirements imposed by law and the foundation board.

The founder and wealth creator is often a visionary, focused, type-A personality who commands respect and obedience, and may perceive himself as a "benevolent dictator." As leadership passes down through the generations, the inherent right to command will change to authority that is granted and respect that is earned. Siblings do not confer automatic power and position merely because of age and, by the time the cousins arrive, any notion of entitlement to leadership is lost completely. The consensus builder will become the strongest leader in this environment.

These are all important Human Capital life skills, which they will be able to apply in many aspects of their own lives.

The Intellectual Capital of a *Legacy Family* is enhanced through philanthropy and the foundation as a result of the learning experience that this activity provides. No matter how much education one may gather through undergraduate or graduate school, the life experience that a philanthropist will enjoy may well become the most important learning opportunity of all. One cannot possibly anticipate the effect of seeing and, to some extent, affecting the range of human talents, emotions, accomplishments, and tragedies that are made possible through the very act of philanthropy.

To add significant value to the *Family's* philanthropy requires a level of education and insight that reinforces its emphasis on both formal education and life experience. Members of the *Family* may well be influenced in their career choices as a result, as they see the world beyond their otherwise sheltered existence, many for the first time. Unlike the family business, with its focus on competition and profits, philanthropic activities provide a place for those who prefer qualitative impact rather than quantitative results, and who measure success by the degree of change in the life of others rather than in the return on equity.

Contrary to the perception of many, effective philanthropy is difficult and not without its own set of unique challenges. To make a *real* difference, you must understand the underlying causes and ramifications of the problems that concern you the most. To make a foundation success-ful through the generations requires knowledge about and skills in orga-nizational management, finance, budgeting, tax and compliance, human resources, public relations, world and local affairs, and communications. It often requires a long-term commitment, in many cases lifelong as well. Those who take this responsibility seriously will participate in lectures and workshops; attend gatherings of other foundation leaders and families, and travel to see for themselves the actual living conditions about which they hope to effectuate change.

Combine the skills required to operate any enterprise whose business is to make a difference, and which is expected to continue in perpetuity, with the talent to respond to the demands of an ever growing extended family, and you can understand both the challenges to and the opportuni-ties of the *Legacy Family's* philanthropic initiative.

It may seem a contradiction that philanthropy actually adds to the Financial Capital account of a *Legacy Family*, but it does. When a wealth creator makes the decision to allocate a portion of the accumulated wealth to philanthropy in general and a family foundation in particular, an under-lying message to the family is that beneficiaries will only be receiving a limited portion of the family wealth. It changes the expectation that all the wealth created in one generation will automatically pass to the next. It reinforces the expectation that each generation be responsible for its own lifestyle and economic success. By managing the expectations of the next generation, parents will have done more to liberate them than to restrain them and will have done more to encourage self-sufficiency and counter overindulgence.

The family foundation has its own financial needs. Once endowed by the founder, it's unlikely that others in the family will add significant assets of their own. Though certainly permissible and valuable, future generations are likely to form their own foundations and donor-advised funds, in part because of the greater control that they may have, and in part because their goals may be quite different than those of the founder and the extended family. There is logic to the Rockefeller tradition of establishing new foundations at every generation.

The assets in the endowment are considered the permanent funds of the foundation. Unlike a traditional business, which strives to build new revenues and resources and to grow its capital base as rapidly as may be practical, the foundation must protect the endowment from erosion. Future revenues of the foundation are likely to come from the earnings and appreciation of its endowment, not from contributions or other forms of capital infusion. So, volatility and risk are unpleasant challenges to those responsible for managing the wealth.

Even if well managed and carefully constructed, endowments can suffer as the economy falters. In late 2008, the economic collapse in the coun-try caused a nearly 30% drop in the value of the endowments of many foundations. But some foundations were virtually wiped out because of the lack of care, prudence, and skill of the board or the financial advisors. The Ponzi scheme perpetuated by Bernard Madoff, which resulted in a $50 billion loss of wealth, caused the collapse of dozens, perhaps hundreds, of foundations, including the Picower Foundation, one of the largest foundations in the country, which had funded groundbreaking brain research at the Massachusetts Institute of Technology and diabetes research at Harvard Medical School. The Picower Foundation closed its doors in 2009. These results would have been avoided with proper due diligence.

Most family foundations are required to distribute a minimum of 5% of the average monthly value of the endowment. This distribution is due within 12 months following the end of the year. So, the management of the portfolio requires producing enough liquidity to meet this distribution obligation, plus any costs that may have been incurred and the payment of any excise tax (which is 2% on the earnings of the foundation) that may be due.

Someone has to be in charge of this process. Even if the foundation has hired an investment manager or consultant, selecting that individual or firm requires insight, knowledge, and experience. The board of the foundation or selected members of the board must oversee the investment activities and monitor performance, but *all* the members of the board must have sufficient knowledge of investing to exercise their responsibilities as fiduciaries of the wealth.

Education learned on one's own is education retained for a lifetime. As the directors and those who aspire to be directors of the foundation learn about asset allocation and diversification, risk and return, inflation and investment expenses, they will be better able to apply this information to their own lives as well. It's no surprise that the poets and English teachers in the family often volunteer to serve on the investment committee, along with their Wharton graduate sibling or cousin, because this is where they will learn.

The family foundation institutionalizes the *Legacy Family's* core values and its focus on the Social Capital. It will shape the *Family's* reputation and legacy within the community. Years after everyone has forgotten how you originally made your wealth, your philanthropy and your family's commitment to their community and public service will define who you are and what you have stood for. While we won't go so far as to call it your family's "brand," there are certain branding characteristics to consider when putting on a unified family front.

A classic example of this effect is the legacy of Andrew Carnegie, at one time the richest man in the world. Carnegie lived the rags to riches story, born from Scottish parents who immigrated with their "young Andrew" to the United States. His first job at age 13 in 1848 was in a cotton mill where he was responsible for changing spools of thread twelve hours a day, six days a week. His wages were $1.25 per week. As his fortune increased, but while still a very young man, he wrote, "I propose to take an income no greater than $50,000 per annum! Beyond this I need never earn, make no effort to increase my fortune, but spend the surplus each year for benevolent purposes!" Good intentions notwithstanding, this internal memo didn't stop him from building his wealth. At the age of 66, he formed U.S. Steel and created the first corporation in the world with a market capitalization in excess of $1 billion.

In one very large family meeting, with over 25 adults gathered together for this discussion, the question was asked who Carnegie was and what he did in his lifetime. The answer from all but one member of the family was unanimous: libraries. Of course, these answers reflected the philanthropy of Carnegie himself, who established over 3,000 libraries in 47 states during his lifetime. No one offered the answer "he built United States Steel Corporation" or alluded to the fact that he was widely known (in past generations) for his low-paying jobs to steel workers and vehement antiunion stance. His lifetime philosophy of doing well and doing good continued long after his own life ended.

That is why we speak so often to the 100-year arc of the *Legacy Family* and why we encourage every generation to become involved in creating a legacy of which you can be proud. If the children, grandchildren, and great-grandchildren aren't proud of the way in which the family wealth was accumulated—the son of the founder of the R. J. Reynolds tobacco company has fought against the tobacco industry for years—there is time to change these feelings through generosity of both capital and compassion in years that follow.

There are many ways to add to the Social Capital of your family. If your generosity begins at your death and appears to be drawn at the expense of your children's inheritance it will not have the same impact as when the family is involved with philanthropy all the time. *Legacy Families* reinforce the belief among family members that, since they are fortunate to be in a position to do so, they have the opportunity and perhaps even the *responsibility* to make the lives of others a bit better.

The tools of the Legacy Family's *Social Capital* include the Donor Advised Fund and the Private Foundation

The Donor Advised Fund (DAF) is actually a fund within a larger public charity, administered by a third party for the purpose of facilitating the charitable gifts of individuals, families, and organizations. Because it is already part of an existing public foundation, it takes very little to establish or maintain. It has all the tax benefits of a public charity, which are often better than those available to private foundations. The host foundation is not obligated to follow the request of the donor, but will usually do so as long as the donor's wishes are consistent with the host foundation's guidelines. The host foundation will often have experienced foundation advisors who can assist the donor in providing recommendations and due diligence.

Many DAFs have a limited duration. Some will only honor the request of the donor or the designee of the donor over two generations. Thereafter, the funds are reallocated to the general endowment of the foundation. The DAF is an important component of institutionalized philanthropy. There are more than 100,000 donor advised accounts today, some of which are hosted by over 700 community foundations, and others sponsored through foundations established by financial service companies like Fidelity Investments and Vanguard Funds, with an estimated combined $17 billion in assets.

The private foundation has been a part of American philanthropy even before there was an income or estate tax. Benjamin Franklin set up two trusts in his Last Will, written in 1788 and that became effective in 1789, each of which allocated 1,000 pounds sterling for the purpose of providing low-interest loans to "artificers" (former apprentices in various trades), with funds to enable them to go into their own business. He directed that, after 100 years, about 70% of the trust was to be distributed to Boston and Philadelphia to support public works, such as bridges, aqueducts, fortifications (especially against the British!), and public buildings. After 200 years, estimating that the trust would then be worth about 4 million pounds, he directed that it distribute the balance to the two communities. In 1991, the trust in Philadelphia distributed over $2.2 million to the community foundation and various charitable organizations, including the Franklin Institute.

Imagine, the Revolutionary War had only ended a few years earlier. There was no certainty that there would even be a United States, let alone formal cities to benefit from his redistributed wealth. Nonetheless, Ben Franklin was thinking 200 years ahead to the needs of a society he could not even dream about, but was fervently intent on funding nonetheless.

Some foundations are established by a founder and left to the control of friends, colleagues, and business associates. The Ford Foundation was initially run by a nonfamily member and, to this day, still has no member of the Ford family on its board. These "independent foundations" actually exceed by a wide margin the number of foundations controlled by the founder or family members. Those foundations, which continue to be controlled by members of the founder's family, are known informally as "family foundations."

The era of big foundations began in earnest after the turn of the last century. Andrew Carnegie's foundation was formed in 1911 (Carnegie Corporation of New York). Carnegie, who died in 1919, gave $350 million in his lifetime. The value of his gift, in today's dollars, is about $3 billion. John D. Rockefeller gave $540 million in his lifetime; he died in 1937. In today's value, the gift would be approximately $6 billion.

The number of foundations and the value of the assets already contributed to them have grown immensely. In 1978, there were 22,484 foundations identified in the United States with a combined value of $37 billion. By 2007, there were over 72,000 foundations in the country with a value of $615 billion. Of these foundations, over 42,000 are controlled by individual donors or their families, rather than by nonfamily directors or corporations. Of these family foundations, 56% have assets less than $1.0 million and nearly 86% have assets under $5.0 million. A third of these foundations have been formed since the year 2000.[1] The largest 100 foundations control more than half of the assets; the small family foundations are more pervasive and diverse. Many of the small foundations are still in the early stages of their funding. The founders are often still living and much of the wealth they anticipate contributing is still held personally. So, over time, these foundations are likely to grow dramatically.

The increased flexibility and continuity of a private foundation is not without some cost. It is more expensive to create and often more expensive to maintain the foundation than to contribute to a DAF. The offset is that it enables the founder to shape the legacy of his or her philanthropy for generations to come.

There are many reasons for this rapid growth. Of course, tax planning plays an important part. Contributions are income tax deductible and pass estate tax free. Appreciated assets contributed to a foundation and then sold by the foundation avoid personal capital gains taxes.

But beyond the tax implications, one of the most common motivations is that, contrary to the perceptions of many family advisors, wealth creators often choose to cap or limit the inheritance of their children and grandchildren. Many estate owners have come to a conclusion, discussed in Chapter Six, that their heirs need only so much wealth to assure their security and maximize their opportunities and personal achievement.

They have determined that too much inherited wealth may be counterproductive, distracting the beneficiary from completing his or her education or pursuing a career, undermining his or her determination to become self-sufficient and actually impeding the beneficiary's self-esteem. During the lifetime of the wealth creators, and especially after a major liquidity event, a significant portion of the estate is increasingly being allocated to new or existing foundations.

Equally important for the creation of a family foundation, is the ability to preserve capital and to maintain family control over the accumulated wealth. *Since there are many benefits to the personal growth and development of family members through their involvement in the philanthropic initiative of the family, many wealth creators feel this is of greater benefit to the family than just transferring the maximum wealth to beneficiaries.* If the family cannot or should not inherit all this wealth, it can and should, in the mind of some founders, at least retain control over it.

Economics are only part of the story. As families grow in size and spread out geographically, it becomes increasingly difficult for the members of the various branches to really know one another. One of the great

---

[1] "Key Facts on Family Foundations," published by the Foundation Center, January 2007.

benefits and challenges of the family foundation is the opportunity to bring the extended family back together.

But merely establishing and generously funding a foundation does not mean that philanthropy will automatically be well-served, nor does it mean that the family will enjoy the experience. There is much work required to make this initiative effective, efficient, and fun. If the family is torn apart by bitter rivalry, frayed relationships, or broken communication, the likelihood that the family foundation will successfully overcome these impediments and create harmonious family relationships is very slim.

Dysfunction in the living room will naturally repeat itself in the board room. *Legacy Families* are distinguished not by the amount of the wealth they annually contribute to charity, but by the quality, consistency, and impact of such philanthropy, and the positive experience enjoyed by *family* members who actively participate in these philanthropic efforts. There are some critical steps required to enable this to happen through the generations.

Step 1: Create the Foundation's Strategic Plan

In both the commercial for-profit world and throughout the public not-for-profit sector, it is common to develop and follow a thoughtful and comprehensive strategic plan that defines the organization's mission and vision, leadership and structure, internal and external resources, products, programs and services, and a host of other features needed to attain its financial and nonfinancial goals. Strangely, the very business leaders who routinely drive this planning process for their own companies, and often the very same people who chair the boards of the most prominent public charities, fail to apply this critical step to their own family foundations!

This is especially true with an enterprise intended to continue and thrive for generations. It can be complicated, especially because of the family dynamics and because it's intended to formulate a process that will respond to changes. Some of these changes may be dramatic and unanticipated, in the family structure, lifestyle and economics, as well as the needs, conditions, and circumstances of society. But regardless of the resources of the foundation, it is important to have a strategic plan that guides the path for the future.

Step 2: The Vision of the Founder

What is it you're hoping to accomplish, whether in your philanthropy or for your family? Is the foundation merely a vehicle to avoid taxes or is the goal to accomplish important things with your resources? If only the former, there are many less complicated strategies available. If you really want to be successful in this initiative, you need to articulate your broad goals and visualize what success looks like.

How would you define "success" over the next 25–50–100 years? How will you or those who follow you know that the foundation is on the right track and accomplishing what you intended? Be specific; write the answers down and look at them objectively to see if they're realistic or not. Remember Ben Franklin and follow his wisdom when setting out a future path for yourself and the foundation.

A foundation without a clear vision and stated mission is like a ship without a rudder; it may have smooth sailing for a while but eventually, inevitably, it will glide off course with no one at the helm to steer it back to shore. Wealth is rarely created without a focus. As in any other business, your foundation needs to focus on your vision.

A vision statement may be the hardest part in the formation of the foundation. Identifying and articulating success requires that you narrow down all the things in life that you feel are important to those concepts that you consider to be the *most* important. After all, no matter how much wealth is set aside to benefit others and the community, you cannot solve all the problems of the world. Furthermore, if your vision is too broad and undefined, it will be impossible to know whether the foundation has been or can ever become successful.

In addition, many family foundations actually have two separate visions. The public and stated mission, which guides the philanthropy and grant-making programs, is known as the "external vision," while, its "internal mission" may be to encourage the philanthropy of the family, create a vehicle for the collaboration of family members, and provide a platform for perpetuating the founder's core values.

Framing the external mission can be an involved process. This is an excellent topic for a family meeting, during which time the dreams and priorities of the founder(s), the next generation, in-laws, and perhaps even older grandchildren, can be expressed. During this process, the founders will often discover with great pleasure that many of their strongest and most fervently held values are shared to the same extent by their closest family members. As you begin to narrow down these values to those that will shape the foundation, you may struggle on wording and selection. But, when you have arrived at the language that best articulates your collective goals, you will find a sense of shared purpose that will support the long-term success of your foundation.

The following is a sample of one vision statement created by the Charles family:

> *We believe that...*
> - *Respect is earned, not given;*
> - *Self-esteem comes from personal achievement, not inheritance;*
> - *Education creates opportunity, not guarantees;*
> - *Success is measured within, not on a balance sheet;*
> - *Opportunity denied is tragic; opportunity wasted is inexcusable.*

Our Foundation is designed to support those individuals in our communities most committed to achieving personal success, but whose financial or family circumstances make such effort beyond reach.

This statement is a reflection of the founder's deeply held belief that creating opportunity for those for whom opportunity has been denied is the greatest gift he can offer. He has chosen to use his foundation to overcome those barriers, whether in education or business, for those whose passion, commitment, and determination offer fertile ground that needs the help that funding, networking, and mentoring can provide.

In your strategic plan, your vision statement can be amplified by a clear and specific description of how you would measure your success in this effort. Perhaps it will express the change in the lives of those you have benefited or the change in the condition of the community you have chosen to support. Remember, philanthropy cannot always be quantified or counted. As reflected in the Charles family's vision statement, often the most important changes are about quality, not quantity; impact, not statistics.

Step 3: Implementing the
Vision is the Mission of the Foundation

If the *vision* is the statement of what success looks like to the founder, then the *mission* of the foundation is how such success will be achieved. It is, in other words, a statement of the business of the foundation. It is what the foundation is here to do. In carrying out the vision of the Charles Foundation, its external mission statement provided the following:

The primary mission of the Charles Foundation is to support the efforts and opportunities of disadvantaged children and young adults to become independent, self-sufficient, hard-working, ethical, and moral human beings. We focus on formal and vocational education, essential health care, and nourishing and supporting family life through organizations serving these individuals in the communities in which we live and work.

The critical test for the mission statement is whether these types of activities would advance the vision of the founder.

For those foundations that also have an internal mission, the statement might look something like:

The internal mission of the Foundation is to strengthen the Charles Family, through reinforcement of its values, respect for each other and commitment to the community.

Keep in mind that a mission statement is not a broad statement of philosophy but rather a clear, specific, and active expression of goals and tasks. From this statement the grant program of the foundation will be developed, so make it clear and direct.

Step 4: The Business of the Foundation is Grant Making

One essential in a successful for-profit business is awareness of its target market, its product and the delivery of its product. If the business of the foundation is grant making, what makes up its process and procedure for identifying opportunities, evaluating prospective recipients, implementing the grant, confirming the expectations of the grantee and the foundation, and, just as importantly, monitoring the results? Many foundations function more like the checkbook for the founder, implementing personal philanthropy and responding to social pressures without any consistent focus. After the founder is gone, the family tends to continue this disjointed process, scattering its gifts and diluting its impact.

The *Legacy Family* will administer its foundation in the same manner as it runs its for-profit businesses and shared investments. If the goals are strategic, implementation is tactical. The steps are defined, clear, and logical. Participation by the family is encouraged, not commanded, and opinions are invited and respected. Grants are given to further the mission and applicants are vetted through due diligence and thorough discussion. If the foundation is to be successful through the generations, it will be respected by those for whom its support was intended, both institutions and individuals. It will be run efficiently; its grants will have impact; and those who choose to participate will be proud of their efforts and, as a result, closer in their personal relationships.

No matter how effective any program may be, the process will change over time—during the founder's life, during the management by the children, and through the generations to follow. What is the role of the children and future issues in this process after the founder is gone? Will they need to establish new rules? Must they follow the old rules? Have they been involved in setting up these rules?

Among the most common reasons for the failure of a family foundation is the inability to engage younger generations and to prepare them for their foundation responsibilities. There's no magic in creating successful transitions to future generations. It requires paying respect to their opinions, mentoring their skills, and permitting expression of their own passions and concerns. The children of today are no less generous and compassionate than those of yesterday. But their focus has changed and their method of processing and communicating is different.

The philanthropy expressed by today's youth reflects the differences not only in age, style, and culture, but also in technology. A foundation mired in yesterday's dried ink will have a hard time meeting the expectations of tomorrow's high-tech virtual print. This new generation of future leaders and philanthropists look for innovation, accountability and leverage, often at the speed of thought. Now more than ever, if they can think it they can do it. They are anxious to create collaboration and alliances, and more willing to become proactive in implementation. The issues tend to be more global, with much less emphasis on those institutions that shaped the lives of their parents or grandparents.

If an important goal in your foundation is to stimulate the philanthropy of your children and grandchildren, be prepared to hear their concerns and to consider their views seriously, and then follow the process for deliberation and decision making that you authorized in the strategic plan.

Step 5: How Will the Foundation Be Run?

Governance and management will also change over time. During the founder's lifetime, will decisions be made by dictatorship? Democracy? Anarchy? Will there be shared leadership? Is there a process in place for preparing the next generation of leadership?

After the founder is gone, who will choose the successor leadership and what is the process for doing so? Will the foundation leadership be chosen on the basis of age, intelligence, proximity to home, or as a reward for being the primary caretaker of the aging founders? Must the successor actually be a family member, or might it be a nonfamily friend or professional foundation manager?

Is the younger generation being prepared to assume responsibility? Since the future leaders of the foundation should have experience and skill in managing a family enterprise, programs should be developed to train and prepare these younger members of the family in these tasks. The foundation provides an opportunity to mentor the younger generation through the efforts of other older and more experienced family members. This achieves several objectives, including preparing future leaders, teaching important life skills, and building family relationships. But it takes time and effort. If you want this enterprise to be successful, use your time wisely.

Step 6: How Will the Assets of the Foundation Be Managed?

In a tax-free environment, even with modest risk and a diversified portfolio, and notwithstanding periodic volatility in the capital markets, foundation assets can grow rapidly. When J. P. Getty died in the 1970s, his wealth was approximately $1.5 billion. Since then, his foundation spent $4 billion in rebuilding the Getty Museum and acquiring new art acquisitions, and the remaining endowment is *still* over $5 billion.

Since the endowment is the economic engine of the foundation, its protection, preservation, and growth are essential. At a minimum, the directors of the foundation should be striving to meet its distribution rate

(5% of its annual value), the costs of administering the estate and managing the endowment, plus inflation. The typical target return of family foundations is around 8%, allowing it to make its distributions and maintain its purchasing power.

The most important principle to remember, as you establish and operate your foundation, is that accepting the role as a director makes you, and each other member of your board, a "fiduciary." What is a fiduciary? What is expected of a good fiduciary and what are the risks of failing to perform the duties properly? How does one prepare for this responsibility? Anytime there are funds to manage, there is the likelihood of conflict of interest. How does this conflict affect the trustee's ability to perform his or her fiduciary duties?

A "fiduciary" is anyone who holds a position requiring trust, confidence, and the exercise of good faith and candor for the benefit of others. In most cases, this duty is imposed by law and in some cases by contract. Every director of a foundation is considered a fiduciary, as would most corporate officers. The specific criteria may be different depending upon whether the foundation is organized as a trust or as a corporation. But, in either case, the fiduciary is held to a very high standard of care, candor, impartiality, and good faith. The duty is owed to the members of the foundation, and to the public at large. That is why the state's attorney general has the authority to intervene and protect the interests of the public and the state. As one might imagine, if a foundation's assets are extensive but its plans for redistribution and philanthropy are internally and externally "hazy," it becomes ripe for abuse, be it intentional or incidental.

Increasingly, federal and state regulators have begun to focus on the perceived or actual abuses by foundation trustees and officers. In Texas, the state's attorney general seized the assets of a major family foundation and replaced its president, a prominent member of the founder's family, on claims of excessive compensation and breach of duty. Elliot Spitzer, as former New York attorney general asserted, from time to time, his belief that the Sarbanes-Oxley legislation, enacted in part to prevent public corporate board abuse, also applied to public and private foundations.

On the federal level, the Internal Revenue Service has taken aim at excess compensation, self-dealing, private inurement, and other forms of abuse. In response to the concern about excessive compensation, Congress debated for much of 2003, and may still enact, a rule that would prevent certain foundation expenses from partially satisfying its minimum distribution rules.

One can draw a few general conclusions from the various new laws. The legislative bodies and regulatory agencies have become increasingly aware of the duties of a fiduciary and the responsibilities associated with such a position. Modern investment strategies and products have changed the way that we expect a fiduciary to act, and the general public now recognizes its right to demand knowledgeable, impartial, and prudent actions from such fiduciaries. Watch dog agencies are scrutinizing tax returns and annual reports, are rating charities and foundations and, are actively publicizing their findings. Transparency is suddenly a key issue. With increased visibility and scrutiny, fiduciaries can expect heightened pressure from, and demands by, all the stakeholders.

What does this mean to you and your family? It means that you need to have everyone who wants to be involved properly prepared and adequately trained for his or her responsibilities. It means that your board of directors needs to identify, recognize, and follow the rules of governance that are expected of all fiduciaries. It's not only unfair to ask your family to accept responsibilities with unforeseen risks without the proper education and training, but it could also expose your foundation to potentially serious penalties and even disqualification.

Perhaps as importantly, the preparation and training that is appropriate for all foundation directors will provide new insight and skills that can apply to a wide variety of other circumstances, including the role as a trustee over trusts for family members as well as overseeing the investment and management of their own financial assets. In other words, the foundation is another way of providing those who participate with critical financial, as well as life, skills.

Step 7: What Are the Traps That Could Jeopardize the Foundation, Founder, and Family?

With increasing scrutiny from Congress, the IRS, and the state attorneys general, modern foundations must be careful to avoid the tax traps. Self-dealing—paying compensation or rent to family members or purchasing tickets at galas—all raise serious issues. Using foundation grants to satisfy personal pledges, investing foundation assets in family-owned business and projects—these and other transgressions could cost the foundation and its directors significant penalties and even jeopardize its exempt status.

In Other Words ...

A foundation that is formed without a comprehensive plan, clear focus, prepared management, and careful governance will not be able to achieve the true vision of its founder. As noble as it may be to do the right thing, it's just as essential to do things right. Philanthropy was dealt a severe blow because of the Bernard Madoff scheme. We would do well to remember that for those whom our philanthropy affects the most—people in need, the recipients of all those scholarships, grants and funds, and so on—this is not a mere exercise in legacy planning but an actual strategy for the personal survival and quality of life for countless others.

★   ★   ★

"But history will judge you, and as the years pass, you will ultimately judge yourself, in the extent to which you have used your gifts and talents to lighten and enrich the lives of your fellow men. In your hands lies the future of your world and the fulfillment of the best qualities of your own spirit."

~Robert F. Kennedy

CHAPTER TEN

Financial Competency and Life Skills Training

Marty again felt his temperature rising as he saw the monthly credit card bills that his teenage daughters so carelessly compiled. How well he remembered growing up in a home where money was always in short supply. Luxuries could never be considered and many a dinner conversation was fixated on finding the bargains that would help stretch the meager family budget. He realized that this fiscal discipline had clearly contributed to his ability to create his now successful business as he was able to make significant financial sacrifices in the early years of building his business. Maybe he had been somewhat indulgent with the girls. Now that he had money he had to admit that he did enjoy indulging his family in a manner that he had never been able to experience. However, now he worried that his children would never understand the value of money and would quickly dissipate any inheritance that they would receive. How could he turn things around?

What is it that keeps you up at night? Is it the concern that your children will be more successful in their careers than you, or that they are not prepared for the responsibilities of the wealth that may be coming?

National studies have confirmed that one of the most critical fears of financially successful families is the lack of financial skills of their children. But our children have expressed similar concerns. In a poll conducted for the Charles Schwab Foundation and the Boys and Girls Clubs of America, reported in USA Today (May 2005), 80% of teenagers believe that money management should be a requirement in high school.

In a 2008 nationwide survey sponsored by the Federal Reserve, high school seniors answered correctly on 48.3% of the questions dealing with economics and personal finance. This was even lower than a similar study conducted in 2006 (Associated Press, April 9, 2008).

The problem is not new to parents or their children. Most of us learned our financial skills the hard way. We lost a lot of money making expensive mistakes. But, for many of us, we started with little, grew our wealth on our own, and learned as we earned. The price our children will pay is likely to be much greater. Salaries are higher. The cost of goods and services are higher. Over the last decade, credit became more available than at any time in history. Bankruptcies are at their all time high. Divorce affects nearly 60% of marriages. The amount of wealth that will be transferred to the next generation is the greatest ever seen in history.

The lack of financial skill is more than just an economic problem. Whether as a child or an adult, an individual's sense of self-worth, what we know as self-esteem, is the result of two key conditions—competency and confidence.

Competency is not an inherited trait. It cannot be transferred by gift. No estate plan can provide it. You can't mandate that your children will be competent. If a classroom could fill the gap in financial competency and life skills, we would have solved the problem long ago. Our children would graduate with more than a degree. They would be able to function well in society and in their own personal lives. Unfortunately, that is often not the case.

To be competent first requires knowledge and skill. Knowledge is acquired through formal and informal education, reading and listening, mentoring and coaching. We know that our primary and secondary schools have failed to focus on financial literacy, so it's little wonder that our college students are so ill-prepared for their first experience away from home. Remarkably, even those students who graduate with undergraduate and graduate degrees in business or finance often have little fundamental knowledge of personal cash management, credit, or income tax. They may know how to read a company profit and loss statement or balance sheet but have never created their own budget or balance sheet. They are unprepared for the tasks of purchasing a car or a home and their experience in negotiations may be limited to coaxing dad to give them the keys to the family car.

Skill is the result of practice and experience. To learn theory is a good foundation for competency, but knowledge without application or hands-on experience is usually inadequate in dealing with real-life challenges. Often, our greatest learning comes from the mistakes we've made. Teaching budget and risk management is important, if not essential, but living within a budget and implementing risk avoidance and risk shifting strategies is what is required to fully comprehend and apply that knowledge. How can we expect our youth to become responsible financial adults if we do not teach and model that behavior?

Confidence is the result of these trials and errors. And it's not without risk. Every parent can relate to the day the training wheels came off the child's first two-wheeled bicycle. On that first ride, most children will tumble into a tree, bush, or cement sidewalk. But, after a few harrowing rides, balance is achieved and your child experiences a newfound freedom. When your child looks back at you after that first successful ride, the expression on that youngster's face is the sign of self-esteem. It says "I can."

Adults who lack financial literacy and skill and who find themselves dependent on parents, advisors, trustees, and salespersons for all things financial will never feel self-reliant and independent. They will never know the freedom of riding without those training wheels. Mistakes will be repeated and the costs of each mistake will likely grow.

Good parents are eager for the success of their children. They are continually organizing, guiding, directing, and assisting in all activities. In their absence, nannies, governesses, tutors, housekeepers, and so on are hired to perform these functions. In fact, well-meaning parents become so intrusive in the lives of their children, that they create permanent dependency and passivity.

With this flurry of adult activity, how is a child to become competent? Competency is not something that occurs at chronological milestones. Children become competent because they are permitted to do so. This means that they physically take care of themselves as much as is possible, are permitted to make choices and their thoughts and opinions are solicited and respected. When a child asks for help, whether physical or intellectual, before any type of assistance is forthcoming, the responsible parent will ask himself, "Can my child do this activity or any part of it independently?" If the answer is, "yes," step back and let the child experience the exhilarating feeling of mastery. Don't do it for them or rescue them. This is as true in the child's financial life as it is in other daily life experiences.

Ironically, with very successful financial families, routine and candid conversation with children about money is rare. Dads are often known for their sage financial advice "money doesn't grow on trees!" and moms are often heard to say "ask your father!" Sometimes the roles are reversed, but the result is usually the same. Money isn't discussed because somehow it appears "unseemly" or might encourage the children to slack off. In some cases, the notion of having a personal financial budget is so foreign to the parents that they don't even consider the concept when their children move away to college and independent living. It's no wonder that college students graduate with enormous credit card debt, poor FICO scores, and virtual ignorance of their financial conditions.

Unusual as it may be for some families to develop and follow a financial budget, it would be rare to find a family business that didn't operate within a budget. If it had done so, the likelihood that it would succeed over time is slim. The business that spends beyond its means, that doesn't track its cash flow and debt, will not long survive. The same is not true to children of affluent families. There's always home to come back to.

When children go off to college, the opportunity, indeed the necessity, for financial training becomes apparent. No matter what the stated "budget" is for the student, invariably there will be an urgent call for "emergency" funds. In the era of ATMs, the call home has been replaced with repeated withdrawals from a machine that appears to have a never-ending supply of money.

With this backdrop, it's no wonder that wealth is often created and lost within three generations. The phrase "shirtsleeves to shirtsleeves in three generations" is actually a worldwide phenomenon. In Asia, you may hear distraught parents worry about "rice paddy to rice paddy" and in the Netherlands you may hear the phrase "klog to klog." Where affluence is taken for granted and where the financial skills required to build, preserve, and shift wealth are ignored, the results are likely to be the same.

Financial competency requires knowledge and experience in four distinct quadrants, what we call the "pillars of wealth"

To deal with this apparent vacuum, parents must accept responsibility to guide their children to become financially competent. This means the children must understand the language of financial affairs. They must be "financially literate" in the concepts, issues, and most fundamental principles. It also requires that the children gain real-life experience through hands–on activity. It may take coaching and mentoring, but it will most certainly demand practice. Few will become financial experts. That's the territory of the professionals who devote a lifetime career to their field. But those who are willing and able to partake in this process will become informed consumers and users of the financial marketplace. They will become the chief financial officers of their own lives.

Managing Wealth

Managing wealth focuses on the cash management aspect of wealth. It means that the wealth owner can set financial and lifestyle goals, which are consistent with and appropriate to the individual's resources for both the short and long term. Money as a finite resource is a concept clearly understood by all members of poor or middle class families. However, in financial families, material items are rarely constrained by cost or budget.

Financial parenting begins with an allowance that should not be so small that the child cannot make choices, but not so generous that everything is possible. Give allowances in three parts, one for immediate spending that includes designated weekly fixed expenses (such as school lunches, and so on), the second part for long-range saving, and the third part for charity. Teach the use of checking accounts and the obligation to balance monthly statements. Give stock as presents. Encourage work experience. Since these individuals will someday be responsible for financial decisions, develop proactive family financial learning programs that teach age–related aspects of budget, credit, investments, and the family business.

For young adults, especially those who have completed their college education and are now entering the workplace, they should be educated and prepared to demonstrate competency, if not proficiency, in each of the following:

- *Creating and following a budget.* Do they understand where their revenues come from and where the cash is going? Do they at least meet their obligations monthly? If not, and you are the source of the difference, is there a plan to reach equilibrium? Are you content to cover the shortfall indefinitely? At age 25, the cost of housing, food, health care, transportation, clothing, and other necessities may well exceed the earnings from employment or passive investments. But at age 40, this condition should be unacceptable. The budget should define the acceptable gap and the timing of closing that gap.

- *Understand and managing credit.* Does your young adult know his or her credit score? Is that score where it needs to be, somewhere above 720, or is it languishing at a level that might identify your child as not credit worthy? A poor score will not only cost your child considerably more in interest on every consumer or commercial loan, but may make obtaining such a loan impossible. In today's world, access to credit is a necessity, not a luxury. It will not only make the difference between being able to buy a home, but it may affect the ability to get a job. Employers routinely request a credit report on applicants. They don't want financially irresponsible individuals, in part because it says something about the individual's character and sense of responsibility, and in part because poor credit is a telltale sign of a security risk.

Building Wealth

Building wealth refers to increasing the financial assets of the wealth owner, whether that is to assure the long-term security of the individual, or to maximize the wealth that might ultimately pass to future generations or to philanthropy. It considers the spending needs and desires of the wealth owner, market risks, costs, and inflation.

The financially competent adult is capable of building wealth, perhaps through his or her labor and employment or perhaps through investments initially seeded by others but that have grown by prudent and thoughtful strategies.

- *Business.* If your wealth was created through business, you may naturally expect your children and future descendants to continue that path. It may happen. Some of the greatest fortunes built by *Legacy Families* were launched, however modestly, by the first generation of the family wealth creators and then magnified many times over by subsequent generations. The Anderson Family, with whom we've visited throughout this book, began its rags to riches story in the late 19th century. But, it wasn't until Generation Three, well into the 20th century, that the wealth became significant.

- *Investing.* Regardless of whether you have built a business or not, you will be responsible for overseeing and perhaps taking an active part in building your financial assets and other investments. This may require your knowledge about and attention to such diverse asset classes as stocks, mutual funds, bonds, real estate, and perhaps a variety of alternative investments, such as collectibles, private equity, hedge funds, and derivatives. You understand the principles of asset allocation, diversification, risk, and return. You can read the appropriate economic indicators.
- *Working with advisors.* One thing is clear. You won't be able to do this alone. You'll need the help of the best professional advisors you can assemble to help you. Identifying, evaluating, selecting, and monitoring your advisors, whether involved in your business or investments or your personal life, you will to know what these individuals can do and what they cannot do, and you will to understand the advice given if you are going to make an informed and educated decision. Relying blindly on advice, regardless of the source, is nearly as dangerous as avoiding or refusing to hear such advice.

Protecting Wealth

Protecting wealth focuses on managing the various types of risk to that wealth, including the obvious ones—calamities (such as fire, accident, and health), personal and business creditors, and disgruntled or former spouses—and the less obvious ones, such as income and estate taxes.

- *Managing risk.* Life is filled with risk, from the time of your birth through the moment of death. Risk can come in the form of natural events and disasters as well as man-made ones. The financially competent individual realistically assesses the sources of risk, then works hard and continuously to minimize each, isolates each to the extent possible, shifts some of the exposure by virtue of contracts with other or through insurance, and then deals with the consequences. It requires an understanding of where risk may arise—health, disability, death, natural calamities, business mistakes, and so on. It also draws on the principles of law, economics, finance, and credit. To get a handle on the range and depth of risk, you will seek and consider the advice of the most capable attorneys and accountants, insurance agents, and financial advisors.
- *Personal exposure.* Unfortunately, one of the greatest risks to your wealth may be divorce. Nationally the divorce rate is nearly 40%. In some areas of the country the rate may be as high as 60%.

Understanding this reality should motivate you first to make wise choices in your spouse. Then it should encourage you to work hard at maintaining that relationship for life. As with most of the best things in life, you cannot take your marriage for granted. But, divorce happens, so understand that as you prepare yourself and your children for wealth.

Transferring Wealth

Transferring wealth refers to those planned gifts of wealth, such as lifetime and deathbed transfers to family, friends, and philanthropy, and unplanned transfers, such as that which comes from divorce.

A reality of life is that we are only stewards of the wealth. No matter how successful we are, the wealth is not likely to go with us when we die. So, it is both inevitable that you will transfer wealth and a privilege.

- *Estate Planning.* You need to understand both the principles and strategies of transferring wealth to others, including a spouse, children, and other possible beneficiaries, as well as the rules and responsibilities of inheriting such wealth. We spent considerable time discussing these issues in Chapters Six to Nine. The message we hope you heard was responsible stewardship is fundamental to sustaining your family through the generations. Regardless of the extent of your wealth today, you owe it to yourself and your descendants to thoughtfully consider how that wealth is transferred.

In the Appendix, we have provided you with a checklist of the topics that you should be able to master. Try it yourself, then ask your adult children to give it a try. If your child can demonstrate proficiency in most of the topics, he or she is well on the way to financial competency.

> *How you model, teach, and mentor the financial training of your*
> *children is just as important as the content of what you offer*

It's not enough to identify what must be taught. It's essential that the teaching process be relevant, age-appropriate, and geared to the learning style and capacity of the learner, whether a young child or mature adult.

We know that young children learn differently than mature adults. And adults just out of college have a different learning style and interest than those who have been in the work force for many years. This doesn't mean that the knowledge needed is different, but how that knowledge is acquired, retained, and applied may be very different. What is relevant to a 35-year-old may not seem as important to a 25-year-old, at least at that point in his or her life. Purchasing a car may be the most important major purchase of the younger adult, while purchasing a home may be more pressing to the older adult. A young child may need to know how to earn, spend, share, and save allowance, but a mature adult will need to know how to manage, build, protect, and shift wealth.

We also know that all individuals have their own learning style. Some individuals are auditory learners. They learn by listening. Others are visual. They must see the picture. Members of your family may be kinesthetic learners. These individuals must do something physically to learn and retain. Most of us have combinations of these learning styles. How you teach and mentor should adapt to fit how your child learns best. The speed with which the child will learn and the pleasure experienced in learning will depend on this.

How rapidly we learn is another factor to keep in mind. Madison Avenue recognized long ago that we remember what we hear seven times or more. Few educational institutions offer their students seven chances to learn their material. Remember when your primary school teacher used to bark out five sets of instructions in a row. "*Open your book to page 242. Read the example in the middle of the page. Write your answers on a sheet of paper and hand it to the student behind you. Stand up when you're done.*" For some of us, perhaps one or more your kids, we're still on which page number the teacher wants. Try asking the teacher to repeat seven times!

This is especially true with individuals who are challenged with attention deficit disorder (ADD). Their ability to concentrate and focus is impaired, causing them to miss information. For those of you who pick up and process information quickly, this delay can be frustrating. It's no less frustrating, however, to the individual who has ADD when critical information is missing. It makes learning much harder and often embarrassing. Wouldn't it be simpler if the teacher also handed out the instructions or perhaps wrote them on the board?

In some families, the notion that learning and competency in financial affairs is the responsibility of everyone is foreign. For many generations, girls and young women were discouraged from pursuing mathematics, science, engineering, or medicine. In some cultures, only the oldest male child is expected or encouraged to go to college. The physically or mentally disabled have long endured society's assumption that sophisticated learning was unnecessary or wasted. Someone should have told Beethoven that a deaf person can't hear or write music. Helen Keller ignored society's norm that the blind can't read. Today's university graduate may be 22 years old or 82 years young.

In other words, the skills essential to financial competency can be learned by most anyone, regardless of their age or IQ, and regardless of whether they were achievers in school or struggled throughout. It can be learned by poets and English majors, as well as math wizards and science fanatics.

Competent adults are prepared to handle life's daily challenges, work collaboratively with others, and communicate effectively

These skills range from learning how to really listen to dealing with conflict and anger. It requires skills in leadership and insight into building a career. It takes understanding your relationship to money and how that relationship affects your expectations of yourself and your children.

We sometimes take for granted that an educated adult will have picked up these skills. The reality is more sobering. Many families still have a hard time talking to each other about the tough challenges in life. After all, in my family, so the thinking goes, we're supposed to know these things.

But if you are really going to prepare your children, and set the model for generations to come, you'll spend time on communications, team building, patience and understanding, tolerance and respect. If your family is to cherish its life together and take responsibility for preparing those to follow, these life skills will become part of your DNA.

★   ★   ★

Remember . . . Self-esteem is earned, not inherited.
Learning is life long. It's never too late.
Knowing the answer is not nearly as important as wanting to learn.
There is no possibility for success unless there is risk of failure.
                                        ~Douglas K. Freeman

CHAPTER ELEVEN

Family Business Succession

Family business wars never fail to capture the imagination of a tabloid-hungry public and grab the headlines of a curious nation. We seem to enjoy the exposés over the way family fighting can destroy both the business and, in many cases, the family itself. When members of the Shoen family, including the company's founder, Leonard S. Shoen, and six of his children, sued U-Haul's privately held parent, Amerco Inc., the action was really against Leonard's third son, Joseph. Brent Redstone sued his father Sumner, and Henry Ford II took over Ford Motor Company through a lawsuit against the founder, his grandfather and namesake. Needless to say, Thanksgiving dinners were never quite the same in those families!

But not all family businesses suffer the fate of the family war. The Tuttle Farm was established by John Tuttle in New Hampshire around 1640 and is still in business after more than 350 years. Zildjian Cymbal was founded in Constantinople, Turkey in 1623, and moved to Massachusetts in 1929. The Wall Street Journal described this music company as "the oldest family business in America."

Levi Strauss & Co. was at the Gold Rush in California and Antoine's Restaurant in New Orleans has been serving dinner since 1840. The Strohs family has been brewing beer in Michigan since 1850 and, about 23 years later; Adolph Coors did the same in Colorado.

One of the most fascinating family businesses, and a model that many families have tried to replicate, is the House of Rothschild. Mayer Amschel Rothschild began his rise to wealth during the Napoleonic Wars, financing the British war effort. He established a finance house and grew the business by placing each of his five sons in European cities to run their own, but interrelated businesses. Rothschild recognized then that their success was tied to maintaining family control.

Family businesses represent a substantial portion of the U.S. economy and have a massive impact on the economy as a whole. Although exact numbers are hard to ascertain, researchers estimate that at least 80% of the businesses in the United States are family owned (*Family Business Review*, Summer 1996); and, 60% of total U.S. employment, 78% of new jobs, and

65% of all wages paid come from family businesses (*Financial Planning*, Nov 1999). Among the companies listed on the Standard and Poor's 500 Index, 34% are family businesses. It was projected that, in the five years between 2003 and 2008, 40% of family businesses in the United States. will pass to the next generation (*Business Week*, August 11, 2003). Unlike nonfamily business, the shift in power often has ramifications beyond the annual shareholders report.

What, exactly, constitutes a "family" business? A family business may be defined as an organization where two or more family members influence the direction of the business through their personal relationship, management roles, or ownership rights. Clearly, with such economic clout, this population is a desirable type of client for the financial services industry. Family businesses are, however, an endangered species.

Statistics reveal that only 40% of such businesses successfully transfer to the next generation, 12% to the third, and a mere 3% to the fourth (*Boston Globe*, May 4, 2003). Fortunately, those institutions that develop a sensitivity to and expertise in managing the challenges inherent in all these types of businesses will certainly have a competitive advantage in being the choice service provider and retaining the relationship with these family businesses in the face of increasing competition.

The reason for the high failure rate in family business succession
is more about culture than cash

Families in business want business prosperity, as well as family harmony and personal well-being. Instead, they often have underperforming businesses, unresolved conflicts within the family, and ambiguity about roles and responsibilities. The disappointing results are caused by significant differences in the values that are important to families and those that drive a successful business, different personal and financial goals, varying expectations from spouses and in-laws, and differing definitions of personal well-being by the business stakeholders.

The family members are born not hired into their roles and will always have emotional ties even when "estranged" physically. You can pick your business partner, but not your parents. Your children are yours for better or worse—and for all time. Whether they work in the business or not, you can't simply "fire" your old kids and hire new ones! Your family relationships are imposed or acquired, and they rarely change.

In the family, you expect to be treated equally. There are emotional as well as financial connections. Families focus on security for their members. Financial benefits and leadership are most often based on lineage and heritage. And, for better or worse, families tend to prefer the status quo rather than change.

But, in a successful business, employees are hired based on experience and need and can walk away (or be fired) from the enterprise. It's competitive, not a "given," to enter and be promoted. Employees expect to be rewarded based on results, not genetics. They expect fairness, know that respect is earned, not inherited. Leadership is based on merit, and success is often the result of overcoming risk not striving to maintain the status quo. Business expects and plans for constant change.

Because of these differing values and personal expectations successful transition from generation to generation requires recognizing and resolving a host of issues that do not affect the traditional business model. Since the odds are clearly against multigenerational transition, the planning must be even more thorough and the execution must be done right.

Succession

Who will be able to carry on the dreams of the founder? Sometimes the founder has predetermined, in his or her own mind, who should direct the business for the future. Not always, however, is the anointed one the most capable, or the most committed, or even the most willing to accept his or her role as leader in waiting. Often the founder will look for characteristics in the successor that match those of the founder, even though at the current stage of business development a different set of skills may be required to sustain the success of the enterprise. How often have we heard from the designated successor that, if asked, he or she would have preferred to devote time to other pursuits? Generational differences sometimes prevent the founder from recognizing that the passions of the next generation are as different from those of the founder as to be nearly foreign. In some cases, there is distinct gender bias; in other cases, it may be age bias.

What type of preparation is undertaken so that when this leadership role is passed to the successor generation there will be a smooth transition? Even if the successor is willing to assume responsibility, is the individual prepared for the responsibilities of both management of the business as well and the challenges of dealing with stakeholders who have equal financial interests and competing objectives? Will the managers and rank and file employees feel the same loyalty to the successor generation leadership that they had with the previous one? Leadership can be delegated, but loyalty and respect is earned.

Are there family members currently competent and being groomed for the responsibilities of management? A family business can be owned by family and operated by nonfamily. Has the decision been made that, regardless of talent and experience, and irrespective of the interests of the stakeholders and owners, a family member will assume control and management?

If there is more than one heir-apparent, how is the choice to be made or how can an office of the president be created and monitored? Some families cannot reconcile the competing demands of management and ownership, so they create an "office of the president" with several individuals sharing the position of responsibility. For the short term, this reconciles competing egos and ambitions. In the long term, lack of clear authority is likely to result in confusion, disagreement, and stalemate.

If there are no obvious candidates, are there individuals who could be sufficiently mentored within an adequate timeframe? If the current management prepares strategically for the future, the pipeline should be filled with candidates, both family and nonfamily, and a plan implemented to provide the training, opportunity, and experience to judge performance and attitude. Objectivity is required for such decisions. If the current owners are prepared to separate their role as "family" from their criteria for "management" the decisions about identifying candidates and their training would be easier.

If there is no direct family member qualified for the top leadership position, are there family members who have the requisite skills to function as responsible members of a board of directors who will hold the nonfamily CEO accountable? Separate from the responsibilities of active management, the task of an engaged owner requires preparation and training as well. How does an active board of directors set strategic direction, approve budgets, and oversee the activities of management? These responsibilities are learned, not inherited, and require preparation and mentoring.

Employment

Many family business owners dream of the day when their son or daughter comes to work in the business. There are often high expectations that this step is the first in a long line of steps to transitioning the business through the generations. But, like most first steps, there are challenges. If the process is sound and fair and the expectations of parent and child are realistic, the experience can be extraordinary and the bonds of family can be strengthened for generations.

But, if the opportunity of working together is to be a positive one for parent and child, and the format for others in the family to follow, then this first and critical step must be thoughtfully considered and carefully implemented. The downside risks can range from mild disappointment to permanent separation. What was a dream can become a nightmare. Families have fractured over relationships broken by working together under conditions that were far from ideal.

Success starts with a clear understanding of who might be eligible and qualified to work in the family business. Is it sufficient just to be related to the founder? What does it mean to be related? Are only blood relatives considered "related" or might that term include in-laws and step-children? What are the criteria for employment or do family members prequalify, regardless of maturity or experience, just because of their family status?

Will the family business be seen as a "welfare state" for family members who are unemployable elsewhere or will it be seen as a meritocracy only employing those family members who are qualified for the position to which they are assigned?

Successful businesses attain that envied status because they are operated by talented individuals. Ask any business owner about the secret of success and, in addition to hard work, they will quickly share, "*I have great people*" or "*I surround myself with the best.*" If the business becomes a safe haven for the poorly prepared, unmotivated, and over indulged descendant of the founder, it will likely affect profitability and drag down performance of other nonfamily employees. Rank and file employees understand the special position of family, but they *do* want to feel that merit is rewarded regardless of family status. In order to lead, you need followers. If employees resent managers who lack the minimum talent and drive to perform their appointed duties, and who are anointed rather than who have earned their responsibilities, it will affect morale and performance company wide. Additionally as soon as talented employees have the opportunity to leave, they will quickly do so.

To avoid this problem, *Legacy Families* make the opportunity for employment in the family-owned business available but not guaranteed. The criteria are clear and most often require that the applicant have related experience, through nonfamily–owned businesses. So, in the Family Constitution, the provision may state something like:

> *In the Smith Family, a family member is eligible to work in a full-time position for the Smith Company provided that . . .*
> - *There is a position open in the Company;*
> - *The candidate completes the Company's standard application procedures and meets all its general standards of age, education, credit history and prior related experience.*

Some *Families* require that the family member report to a nonfamily manager and compensation decisions must meet standard company policies. In other words, family members may have a priority for consideration over nonfamily members, but they will still need to meet the objective criteria and hiring process that all employees have met. Under these circumstances, the road to the top is visible but not guaranteed. Leadership is earned, not bestowed.

The business wins because the new employee has been hired through proper channels. The employee wins because the decision was based on a fair and objective process. The impact on the family member's self-esteem cannot be underestimated.

Accountability

In business, unlike in families, performance is measured and monitored. Positive performance is rewarded and poor performance is punished, sometimes financially and sometimes with severance. So, it is normal and expected that employees will be held accountable for their actions. How will family members be held accountable for their job requirements within the family business? Who will be delegated this uncomfortable task?

Holding a family member accountable for poor performance is much more difficult than recognizing achievement. Demoting or firing a sibling or in-law, or a son or daughter, may be the right business decision for the company, but it will have emotional costs for the family that cannot be discounted. As long as the founder is living and active in the business, this process falls naturally on his or her shoulders. This decision is more readily accepted by the family since the founder earned that right by the very creation of the entity. However, when leadership has passed to the next generation, this inherent authority to make the "tough call" may not exist. A child will take orders, however unpleasant; from a parent with greater acceptance than if those orders are issued by a sibling or a cousin.

Who is holding the family members employed in the business, now CEO, accountable for performance? If the company is publicly traded, there will be a board of directors, including nonfamily members and outside major shareholders, who can hold the CEO accountable. But in the closely held family business, the oversight of a governing board is often missing in reality, even if in existence for legal and compliance purposes.

Failure to hold family members accountable in the same way—and to the same extent—as nonfamily members will lead to dissension within the company and suspicion by family stakeholders not active in the business. The perception that a family member is protected from scrutiny and will be rewarded regardless of performance will inevitably lead to erosion in productivity, profitability, and confidence. It's the early stage that will cause the business to ultimately collapse.

It's not easy being "dad" and "boss." In the Franklin family, Paul Franklin, founder and CEO, had to face this very dilemma. The company was a highly respected aerospace manufacturer. Its products were purchased for use in both commercial and military aircraft. Performance either met or exceeded minimum standards or the product would be rejected. Bids were competitive and survival depended on beating the competition more often than losing.

When dad realized that his son was not working at the desired level of competence despite repeated warnings, counseling, and the additional training that was provided, he knew the time had come to make a decision that would affect both his family and his company. Though the decision was the same as he would make for any *non*family member, Paul knew he couldn't deliver the message quite the same way. So, he invited his son to dinner one summer evening, and suggested he bring his bathing suit.

After dinner, Paul and his son, Rick, went outdoors for a refreshing few minutes in the hot tub. After plunging into the tub with his son, dad produced a hat with the embroidering "Boss" on the brim. "Son," he began, "you know that I've been concerned about your performance at the company. Well, it hasn't improved. So, I'm sorry, but I have to let you go. You'll get the same two week separation as we offer everyone. I'm so sorry it didn't work out."

Rick was astounded as he listened. After all, this was his company, too, or so he thought.

Then, Paul took off his "boss" hat and put on a second hat, this one with the name "Dad" embroidered on the brim. And with a hand gently on his shoulder stated "Son, I understand you've just been fired from your job. Mom and I will be as supportive as we can."

Understanding which hat you are wearing in your dual role as head of the family AND head of the family *business* is critical for the continued success of the business as well as the long-term emotional well-being of the family.

Legacy Families hold themselves fully accountable to each other and to governing boards. The standards for performance are often higher because the family members represent ownership. If nonowners are expected to stretch their efforts to achieve success, then the owner-employees and managers must set the example and keep the bar raised high.

For this reason, in the most successful multigenerational family businesses, there will be a fully functioning board of directors composed of both family representation as well as nonfamily expertise with sufficient authority and responsibility to hire and fire even family members.

Compensation

One of the most difficult challenges within the family business is determining appropriate compensation for owner-employees. During the era of the founder's active management and control of the business, the amount of compensation paid for employment and the profit distributed because of ownership are often difficult to distinguish. Companies frequently bonus out profits to the owners to avoid incurring tax at the corporate level. The founder assumes, rightly so, *it's mine to take, so what difference is it how I choose to take it?*

This pattern is not easily replicated in Generation Two and beyond. In those successor generations, there are many stakeholders. Some of the inheritors are actively involved in the business, and could share in the style of blended compensation and profits. But it is likely that some of the inheritors are not engaged in the business whatsoever. For them, the economics depend on the distribution of profits. If employee-slash-brother Henry is drawing out the profits in bonuses to himself, the share available to his schoolteacher brother, Michael, will be less. As family members become responsible owners and recognize the implication of the bonus versus salary issue, the less tolerable this pattern will become.

The question to be answered . . . *Is the amount of compensation commensurate with the type of work and job responsibility?* There appear to be two extremes observed within family businesses, both creating potential problems:

- family members are overcompensated for their positions, merely because of their family relationship; or
- family members are not fully compensated, with the rationale that someday the company will be theirs.

Neither of these conditions is viable for a long period of time. Some stakeholders will begin objecting, and those objections will fester and grow unless successfully resolved. Ultimately, if either alternative is allowed to persist over a long period of time, there is serious risk of a rupture in the fabric of the family.

How should a family member be compensated for his or her services in the company? The obvious answer is the same as a nonfamily member would be compensated. In this regard, the family member CEO should receive the same compensation package of salary and benefits as would be paid to a nonfamily member. If the company doesn't have the expertise within its management team to make that determination, it should use outside experts to help.

"Fair is fair" should be the family rallying cry. The process of determining base compensation, the metrics for measuring performance, and the financial incentives and rewards for meeting or exceeding expectations should be applicable to both family and nonfamily employees. Only if this system is perceived fair and competitive will both active and passive owners be satisfied.

This is just one of the many decisions that a governing board must make and, at its heart, underscores the importance of impartiality and independence.

Retention of a Nonfamily Executive

If the family business leadership agrees to recruit a nonfamily CEO, it will then have the challenge of attracting a competent executive to serve. The family fights that often erupt over the family member CEO are not necessarily avoided in those businesses led by a nonfamily CEO. Freedom Communications, a family controlled company that owns *The Orange County Register*, 27 other daily newspapers, and 8 television stations, was founded by R. C. Hoiles in the 1930s. In 2002, its nonfamily CEO found himself in the middle of a "family feud" between the third generation and fourth generation owners over the future of the company. Not surprisingly, the first victim of the fight, which ultimately led to his resignation, was the nonfamily member CEO. In a family feud, there are no sure winners and collateral damage is inevitable (particularly when nonfamily members become the go to "fall guy or gal").

The prospect for this position must meet the test of experience and the talent to manage family dynamics. But, even if this unique individual can be found, to attract the person to the company will require a consensus by the decision makers on the responsibilities and authority of the CEO, expectations and metrics, compensation and incentives. Just going through this exercise is an effective way to frame the job description and its attributes, and is as applicable to family executives as it is to nonfamily.

The decision about employment criteria in the family business will have significant impact on the recruitment and retention of senior managers as well as rank and file employees. If it appears that positions of importance, whether management or otherwise, are reserved for those whose primary qualification is birthright, key nonfamily members will quickly look around for other employment opportunities and attracting new employees to fill that pipeline will become even more challenging.

However, if the family business invites and encourages competent family members to participate, and if positive performance is acknowledged and fairly rewarded, the chances of beating the transition odds will grow dramatically. We know from academic study, statistical records, and anecdotal stories, that family-owned businesses are more successful than independent businesses because of the commitment and loyalty of the family employees. The key is to combine the talent and passion of family members with the benefits of security and stability that characterize family enterprises.

Ownership and Succession

Will ownership be gifted to members of the family who are employed? Or will these individuals be required to purchase ownership shares so that the family members who are not actively employed are not disadvantaged, particularly when the family business is the primary asset in the estate?

Be careful what you wish for, as they say; you may just get it. If one heir received the business and another received passive assets, the new business owner may one day wish the shoe was on the other foot. Ownership of a family business carries the inevitable risks of any business, including fluctuation of income, long hours, and personal sacrifices. The heir of the passive assets is often seen as clipping coupons for the same or even greater income.

One of the reasons that the life insurance industry is vitally interested in family business is that, through this product, the estate may be more easily divided between the family members who are active in the business and those who are not. The liquidity available through life insurance may help to create a degree of financial equivalency, permitting those in the business to retain ownership and control and those not actively involved to be able to receive their fair share of the estate assets through the equivalent cash distributions from insurance. The difficulty in this approach, of course, is that the business value is a moving target, while the cost of insurance may make it impossible to create true economic equality.

Ownership transfer, particularly from the founder or wealth creator generation (referred to as "G1") to the successor generation (referred to as "G2") is fraught with challenges. If succession is managed as a process of six orderly transitions, the chances for the successful continuation of the business significantly increases. (For a thorough discussion of each transition, you may wish to read Dr. Lee Hausner's book, which she coauthored with Ernest Doud, entitled *Hats Off to You 2.*[1])

In brief, these transitions involve the following:

Transition #1—Founder Transition

Make no mistake—without the willingness of the founder or current CEO to relinquish control, there can be no succession. Specialists in family business planning will tell you that the emotional state of the founder can be a greater impediment to its sale or transition than any financial hurdle. The founder struggles with such questions and/or issues as:

- What will I do with the rest of my life?
- How can I live at my current level with only passive income to provide for me and my family?
- What will happen to my employees and key managers?
- I can't choose between my kids.
- They may run it *better* than I did.
- Nobody can run it as well as I can.
- The kids want to change "my" business.
- I need someplace to go every day.
- Without the business, I am a nothing.
- Without me, the business is nothing.

Behind every one of these questions or comments is a deep emotional need or concern. Dealing with them long before transitioning the business becomes necessary or appropriate will greatly facilitate the process.

Transition #2—Family Transition

Family dynamics also have an effect upon the successful transition of the family business. We've focused on these issues elsewhere in this book, and

---

[1] *Hats Off to You 2, Balancing Roles and Creating Success in Family Business* by Ernest A. Doud, Jr., and Lee Hausner (Doud Hausner Vistar, 2004).

you may recall that they include the following:

- Effective communication between family members;
- understanding the different rights and responsibilities of management, owners, directors, and nonmanagement employees;
- conflict resolution; and
- alternative governance structures for successor generations.

Transition #3—Business Transition

Family businesses rarely engage in long-range strategic planning on succession. While we are familiar with traditional business planning, the most effective planning will also include such questions as:

- Should this business even continue into the next generation?
- Should the business be retained regardless of its economics but because of the founder's legacy?
- Is a sale a feasible option given current economics?
- How much is the business really worth, disregarding the emotional attachment the founder may have?

The voices of all the key stakeholders, including nonfamily senior management and the family's trusted advisors, its "brain trust," should be expressed and considered.

Transition #4—Management Transition

Even though family businesses like to look to members of the family to assume major leadership roles, there may not be qualified family members (or enough qualified family members), or they may be potential members who, with mentoring and more experience, would be ready to assume a major leadership role in the future. We've already explored the issues of employment, but the other challenges that must be resolved during this transition include:

- How large is the universe from which to make a selection? (Blood family members, in-laws, spouses, adoptees, and so on)
- Can the business use an interim nonfamily leader while family members receive more training to get up to speed?
- Can the family adjust to a new management model, particularly if the transition is from a strong entrepreneur who was a sole decision maker to an individual who must now answer to partners in ownership?
- What kind of leader does the business now need at its current state of development?

It's one thing to focus on day-to-day operations and the source of the talent required to grow the business over the next several years. It's another thing altogether to consider leadership over a long period of time. The company's business plan must address both.

Transition #5—Ownership Transition

An analysis has determined that the business is viable for the future, a new management team has been assembled and now the key issue becomes: who will own this business? Within the family's strategic plan, as well as in the corporate business plan, you will need to consider such questions as:

- Should ownership be vested in the family members who are active in the business?
- Should ownership be a gift to family members working in the business or should they just be given the right to purchase shares?
- If ownership is divided between active and nonactive family members, how are the financial interests of the nonactive members protected? How will profits be allocated and distributed? How will *related*, but not necessarily directly *connected*, business opportunities be spread fairly amongst the family owners?
- How are the needs for decision making on the part of those family members running the business being protected from the nonactive family members whose interests might not be in sync with business strategies?
- What is the educational process necessary to insure that nonactive owners are responsible owners?
- How will financial information be distributed to nonactive owners, and yet be protected from inappropriate disclosure to others?

We've covered many of these points in Chapter Eight, dealing with Shared Assets. You'll want to adapt these suggestions to the reality of business. But don't overlook them.

Transition #6—Exit Strategies

As was discussed in the chapter dealing with Shared Assets there is an axiom in business that you don't enter into a business relationship without knowing how you can exit that relationship. This is even more important in a family business, because personal relationships are often as or more important than the economic ones. Passing ownership to the second generation may be the easy step. But how long will that shared ownership continue and at what price to the family harmony? Every generation past the founder must confront the exit strategy issues, including:

- At some point, one or more of the members of G2 or G3—or beyond—may wish to sell the company. Who has the power to decide? What happens if others don't agree? Receiving a share of the business may have been the easy part.

- If the option to sell the company is rejected, how can the reluctant owner force the remaining owners to buy out his or her interest at a fair price and reasonable terms? Traditional rights of first refusal do not resolve the problem, because that tool is only valuable if an outsider wishes to purchase the member's fractional interest, a circumstance rare in a family-owned enterprise.
- However, the remaining partners may conclude that the time has come to remove one of the family owners and force him or her to sell. But, absent a carefully designed "put and call" option, there is often no more power to force the sale than there is to force the purchase.
- Price is the battleground for many intra-family sales. Who determines the price? What, if any, discounts are appropriate? What if the true value is illusive because of undisclosed business opportunities or risks, understated inventories or inflated receivables? Asking competing sides within the family to agree on price at the time these issues become relevant is likely to prove unrealistic at best and calamitous at worst.
- Payment of the purchase price is not easy, especially when one party expects all cash and the other insists on extended payments. Is there security for installment transactions? If the company or remaining business owners are acquiring a family member's share, will such purchase affect the availability of the commercial credit lines necessary for normal business operations? These are always challenges in any purchase and sale, but magnified many times because of the family dynamics when the sale is triggered between family members who want to terminate their shared ownership.

If a process is not formulated early, before conflict arises, then even a family business as respected as the Dow Jones & Co., owner of the *Wall Street Journal*, which had been in business and family owned since 1889, can find itself on the block, with family relationships strained and even shredded.

As they say, "fail to plan...plan to fail." To beat the odds of failure and to ensure that the family retains both its cohesion as a family and the economic benefits of the business, the founder and family must resolve these and other issues through a comprehensive business succession plan.

The family business is the great economic engine in this country, whether through an operating entity, real estate company, or other form of capital creation. It's not surprising that the wealth creator would like to pass this venture on to future generations. But seeing the possibility is not the same as attaining it, especially when family is involved.

★   ★   ★

"Success" in "succession" is possible but, in the words of that great philosopher, Yogi Berra,

> *"If you don't know where you're going, you're liable to end up someplace else."*

CHAPTER TWELVE

Managing Conflict

As a result of the alcoholism of both her parents, Louise grew up in a family where chaos and violence were a way of life. As the youngest of four children, she quickly learned a defense of passivity and "invisibility" as a method of dealing with the volatility, unlike the aggressive defiance of her two older siblings. When she and Steve married, she was committed to making sure that her children would never experience what she did growing up. Arguing or any type of normal disagreement among her children was not permitted. But what Louise didn't realize was that conflict is a relatively normal occurrence when differences of opinions occur and this does not necessarily mean that the explosions she witnessed as a child would immediately occur.

In fact, avoiding conflict altogether could do more harm than good. Without learning an appropriate method of dealing with conflict, anger and hostility build up internally and then a relatively trivial situation can cause a major disruption in relationships. This was the presenting situation when this family sought help in dealing with transition within the family business. All three young adults were working in various departments within the company, but it was clear to all around them that sibling tension was always boiling just beneath the surface and chances of a successful partnership when Dad and Mom were out of the picture were seriously compromised.

It's an old and far too common story: fairy tale turned to nightmare. Famous families battling over their parents' inheritance, high-profile family infighting, and even violence within the family has become common tabloid fodder. Then there is the unadvertised story that rarely sees sensational headlines—great families transitioning the next generation to greatness.

- What makes the difference?
- Why does a family legacy transfer for some, but not for others?
- How do you develop strength, character, responsibility, and competent family leadership?

Families who are able to become *Legacy Families* have concentrated on building the skill of conflict resolution. They have learned how to apply effective communication practices and to create structures and processes for disputes to be handled as soon as they develop.

What is Conflict?

Some would say "you'll know it when you see it." But mental health professionals define conflict as a disagreement perceived as a threat to needs, interests, or concerns resulting from individuals or groups that differ in attitudes, beliefs, values, or needs. Each person's attitudes, intentions, intuitions, awareness, context, and capacity for empathetic and honest emotional communication have a significant impact on his or her experience of conflict and the capacity for resolution. What distinguishes conflict from mere disagreements is the presence of what are commonly referred to as "negative" and lingering emotions such as anger, fear, guilt, and shame. Within this definition there are some important points to consider.

The true disagreement might be different from the perceived one
Since conflict often involves misunderstandings and misinterpretations, the perceived disagreement may become considerably exaggerated, be it in the heat of the moment or simmering over time. Therefore, it is important to understand the true area of disagreement—and not just the "flash point"—since this will help to solve the actual problem as well as solve the true needs of the parties.

Who are the parties involved in the conflict?
Who owns the problem? Particularly in families, many individuals can become involved in the conflict when, by themselves, they would not have been involved in any disagreements. It simply would not have been their issue. They are influenced or pressured to choose sides based on their relationship with one of the parties involved and it is sometimes a challenge to identify who really has the basic problem. In a multigenerational extended family, this may take the form of one entire branch of the family pitted against the other as a result of a personal conflict between one of the members in each branch.

A perceived threat is very different from an actual threat
The perception of a threat is significantly influenced by past experiences and "headsets," discussed in Chapter Three, which are created by variables such as culture, values, beliefs, past experience, and gender. What is the real issue? What's at stake? What is actually being said? People in a conflict situation will respond to these questions and dozens more based

on their perception of the situation rather than an objective evaluation of the issue. When the true threat can be identified, it becomes easier to find solutions and constructively manage the conflict.

*Needs are things that are essential to our well-being
and are not to be confused with wants or desires*

Conflict arises when we ignore the needs of others, our own needs or the group's needs. It is more than a simple disagreement. The individuals involved perceive a threat to their well-being and therefore it cannot just be dismissed by an attitude of "it will pass if we just ignore it." There are psychological needs to be addressed within the conflict in addition to the objective needs that might be initially presented. Any solution to the problem must take all these types of needs into consideration.

The potential for conflict is constant

Conflicts are normal experiences that can easily occur when two or more individuals are placed in a situation that offers differing choices. Therefore, it is important to develop methods for identifying the potential for these conflicting situations, such as we discussed in Chapter Eight (Family Shared Assets), as well as systems for constructively managing existing conflicts so that, instead of the conflict creating permanent disruption in interpersonal relationships, it can become a productive learning situation instead.

Interpersonal conflict can take a wide variety of forms, ranging from verbal criticism to physical fights, and from active confrontation to passive aggression. Some individuals will release their anger and try to impose their will, while others will shut down and say nothing, but seethe internally. Their opposition is sometimes hard to spot. When you just can't get an answer or, perhaps, even a meeting to come to a conclusion, you may have a participant demonstrating passive–aggressive behavior. Unfortunately, conflict is part of everyday life.

Husbands and wives disagree about a multitude of choices, ranging from which restaurant to patronize to issues relating to child rearing. Siblings can engage in conflict on an hourly basis (or so it seems). Teachers and students have intellectual conflict as well as clashes over behavioral choices. Best friends can disagree frequently while still retaining the friendship. We experience conflict dealing with colleagues in the workplace, interacting with members of both the professional and volunteer boards upon which we serve as well as in dealing with the service providers in our lives. In other words, interpersonal conflict can be experienced everywhere so it remains to be seen that conflict will definitely be a part of even the strongest *Legacy Families*.

As successful as your family is or may be, if you aspire to create a real *Legacy Family,* you'll need to master the process of conflict resolution.

Benefits of Conflict

It is not the act of conflict in and of itself that is so problematic and destructive. In fact, there are some very positive outcomes of conflict.

- Conflict helps to surface problems. One of the reasons that "in-laws" can be seen as "outlaws" is that they often are the objective "agent" identifying problems existing within the family system into which they have married that have been festering for years but ignored. A fresh pair of eyes might see the family dynamics and potential for conflict much more clearly than an "insider." After all, an outsider often has a more objective perspective of family dynamics than those individuals who have been a part of the problem for a prolonged period of time.
- Conflict can lead to creative ways of solving problems as the best of opposing viewpoints can be combined to end up with a far more favorable solution.
- Conflict is a process by which feelings ultimately can be aired openly and honestly, thereby promoting more authentic communication.
- Conflict provides an opportunity to obtain a greater understanding of the opposing parties and how they think, act, and feel. It gives individuals a chance to demonstrate an acceptance and respect for the unique ways in which others think, act, and feel.
- Conflict can breathe new life into a relationship that is stagnating and provide moments of honesty that can result in a lifetime of improved communication.
- Conflict can provide the venue to clarify our expectations of others and a time to modify existing rules or sanctions based on our expectations.
- Finally, conflict gives all participants the chance to apply the effective communication skills that we outlined in Chapter Three.

Thus the isolated act of conflict is not by definition "bad" or something to be avoided at all cost, necessarily. How an individual or a family chooses to deal with conflict is the critical test. Unresolved conflicts are like psychological cancer cells in families, growing and spreading until they erupt with such intensity that a family can become permanently estranged. This certainly is the case when the matter finally has to be resolved in hostile litigation. Once Humpty Dumpty is so broken, it is impossible to put the pieces back together as they were originally.

When Mary and Sam become angry with each other, the negative feelings don't just disappear because nothing further is said or they are admonished to just "forget it." They don't forget it and, in fact, these emotions just get buried deeper and deeper in the invisible "psychological gunny sack" we all carry around. These feelings often become the filter through which future behavior is interpreted. The gunny sack becomes that "emotional baggage" self-help books are so fond of saying we all carry around through life; the more emotional baggage, the more "ammunition" we bring to each new conflict. This can lead to even more hostility. If this occurs only infrequently, then the psychological gunny sack does not become burdensome. But if the conflicting situations continue to occur, the pent up anger will eventually overflow the gunny sack and the outburst may permanently damage the relationship.

Did you ever wonder why a simple poorly worded statement to another, or a forgotten birthday, or a noncontentious issue, suddenly became the flash point for a bitter, divisive, and serious argument? It may have been the result of a prior, unresolved, but festering problem or accumulation of problems hiding in that set of emotional baggage you've been dragging around for years.

The Elements of Conflict

In every situation of conflict there are emotional, cognitive, and physical responses. The emotional responses are how we feel in the face of the threat and can range from rage to fear, despair, and confusion. Cognitively we give ourselves messages about the situation. At a party, an unknown guest makes a sarcastic comment to you. You can cognitively give yourself one of the following messages:

"What a rude jerk. I am going to immediately find someone else to talk to."
"How dare he? I am going to give him a piece of my mind!"
"I should never have voiced my opinion on that subject. Now everyone thinks I am an idiot."

Based on the cognitive messages you give to yourself, you will experience a range of physical reactions that might include bodily tension, rapid heartbeat, flushing, perspiration, and anxiety.

A family was once referred to our practice for the purpose of facilitating their first family retreat. The interview with the patriarch was notable for the numerous times he stated, *"We are a very nice, quiet, close family and we don't want any Pandora's boxes opened."* A truly close family doesn't keep boxes filled with turmoil, pain, and suffering. It did not come as a surprise, then, when we heard a torrent of frustration, anger, and hostility expressed from each of the three adult children, as well as from their respective spouses. In their private conversations with us, the members expressed clear examples of unresolved conflict and evidence that this was not the close family the patriarch idealized.

This was a classic example of a family in which there was no productive outlet for the negative feelings that naturally resulted from the normal, everyday disagreements life presents. Instead they struggled to keep their conversations and interactions "safe," burying the hard feelings just below the surface. The fact that the patriarch was willing to initiate facilitated family meetings was a sign that he at least had *some* recognition that his family was not the picture perfect image he was trying to project, though he didn't know how to go about changing the situation.

He could have continued on, trying to convince himself and others that his was the iconic Norman Rockwell family blissfully celebrating a Thanksgiving dinner together, but, since there were significant assets, including a substantial business, to be managed collectively by his children, he recognized the need to create a healthier family team. Fortunately he acted in time, and this story has a positive ending. The family business has been successfully transitioned to the next generation. It was important to deal with emotional issues, cognitive messages as well as the physical responses that were stimulated by stress and conflict. It took work and many meetings over a period of time to build effective communication skills and to create an environment of open, honest dialogue so that disagreements were not something to be feared and could be positively resolved.

Conflict Styles

Everyone's emotional makeup is different, and thus everyone comes to the conflict in different ways, bearing various styles of how, when, and why they conflict. Conflict may be more easily understood by examining the consequences of various conflict styles. Each style is a way to meet one's needs in a disagreement but may impact other people in different ways:

- *Competing.* Competing is a style of conflict in which one's own needs are advocated over the needs of others. It relies on an aggressive style of communication, low regard for future relationships and the exercise of coercive power. Those using competitive styles of conflict tend to seek control over a discussion, in both substance and ground rules. They fear that loss of such control will result in solutions that fail to meet their needs. Competing tends to result in responses that increase the level of threat, prolong conflicted relationships, and exacerbate anger and hostility. Individuals who utilize this style will love accommodators (see next).
- *Accommodating.* Accommodating is also known as "smoothing," which is the opposite of competing. Persons using this style of conflict yield their needs to those of others, trying to be diplomatic. They tend to allow the needs of the group to overwhelm their own, which may not ever be stated, as preserving the relationship is seen as most important to the accommodator. However, all is not as diplomatic as it may seem; after a prolonged period of this type of behavior, anger over the unmet needs of the accommodating individual will begin to spill out.

- *Avoiding.* Avoiding is a common response to the perception of conflict being something bad and to be avoided at all cost. "Perhaps if we don't bring it up, it will blow over," we say to ourselves. But, generally speaking, all that happens is that feelings get pent up, views go unexpressed and the conflict festers until it becomes too big to ignore. Like a cancer that may well have been cured if treated early, the conflict grows and spreads until it kills the relationship or is evidenced in an overly emotional outburst that can ultimately lead to violence. Because needs and concerns go unexpressed for so long, only to blow up over a single, often unrelated "flash point," other people are often confused when this ultimately happens, wondering what went wrong in a relationship. Adults who were raised in a family of abuse and violence will often tend to use this approach to dealing with conflict, fearful of exacerbating the situation and creating the fearful outcomes they experienced in childhood. It is only helpful to use this type of reaction to conflict when the issue simply is not worth the effort to argue.
- *Compromising.* Compromising is an approach to conflict in which people "gain" and "give" in a series of tradeoffs. While often satisfactory, compromise may ultimately not be satisfying enough since each party remains shaped by individual perceptions of needs and don't necessarily understand the other side very well. This results in the retaining of a lack of trust and the avoidance of the risk-taking involved in more collaborative behaviors. Compromise works when both parties are willing to reduce some demands or, as an intermediate solution, saves time and effort for both sides.
- *Collaborating.* Collaborating is the pooling of individual needs and goals toward a common goal, which is often called "win-win" negotiation. Collaboration requires assertive, honest communication and cooperation in order to achieve a better solution than either individual could have achieved alone. It offers the chance for consensus, the integration of needs and the potential to exceed the range of possibilities that previously limited one individual's view of the conflict. It brings new time, energy, and ideas to resolve the dispute meaningfully in a positive "two heads are better than one" scenario.

Understanding your own style of dealing with conflict as well as the natural orientation of those involved in conflict situations helps to develop a more effective resolution. You can become more effective in conflict situations if you consciously select appropriate behavior instead of reacting according to habit.

To manage conflict, you need to understand the way you currently act and then learn alternative ways to cope. If you recognize the way you normally react in a conflict situation, ask yourself, "Is that the way I *want* to respond?" Knowing other ways that might better solve conflict, you may be motivated to change. Remember, only *you* can change your behavior. Changing the *way you act* often affects the *way others react* to you.

Behaviors that assist in conflict resolution

Conflicts are only resolved successfully when both parties commit to working actively to solve them. With so many styles of conflict it is easy for one style to assert itself over the other, that is the accommodator rolling over for the competitor. However, such accommodation only works in the short term and may not work at all if the accommodator is rolling over for the wrong reasons. But, as we shall see, conflict can be resolved effectively by working together regardless of your conflict style. Over the years we have identified several behaviors that assist in conflict resolution.

Clearly define the problem you are trying to solve

Different underlying needs, interests, and goals can cause people to perceive problems very differently. Do not assume anything. We teach young children to "use your words" in dealing with their problems. However, as we emerge into adulthood we forget that very simple, yet powerful adage and assume we know or they know or should know what we're feeling. Additionally, be honest with yourself. If you are feeling in a way you think you must or in a way the others want you to, that is not "being yourself," then you will not be clear in defining the problem and any resolution of the conflict will be a false one. In the end, you waste your time and energy and end up feeling failure—or guilt—rather than growth.

Express your concerns from your perspective utilizing "I" messages rather than "You" attacks (See Chapter Three.)

In a controlled, assertive manner communicate your feelings regarding the conflict. Avoid generalizations about the other party, your relationship, or the conflict itself. Keep statements focused on how *you* are behaving, thinking, and feeling rather than how the other is acting. "You" messages suggest blame and encourage the recipient to deny wrongdoing or, just as often, to blame in return. However, "I" messages simply state a problem without blaming someone for it. This makes it easier for the other side to help solve the problem without having to admit they were wrong.

"I feel angry when our family decides upon an action plan and the plans are derailed by lack of cooperation from one member."

Utilize assertive behavior techniques rather than aggressive behavior

When you are assertive (as opposed to aggressive), you identify specific behaviors that are causing you personal concern and express them in a clear, controlled manner.

For instance, you might say, "I feel that my opinions are not being considered when decisions are made without any input on my part."

Not, "I will not stand for your bossy, overbearing behavior anymore."

If your statements are met with resistance or an attempt to divert your attention to other issues, (e.g., "I understand more about the financial implications of these choices than you do"), hold firm to your original statements, repeating the exact words if necessary until your concerns are at least acknowledged. This technique is often called the "broken record" technique. Just as the stuck needle keeps playing the same passage of the record over and over again, so will you continue to express your concern in exactly the same way until there is some indication that the other party understands your position. Be careful not to express hostility in your posture, facial expressions, or tone of voice.

Aggressiveness involves threats (overt or implied), labeling the behavior of others (*"you're being childish"*) or playing armchair psychologist by trying to negatively diagnose the motivation behind the troublesome behavior of the other party ("you are just enjoying all the attention you are receiving from being so negative and argumentative"). Don't corner the opponent with absolutes or threats. All parties need to preserve their dignity and self-respect, even if you are right in this case. Aggressiveness either exacerbates the verbal mudslinging or causes the other party to retreat without resolution, thus permitting the underlying conflict to continue to fester and grow. Remember, if the other party simply withdraws from the conflict this does not mean you have won and the conflict is over. The unresolved issues will surface at a later date with greater intensity and the potential to cause irreparable damage to family relationships.

Communicate in a calm, respectful, rational manner
We often think that emotional outbursts are the only way the other party will pay attention to us. Usually, just the opposite is true. Talking calmly, respectfully, and rationally creates a more favorable environment for being heard and you will be able to maintain better control of yourself. Do your best to be courteous to one another, no matter how tempting it is to revert to aggressive, disrespectful, and childlike behavior. It does not help a conflict situation to be discourteous. It will only make the others angry and less likely to listen to what you have to say or do what you would like them to do. This also applies to what is written, especially utilizing email with its instant transmission. If it is necessary to write something in anger, wait for 24 hours and then reread the document before sending it when you are in a calmer frame of mind.

No matter what you think of another person, if they are treated with respect and dignity, even if you think they do not deserve it, communication *will* be more effective and the chances of successful conflict resolution is increased. Remain constructive under pressure. If you feel that you are beginning to lose control, it is perfectly acceptable to take a time-out break and physically remove yourself from the conflict until you can regain control. Excuse yourself with comments such as, "I need some quiet time to reflect on what we have just been discussing. Let's take a short break and continue this discussion in 20 minutes."

Conflict resolution is severely compromised in an overly emotional confrontation and things are said that the speaker later regrets. If you know that anger management is an issue of yours, get help for it or "practice" being calm and rational by resolving smaller conflicts successfully before you work up to addressing a truly important family issue.

Avoid blaming

This will keep the communication flow going. When you avoid blame by admitting personal responsibility for your own actions, it encourages understanding and empathy for each other's feelings. Remember that in a conflict there are at least two parties who are adversely affected and feel some justification in their positions.

Of course, some people equate avoiding blame by going in the opposite direction and being too accommodating, accepting blame for all aspects of the conflict when you may or may not be at fault. While avoiding blame it is important to be clear on just what, and how much, responsibility you are willing to take for the conflict.

Listen not just for content but, equally importantly, for understanding the needs of the other party(ies)

Effective listening and responding are key elements to the productive resolution of conflict. In his book *The Seven Habits of Highly Effective People*, author Stephen R. Covey introduced the powerful concept of "listen first to understand before being understood." Our natural instinct to just blurt out and explain our case at all costs, before actually listening to vital information that might help us be understood in the process, impairs the process of conflict resolution.

Instead of constantly reacting or even interrupting, listen for the feeling and emotions of the other and reflect upon them with understanding. Ask the opponent to clarify or repeat anything that is unclear or seems unreasonable. Attempt to repeat their case, as they have presented it, back to them. This demonstrates that you are listening and that you truly want to understand what they have said. Everyone wants to be heard and the degree to which each party to the conflict can feel that they have been able to express their feelings as well as their position and feel respected greatly facilitates the resolution process.

Listening creates an atmosphere of being cared for and reduces defensiveness. It then enables the parties to productively look at the issues and seek the most effective solutions. Listening does not mean that you agree to the position of the other individual or are capitulating to their unreasonable demands. But it does acknowledge thoughtful consideration of multiple positions and that in itself helps produce successful outcomes. Resist the natural need to want to explain your side first with the mistaken belief that if they understand your perspective, they will certainly come to the same conclusion as you have. (If that were truly the case, the conflict probably wouldn't exist in the first place.) Additionally, when listening to other parties resist the tendency to interrupt with objections that support your point of view without hearing them out fully.

Put yourself in the shoes of the other party

Why are they taking the position that is in conflict with yours? Why are they angry? How you see the world depends upon your background and the tendency for people to see what they want to see. It is difficult to briefly put aside your point of view and try to imagine how the other party may be viewing the situation. However, the ability to master this skill and, in the process, possibly see some merit in the position of others greatly helps the process of conflict resolution.

Be willing to forget

Grudges are the Achilles heel of conflict resolution; your conflict isn't truly resolved if you're still holding onto the discord and holding a grudge. Instead, once you have "resolved" a conflict and felt that you were heard and understood, then "let go" of the conflict. Once you have reached an agreed upon plan of action, move forward and do not continue to dwell in the past. Don't bring it up in the future as if it had not been resolved. It is often helpful to commit the agreed upon solutions to writing so that you have the written document as proof it is over and can now be forgotten.

Be willing to forgive

During a prolonged conflict, words are often spoken in anger, vindictive behaviors occur and feelings are hurt. Occasionally, even violent or physical confrontations erupt. The act of forgiving demonstrates personal growth and an acknowledgment of the waste of productive energy that is required to hang on to negative feelings over past hurts.

Communicate in person

Technology has made it easier than ever these days to avoid confrontation, but to successfully resolve conflict face-to-face confrontations are a must. Don't send in another party to solve your problems. If you are lacking in confidence to verbalize your concerns or feel that the situation might get out of hand, it is acceptable to ask an individual who has the respect of both parties to the conflict to join the discussion as an observer and peacekeeper, but it's not okay to let him or her intercede on your behalf and "take the meeting" for you. The mere presence of a neutral third party serves to keep emotions in check and the parties to the conflict will put forth greater effort to keep under control in discussions. If the conflict involves many individuals, it might be wise to utilize the services of a professional mediator.

Deal with one issue at a time

There may be more than one issue involved in the conflict at one time. Someone in the group needs to provide leadership to identify the issues involved. Then only one issue at a time can be addressed so the problem is manageable. If there is another problem from the past blocking current communication, list it as one of the issues in this conflict and, if necessary, prioritize that conflict to resolve first. It may have to be dealt with before the current conflict can be resolved.

Choose the right time for a conversation regarding the conflict

When it comes to conflict resolution, sometimes timing really IS everything. Individuals have to be willing to address the conflict. They are likely to resist if they feel they are being forced into negotiations. In order to avoid dictating the resolution and starting off on the wrong foot, begin the process by compromising on a time that is good for both of you. For instance, "I think we should talk about what happened this morning. When would be a good time to discuss this?"

Avoid reacting to unintentional remarks

Words like "always" and "never" may be said in the heat of battle and do not necessarily convey what the speaker means. Anger will increase the conflict rather than bring it closer to resolution.

Avoid resolutions that come too soon or too easily

People need time to think about all possible solutions and the impact of each. Quick answers may disguise the real problem. All parties need to feel some satisfaction with the resolution if they are to accept it. While everyone is eager to put the conflict to bed, conflict resolutions should not be rushed. For instance, rather than settling too soon or too often, instead suggest, *"That's a possible solution. Let's think about it and talk on Monday morning to see if we still feel that way."*

Agree to disagree

Respect for one another and the value of relationships are two good reasons to disagree, but to choose not to allow the disagreement to interfere with the group is something we can all agree on.

Don't insist on being right

Rarely do conflicts hinge on black and white, "you're wrong" or "I'm right" statements. In fact, there are usually several "right" solutions to every problem. There do not have to be winners and losers and dealing with conflict competitively is not a productive course of action.

Understanding the issues involved in principled negotiation

Successful conflict resolution depends upon learning effective negotiation skills. In Roger Fisher and William L. Ury's book, *Getting to Yes*, based on the Harvard Negotiation Project, five important negotiation concepts are introduced:

- *Negotiation Concept #1.* Separate the people from the problem. During the process of negotiation, relationships tend to become entangled with the discussion of the issue at hand. However, it is important to separate the personalities involved and deal with the people as human beings and with the problem on its own merits. Anger over a situation gets transferred to the individual with whom you associate the situation, but it is equally important that participants see themselves as working together to solve the problem and not be diverted by personality issues.

  A mother-in-law might remark to the parent of her grandchild her concern over the amount of candy she observes her grandchildren eating. The actual, measurable issue at hand is nutrition, but the parent might take immediate offense interpreting that statement of fact as a personal criticism of his or her parenting. If the problem, nutritional snacking, could be neutrally discussed, both parties might end up brainstorming healthier snack options. Accommodators will find this particularly hard to do as they are overly concerned with maintaining relationships and not having anyone mad at them.

- *Negotiation Concept #2.* Focus on interests, not position. Your position is something you have decided upon. Your interests are what caused you to decide on that position. Jack and Susan were involved in a standoff regarding estate planning for their only son, Philip. Jack had come from a family of very modest means and thus had worked from a very early age for everything he had needed above and beyond basic food, clothing, and shelter. He felt that this fiscal discipline was a strong factor contributing to his success and was very fearful of "spoiling" Philip. Thus he wanted to provide very little in the way of a financial inheritance for Philip, instead expecting him to work his way through college and achieve on his own as he had done. Jack wanted the majority of their wealth to go to the foundation they were creating.

  Susan, on the other hand, had come from a more affluent background, had all her education paid for by the family as well as travel opportunities with both family and friends. She felt that she had not been spoiled by the generosity of her family and wanted to assure this same type of support to Phillip. Thus they had not been able to complete any estate planning documents. Jack was taking a position of fiscal limitation while Susan was taking a position of fiscal generosity. However, both shared an interest in their son becoming a productive, contributing member of society. By helping each of them shift from their opposing positions to focus on the joint interest, that of the long-range success of their son Philip, it was possible to construct a plan that would provide funds in a controlled manner that would not "spoil" Philip (Jack's main fear) and would be generous enough to support his growth and development both educationally and professionally (Susan's concern). By concentrating on the shared interests rather than their opposing positions, a satisfactory compromise was reached and the estate plan was completed.

- *Negotiation Concept #3.* Brainstorm to generate a variety of possibilities before deciding what to do. Once the problem has been clearly identified, consider a variety of options that might solve the conflicting situation. Objectivity and rationality will be key to your success. To those dual ends, it is helpful to involve other trusted individuals to assist in this step in order to expand the range of possibilities. A brainstorming session is designed to create as many ideas as possible and is not the place for criticism or judgment of the options suggested.
- *Negotiation Concept #4.* Establish objective criteria to evaluate the results. Depending upon the nature of the conflict, an objective standard might be:

Market Value	What a court would decide
Precedent	Moral standard
Scientific judgment	Professional standards
Cost	Equal treatment
Tradition	Reciprocity

- *Negotiation Concept #5.* Formalizing the process. As families grow in numbers, many *Legacy Families* create structures within the family to deal with the inevitable conflicts which will arise (see Chapter Five). These may include:
  - *A Council of Elders.* This is a small group comprised of members of the senior generation who have the respect of family members.
  - *The Family Council.* The council is made up of representatives of the larger family. Membership in the council may be determined by electing representatives from each family branch, or be organized by selecting representatives from each generation.

If conflict cannot be satisfactorily resolved by the individual parties on their own, or through the use of the Council of Elders or the Family Council, then the use of a trained mediator is a worthwhile investment for any family.

One Family's Story

The chain of Tipplers Hardware stores had been established by Phillip Tippler and had grown to 15 different locations under the guidance of his three sons, Stuart, Michael, and Donald. Transition from dad to the three sons proved very successful. For over 25 years, the three brothers were able to work harmoniously and collaboratively together. But the time for succession to the third generation was at hand.

In each of the family branches there was a highly qualified individual who had distinguished himself both academically and through his conscientious work within the company. Each brother felt that his heir should be the successor to the position of Chief Executive Officer or CEO, the role currently held, not surprisingly, by the elder brother, Stuart. Suddenly, the tradition of building consensus and seeking collaboration was threatened. Each branch found itself in a tug of war with the other branches, competing to have its candidate selected. Stuart was accused by his brothers and various members of their family groups of being controlling and overbearing and trying to manipulate the process to ensure that his son would become president. He uncharacteristically became domineering, limiting discussion of the succession process in meetings and inviting professional advisors that he had hired on behalf of the company to provide their recommendations. Not surprisingly, the experts seemed to support Stuart's conclusions.

The risk of the collapse of the business and the permanent fracture of the extended family forced the three brothers to find a new approach. If you look at the underlying causes of the crisis, you'd spot the obvious.

- *Problem one: people.* Each of the brothers shared in the problem, particularly Stuart. He used his position to drive his own agenda rather than to lead the company as a true manager.
- *Problem two: attitude.* Each brother became locked into a position ("I want my heir as the CEO"), losing sight of the mutual interest of the family to select the most qualified individual to lead the company.
- *Problem three: process.* The company had never developed a process for establishing criteria, identifying candidates, or selecting a CEO. Stuart had been handpicked by Phillip who, as the founder and father, had the status and inherent right to make such a decision. As the business transitions through the generations, however, the right and power exercised by the now deceased founder no longer applied. The company had no formal board of directors. The three brothers served in that role, but rarely had official meetings. There were no independent directors. The bylaws of the company were so old that none of the brothers could even find a copy. When they did, the document was, naturally, silent except to say that the CEO of the company was to be picked by a majority of the directors. Not very helpful in this case.

Fortunately, the crisis was resolved through a formal shareholder agreement that established, for this generation and future generations, a process perceived by all to be fair and to ensure that the interests of all the key stakeholders were protected.

The first step was to develop objective criteria for the selection of the next CEO. What were the qualities, background, experience, and personality of the person needed to run this company? Was it essential that the individual be a family member or could unrelated individuals be considered? Who would do the recruiting, screening, and preliminary evaluation?

What were the specific responsibilities assigned to the CEO? What authority would this individual have? To whom would the CEO report and be held accountable? How would performance be measured and compensation determined? In other words, what was the job that was being offered?

Because of the inherent conflicts amongst the brothers and the lack of independent board directors, it was necessary to employ an outside consulting firm with no personal ties to any branch to assist. Through a process of interviews with each member of the management team, including nonfamily senior executives, a job description was developed and the profile of the background needed to be considered was prepared. The three brothers had to agree on the final documents but, having done so, were then able to interview candidates more objectively and with greater focus.

As part of this process, the three family candidates were each asked to submit their own analysis of their strengths and weaknesses and their ideas for the future of the company. When the set of standards were compared to the self evaluation of the three cousins, one individual became the obvious choice for the position of CEO and the election was made without rancor or frustration. Had outside, nonfamily, candidates been considered, then family and nonfamily candidates would have been considered with the same criteria. All things being equal, a family member would likely prevail over the nonfamily candidate. But the process was fair and any candidate who prevailed would have been acceptable to the rank and file of the company.

Though the other two cousins were not selected for the position of CEO, the newly invigorated board of directors created other opportunities for them that would effectively utilize their talents and prepare them further for advancement in the company.

Though this story relates to conflict in business, and not to nonbusiness family matters, it demonstrates the value of process created by consensus. The future of your *Legacy Family* may depend on it.

★ ★ ★

"The quality of our lives depends not on whether or not we have conflicts, but on how we respond to them."

~Thomas Crum

CHAPTER THIRTEEN

The Brain Trust

The Richards Family Office was created more than ten years ago to help oversee and manage the shared assets and overlapping interests of the extended Richards Family. The original wealth creator, A.J. Richards, had formed a very successful business nearly 35 years ago. When it was sold, the Richards Family Office was formed and the proceeds were transferred to it to be managed. The Office is now run by Michael, the oldest son, and owned equally by all four of A.J.'s children and trusts for the grandchildren. The Family Office also was responsible for the commercial and industrial real estate and sizeable financial assets held for the benefit of the extended family. Profits in all the holdings were strong and growing, though sometimes the real estate seemed to be carrying the financial investments, and sometimes it was reversed.

But all was not well. Though one sister, Francine, was employed in the Family Office, along with one of Michael's children and one of his nieces, most of the 12 family stakeholders were passive owners. There was the usual grumbling about too much compensation and too many perks for Michael, not enough distribution of profits, lack of communication and transparency. Though Michael was only one of the many minority stakeholders, he was comfortable with his decisions. He felt that he had put together a strong professional advisory team, although some of the other stakeholders were not altogether pleased.

The chorus of anger and frustration was growing every year. To many of the disgruntled family members, the advisors were biased to support Michael. After all, he hired them. If they disagreed with his policies, he'd likely fire them. Different advisors were involved at different times regarding decisions related to the business or buying or selling investment assets, retaining or distributing profits, setting compensation and benefits, and information distributed or kept in-house. Estate planning lawyers rarely attended business meetings; accountants who advised in the different areas of the Family Office rarely spoke to each other. The financial advisors who managed the extended family's cash and securities dealt only with Michael.

Outspoken family members insisted that the advisors were more interested in keeping the Family Office around and growing for their own benefit and for

*Michael's continued employment than looking out for the needs and concerns
of the remaining stakeholders.*

    *The signs of a pending family crisis were clear. Unfortunately, no one
seemed to be telling Michael.*

We all have mentors we look up to, teachers who instruct us, colleagues
who inform us and friends who inspire us; these people become important allies as we build a *Legacy Family* to weather the generations. Their
influence and intelligence cannot be underrated, nor can their value be
overrated.

The *Legacy Family* Needs a Brain Trust

Every family needs that unofficial advisory board to help see them through
the 100-year arc. Who will make up your advisory board or, as many
Legacy Families call it, the "Brain Trust?" Why is a Brain Trust important? What does it take to create a Brain Trust? Who, exactly, should be
involved? How do conflicts of interest become identified and resolved?
How should the members of the Brain Trust be compensated?

    Successful businesses rely on their board of directors to serve as a
resource of expertise to the management team. The ideal board is created
by first determining the needs of the specific business, and then assessing
the strengths and weakness of both the organization and the members
of the management team. Following this analysis, board members are
solicited who have the needed expertise to help the enterprise develop its
long-range strategic plan and then guide management in its implementation. There are regularly scheduled meetings of this important group
and proceedings, and decisions are documented in minutes that serve as
a reference point of agreed upon action plans. Strong boards invite disagreement on policies and procedures, working through the differences to
develop a consensus for action.

    However when we analyze the organization of the "business of the
family" the use of advisors is a haphazard process at best. There may
be quite a diverse collection of professionals interacting with the family. They are identified when a specific need arises; involved only with
regard to the issues created by the need; and then not consulted again until
another need arises. The advisors comprise a pool of talent, but hardly a
team. They often include a variety of accountants and auditors, business,
tax and estate planning lawyers, investment advisors, insurance specialists,
management consultants, and family office executives.

    Rarely is there a professional experienced in family matters, communi-
cations, or conflict resolution. Their help is enlisted when a crisis arises,
but their proactive skills have not been utilized. None of the existing
advisors are charged with those responsibilities, so all assume that the need
either doesn't exist or someone else is handling it. They almost never meet

as a group, as would a business board of directors. There is no overarching plan for the Family Office or extended family members in which each of the key advisors has contributed, as you might expect for the company's business plan.

It would be difficult to characterize the typical advisor pool as a "Brain Trust." We define the family's Brain Trust as a multidisciplinary group of specialists who have the opportunity and responsibility of working together on an agreed upon set of issues, including the development, implementation, and operation of the family's Strategic Plan and Constitution. They meet together and with the family leaders and family group members to gather critical input, ensure a steady flow of information, and provide integrated and comprehensive counsel.

The Brain Trust Members Are the True "Trusted Advisors"

What constitutes the attributes of the Trusted Advisor? Over centuries, for better or for worse, these individuals were valued for not only their perceived expertise, but for emotional support as well. The personal attributes associated with the Trusted Advisor went far beyond professional credibility and reliability. Their presence suggested that they offered an additional kind of security. The Trusted Advisor seemed to consistently act with integrity and discretion with an acute awareness of the broader picture. Their importance demonstrated a clear understanding that it is nearly impossible for any single individual to alone possess the varied degree of expertise needed to handle the wide range of challenges confronting clients. In today's complex society, Trusted Advisors play an equally important role.

- *Members must contribute.* The operation of an effective "Brain Trust" is dependent upon the understanding that each of the Trusted Advisors has a significant contribution to make and that none are "in control" of the Family Office or extended family members. At different times in the evolution of the family, certain advisors may have a more active role but that does not reduce the importance of the other members of the team. It is important for the individuals who form this Brain Trust to recognize that the team was created to be able to respond to a variety of important needs and that the combination of talent is far more powerful than any one single provider, no matter how capable.

- *Members must be concerned.* In addition to the specific talents of each Trusted Advisor, as a member of the Brain Trust, the Advisor must have the ability to focus on the needs, aspirations, fears, and concerns of the various members of the extended family, each of whom is, at some level, a client. The advice must be made without considering how such decision might affect the Advisor's personal status or compensation. Affluent individuals are often a target for maximum fees and they have a high level of well-deserved sensitivity and mistrust about issues of pricing, even though the advice they are given may be very appropriate. Other members of the Brain Trust will quickly identify an individual member of the Brain Trust who is acting in a self-serving manner. If left unchecked, such conduct will seriously impact the ability of the group to work together effectively.

- *Members must be able to communicate effectively.* Members of the Brain Trust have to be skilled communicators. They need to be sensitive to both the content of what the family members are expressing as well as the emotions behind the words. Often clients will tell their advisors what they think the advisors want to hear without regard for what is really important to them. Effective Brain Trust members must have a depth of understanding and the appropriate communication skills that will allow the important questions to be raised. When the Brain Trust comes together and shares their individual observations, a much more realistic picture of true issues will be evident.

  Additionally, since the Brain Trust is dealing with a variety of personalities that comprise the family unit, they must be able to communicate with each member in the style that elicit the most response. Some family members will be very verbal, some visual learners, and others will need information related in a practical, project-based manner. They will present a variety of ages and backgrounds. Utilizing a specialist in the field of communication to help these diverse professionals understand the challenges of communicating the same information in the most effective manner to all family members would be a very valuable education experience for these specialists. Individuals with this type of skill set may even be invited to be permanent members of this important resource group.

- *Members must be candid.* Honesty and integrity are what is expected of all advisors. There must be a willingness to state that "the emperor is naked" even if that opinion might not be in popular favor. Often individual advisors are hesitant to say what needs to be said for fear of offending and thus losing an "important" client. The ability to have the support of a Brain Trust in honestly dealing with all aspects of a situation provides a climate for the most honest feedback in service of the family.

- *Members must be collaborative.* Understanding team dynamics enables each member to be able to operate cooperatively. Brain Trust members may have historically operated as solo professionals within their individual specialties, and it may be necessary to enlist the services of a consultant to educate this group on the principles of effective group decision making.

- *Members should be curious.* Constant learning and endless curiosity assure that all members of the advisory team remain open, educated, and aware. Those who rest on yesterday's information will be surprised by tomorrow's new developments. Members of the Brain Trust can provide education to the other members of the team regarding their individual specialty. The ideal Brain Trust will be comprised of professionals open to integrating this new information into their daily practices. These individuals enthusiastically engage in lifelong learning.

- *Members should be able to coach.* Coaching and mentoring of members of the younger generation of multigenerational families ensures that the family will sustain the ability to remain productive and contributive for many generations. The unique talents and skills of members of a thoughtfully organized Brain Trust provide the opportunity for these younger family members to form these special relationships. It is important that advisors recognize the value of directing their time and attention not only to the senior generation but to those younger members of the family who can profit from their wisdom and talent.

Complex families have many diverse needs that cannot adequately be accommodated by any singular specialty. A well-balanced Brain Trust incorporates both expertise in quantitative as well as qualitative skills to give the *Legacy Family* the type of powerful resource that will support their multigenerational success.

Every team needs a leader. The greatest challenge in creating a Brain Trust with top talented individuals is to ensure that the team works smoothly and collaboratively together. The selection of a team leader is not a simple process. Each member may feel entitled or anointed to be the leader. Should it be your oldest or closest relationship? Should it be the senior member by virtue of age or experience? Must you designate the leader or can the team designate the individual? Should it vary depending upon the task or project? What are the specific responsibilities that the team leader is expected to assume—setting agendas? Delegating tasks? Holding others accountable?

There is no answer that will apply in all cases. You may choose to serve as that leader. If you have established a family office, as the Richards Family had done, it might well be delegated that responsibility. It is clear, however, that if the Brain Trust is to serve you properly, you must answer these questions for yourself. Do not let this talented group of advisors compete for leadership. Such competition can be divisive and lead to internal conflicts within the group.

Watching a talented and experienced Brain Trust in action can be very instructive. The Richards Family was in crisis, even if Michael didn't realize it. Financial success could actually enable family members to break away from shared ownership and collective management. Whether well deserved or not, the sense of "we don't need Michael or the Family Office anymore" will encourage a breakup of the organization. Unfortunately, many of these breakaway family members will find themselves over-whelmed and underprepared for the responsibilities of managing their own affairs. This, coupled with the damage done to family relationships, is often the end of the road for aspiring *Legacy Families*.

Fortunately this story has a happy ending due to an "uprising" on the part of the other siblings. Joining together, they were able to convince Michael to fire the problematic advisors and to create a functioning "Brain Trust" filled with Trusted Advisors the extended family respected The team consisted of the head of the family office, attorneys with expertise in estate planning, tax and business organization, a financial planner, management consultant, and a mental health specialist with a specialization in family business dynamics. This multidiscipline team was in constant communication, formally connecting each month on a conference call to plan the activities for the upcoming month. The turnabout was not instant. As well as the necessity of focusing on the overall organization, each family branch required individual attention and training. However, within the first year, the extended family was back on track and the Family Office now operates successfully in both its financial duties and family responsibilities.

★   ★   ★

"When there is no counsel, the people fall; but in the multitude of counselors there is safety."

~Proverbs 11:14

CHAPTER FOURTEEN

Taking the First Step

Building the *Legacy Family* begins right now; you are now in possession of all the tools necessary to begin your journey toward leaving a rich, fruitful, conscious, and lasting legacy for your family—through the entire 100-year arc.

Consult this book often; it can be your road map to a successful *Legacy Family*. The tools here were developed, tested, and trusted over decades of experience in dealing with hundreds such *Legacy Families* under our care. What they taught us we hope to share with you; what we've learned you, too, can learn to help you foster the habits, skills, and values of a *Legacy Family*.

Remember that building a legacy is not about how much is in the bank today, but how to build strong teams and alliances and foster true legacy-leaving habits that enrich both the lives and the bank accounts of those involved. By focusing less on the financial and more on the family, you will in turn strengthen both; such is the foundation of a successful *Legacy Family*.

Steps to a *Legacy Family*...

Envision, plan, allocate, prepare, execute, adjust, and move forward . . . or, if you prefer an acronym EPA—PEA. If you wanted to create anything of sustainable and significant value, whether a great business, a successful sports team, a meaningful book, or a *Legacy Family*, you're likely to follow this process. There may be short cuts in some areas of life, but few you can rely upon and fewer still that you would test with your own family.

"E"—Envision the Future

This may be the most important and the most challenging. You have to look past where you are today and see the world and your family as you would like it to be. So, ask yourself that most difficult of questions *"how would I describe the legacy I seek? What would success look like in my eyes and the eyes of my family members 100 years from now?"* We sometimes refer to this vision of the future as a "big hairy audacious goal" or "BHAG." Seem farfetched and out of reach?

In 1966, the Star Trek television series captured the imagination with its call to "To boldly go where no man has gone before." And indeed they did. You must see success in your own mind's eye, articulate that vision well, engage your family members to help shape that vision, and don't let your eyes cloud over with pessimism and cynicism.

Nonetheless, remember the following things:

- *Failure is an option, even if unacceptable.* To assume success is to invite failure. When you realize that success is not preordained or guaranteed, you will devote the time, attention, and resources every day and through the generations to ensure that the option to fail is not the only option that remains.
- *Draw on the collective vision of the critical stakeholders.* You can't impose your vision on others. It must represent the core values and abiding principles of your family. If others can't see or prefer not to see a shared vision, the road forward will be nearly impassable. To put it another way, if your family members help to design it, they will help to build and perpetuate it.
- *Dream about the possible, expect the inevitable, prepare for the unanticipated.* One of the great visionaries of any generation was Walt Disney, who told his own children and the children of every generation "If you can dream it, you can do it. Always remember that this whole thing was started with a dream and a mouse."

"P"—Create the Plan

"Visualize this thing that you want, see it, feel it, believe in it. Make your mental blue print, and begin to build."

~Robert Collier

Imagine designing a great cathedral with a wonderful vision, a lot of heart and enthusiasm, plenty of money and time, but not a single written detail, no calculations, no engineering, no idea about what to start first and when you're ready to take the second step. The end result would likely be very different than your original vision. As important, those who follow you will have little understanding or appreciation of the thought that went into the vision and even less emotional buy-in. So, after you formulate the vision of success, craft the plan that will enable you to get there.

- *The Strategic Plan.* If every successful business relies on its business plan to set the agenda, allocate the resources, and measure its results, then a family that seeks to build its multigenerational legacy can do no less. While the elements of a plan are similar for most families that embark on this course, the content will vary as much as the personalities within the family and amongst families. What's equally important is that the adult members of the family, including the children and in-laws, have an important stake in the results, and so must participate in its design. If it's imposed from on high, the natural response is to push back, resist, and sometimes passively but aggressively undermine it.

- *The Family Constitution.* Again, using the successful business as an analogy, there are rules of behavior, a process for decision making, systematic method of selecting, evaluating and replacing leaders, and a procedure for resolving differences and disagreements. While children are young and dependent, the rule of the parent as the benevolent dictator is appropriate and appreciated. But, as the children mature and become the independent, self-sufficient, and personally productive individuals that parents seek, they feel entitled to be heard and respected. Long after the wealth creators are gone, the leadership in future generations will continue to make decisions that are intended to benefit or at least impact the lives of the extended family members. These leaders need to be held accountable to those members and responsive to their aspirations, especially when consistent with the vision and design of the family's long-range plans.

- *The Family Wealth Plan.* The Strategic Plan will outline the purpose and general allocation of the *Legacy Family's* wealth, including its Financial, Human, Intellectual, and Social Capital. Sometimes within the Strategic Plan and sometimes in parallel with that Plan, there must be a thoughtful, comprehensive plan for the use and deployment of the financial wealth. What assets and income are needed to support the current and desired lifestyle of the wealth creator and, in future generations, the senior members of the extended family? How will financial assets be invested to provide both cash flow and long-term security? How much, when, and under what conditions will assets be transferred, either during the lifetime of the wealth owners or upon death, to younger generations? What are the mutual expectations of the generations? The answers to these questions affect the estate planning of each of the affected family members, as well as their budgets, life style, and perhaps career choices.

- *Cash Flow and Budget Plan.* As you drill down into the details of the planning, you will need to develop and adhere to a budget for yourself, as will your children and future generations need to do so for themselves. The era of "spend what you want—someone else will replace the funds for you," if it ever really existed, won't survive through the generations. The discipline of a budget is a profound change for some families. But it fosters respect for the limitations of wealth and it requires understanding finances, credit, and risk. Many wealth creators live very comfortably without a budget. They do so because, in large part, they are comfortable in creating new wealth that will replace the assets consumed. Of course, when the economic pipeline bursts, as it has in the current recession, the unlimited wealth building capacity ends. Even these entrepreneurs may find themselves strapped, sometimes insolvent, and even facing bankruptcy. Those who understand how to confine their expenditures and live within their means will thrive both emotionally and financially. Those who don't will consume their assets and may never recover their former wealth or status.

Many inheritors will have an even harder time adjusting. Those whose lifestyle is propped up by the distributions from assets created by others will often face more serious challenges. When those distributions are cut back, diverted, or cut off, financial chaos can occur to inheritors. Without a budget, and the discipline of living within one's means, changes in cash flow can result in more than a significant disruption in lifestyle. It can create emotional fear and paralysis. "What will become of me" and "how will I survive" are responses heard from the scions of wealth creators.

- *Transition and Succession Plan.* If the family business is an important component of the wealth creation and legacy of the founder, and if its transition from Generation One to Generation Two or beyond is important, then preparing for transition must be part of the company's business plan as well as the family's strategic plan. Preparing is more than thinking. It's about setting clear goals, establishing fair and appropriate criteria, clarifying mutual expectations, and teaching the critical business and life skills that will be needed. The odds against a successful transition through the generations can be overcome only by thoughtful planning and very good execution.

- *Family Meeting Plan.* Communications within the family is the pipeline through which ideas and strategies, hopes and dreams, fears and frustrations, are conveyed. When the communication process is healthy, open, and supportive, families have the ability to think big thoughts, as well as to anticipate problems and resolve conflicts.

Effective communication is the critical feature found within every *Legacy Family.* Family meetings, from those that involve only the nuclear family of mom, dad, and their children, to those that reach the extended family of siblings and cousins, uncles and aunts, descendants and in-laws, are the most common method of collective communication. But family meetings can also open up old wounds and create new ones. The forum to communicate can be risky, if not well planned and conducted. Follow the guidelines we've given. This is not an area in which to "wing it."

- *Family Bank.* If it's important to you to provide the capital resources that will be needed by members of future generations who seek to go into or to expand their businesses, then creating your own entrepreneurial fund, or family bank, may be an important feature in your long-term wealth plan.

Remember that the drive, vision, and risk tolerance of an entrepreneur will not necessarily present itself in every generation. If you are an entrepreneur, your child may well choose to become a school teacher. The offspring of the school teacher may well become the business tycoon of the third generation. In addition, the resources needed by the aspiring entrepreneur will likely require more than financial support. Entrepreneurs require a range of critical life skills, including those related to leadership, collaborative decision making, and effective communication. They may require specialized education and business-related skill training, mentoring, and practical experience. So, your family bank may have responsibilities far beyond providing funding to start, acquire, or grow a business.

- *Shared Asset Plan.* If your wealth includes any asset other than cash or publicly traded securities, it's quite likely that your heirs will end up owning assets together. It may be the home, vacation property, family business, collectibles, airplane, or boat. But the very nature of shared ownership requires working collaboratively, arriving at consensus on key issues, delegating responsibilities and authority, and resolving differences in a fair and amicable way. If your children have not had experience in doing this through the years, or if you don't prepare them for doing so after you're gone, the risk of friction, fighting, and frayed relationships is substantial.

  The legal structure of the ownership, whether through a corporation, partnership, or limited liability company, or even as joint tenants or tenants in common, will greatly impact how the process will be implemented. But the ingredients of that process, which we outlined in Chapter Eight, are very similar. You don't want to be the cause, or even a contributing factor, of the break up of your family. So, it is your responsibility to design your wealth plan, whether implemented during your lifetime or upon your death, in a manner that will help bind your family together through the generations out of choice, not out of necessity.

"A"—Allocate the Resources

What are the resources—financial, human, intellectual, and social—our family will need to achieve these lofty goals?" Legacy Families make sure that each year they have added to the four capitals of wealth—financial, human, intellectual, and social—and that each of these sources of wealth is integrated into the family's life. Allocating the organization's limited resources makes priorities real. In business, the flow of resources—people and money—is the true indicator of where a company is headed. The same is true in families. Setting priorities without allocating sufficient resources to achieve them tells everyone that you weren't serious about the priorities in the first place. So, if you truly want your family to be connected, caring and competent, make sure that you are continually replenishing each of the following critical capital accounts.

- *Financial capital.* It's not about how much you leave but how you leave it. Too much too soon can be destructive. Too little too late can delay success or even prevent it. But too little at the right time often just makes the recipient work harder and more creatively. So, as you deploy your financial wealth to help your family today and through the generations, think carefully about the effect that such help can have, both positively and negatively. Hunger is a great motivator. The degree of your success is often measured by the extent of the potential failure. If there's no chance to fail, there's little chance to succeed. So fund opportunity for your family and then get out of their way.
- *Human capital.* The degree to which you provide loving and nurturing parenting and grandparenting, teach and model strong values, listen well and communicate clearly, and teach those critical life skills we have emphasized throughout this book, the greater the likelihood that your family will, for the generations to come, feel loved unequivocally and better prepared for the many challenges they will face. Every generation that has enjoyed this experience will be stronger, emotionally healthier, and closer. If this account has been shortchanged, the links in the chain will be weakened and the road to a *Legacy Family* will far more difficult to travel.
- *Intellectual capital.* We live in a competitive world where the prepared and educated will typically prevail over the unprepared and ignorant. It will enrich the spirit as well as the mind. And it will enable the individual to better enjoy and appreciate the beauties of life that are there for those given the opportunities to experience it. But remember that formal education, as important as it may be, is an incomplete text. We learn more by doing than by watching. So, help your children and grandchildren by mentoring and coaching, and by encouraging personal effort and achievement. We learn at least as much from our failures as our successes. Our education is lifelong, and we can learn from our children as well as our parents.
- *Social capital.* "*For everyone to whom much is given, of him shall much be required,*" Luke 12:48. Great and distinguished families are generous of spirit and resources. They give of their time, talent, and treasure. They recognize that their road to success was paved by the efforts of others, many of whom they never knew. If each generation takes more out of society than it contributes back, future generations will live in a hollow, desolate world.

"P"—Prepare

Ben Franklin was right about a lot of things, including noting that "by failing to prepare, you are preparing to fail." We began this book by urging you to start with a plan and we've filled the pages with guidelines on questions to ask, lessons to learn, and skills to practice. But to plan without preparation, and to learn without understanding, will doom your chance for building the family you dream to create and the legacy that you hope to leave. So, leave nothing to chance. Prepare today.

"E"—Execute. Hold Yourselves and Others Accountable

"The way to get started is to quit talking and begin doing." Walt Disney. A good plan poorly executed will end in a bad result. It's more than just not reaching your goals. In the process of creating this plan, your relationship with your family will change. Their relationships with each other and you will change. Expectations will rise. Opportunities that some may have thought impossible will become more attainable. You will, if you follow the concepts we've outlined in these pages, be on the road to a *Legacy Family.*

But, if you don't follow your own plan, carefully constructed with the help and input of your family, the results will be different from what you had hoped. If you establish standards of behavior to which you hold others accountable, then you need to follow those standards. Don't promise what you can't deliver. If no one is accountable, then everyone is to blame.

More important than any of the details of the plan you and your family establish for each other is the commitment to the process of preparing, planning, and executing well. Surround yourself with talented, thoughtful advisors who are committed to doing the right things in the right way. Your brain trust is the key to good execution. Keep them close to you.

How will you know if you're successful? Maybe you'll never really know, unless you have the good fortune to look into the eyes of your grandchildren and see the legacy that you envisioned. The metrics for success in a family are quite different than the way you measure success in business. The balance sheet will have more than numbers. Remember to ask the question... *what would success look like in my eyes and the eyes of my family members 100 years from now?* Be honest and answer that question clearly, because one day you'll judge success by how well you've achieved your answer.

"A"—Adjust and Move Forward

The best of plans will change. "Change is inevitable. Change is constant." Benjamin Disraeli. We're creating a plan for 100 years, but everything that we know and understand will evolve. Four generations from now, the world will look very different. The plan won't look the same either, but your aspirations, hopes, and dreams, are likely to be as relevant and as hard to attain 100 years from now as they may be today.

How will the story of your life be written 100 years from now?
Imagine the story of your life and the lives of the members of your family that might be written 100 years from now. What would you like that story to say? How will your descendants use the gifts that you have given to them? How will they see their own responsibilities for the generations to follow them? Will your family remain productive, competent, and connected through the generations, or will your wealth actually impede that result? The story of your legacy is actually being written now, and you have a lot to say about what it will contain.

★   ★   ★

"A journey of a thousand miles begins with a single step."

~Lao Tzu

Useful Tools: Family Strategic Planning Issues

What Is It That You Want for Each Other and Yourself?

- *Vision*. This is the family's collective view of "success" through the generations.
  - If your family could be all that *you* would have wished for over the next 25–50–100 years, what would it look like? What attributes would it have? How would members relate to each other?
- *Values*. These are the qualitative, ethical, and moral guidelines of the family.
  - How would you describe the fundamental core values that define your family?
  - What do these values mean and how are they reflected in the behavior of your family members?
  - What important family values currently need to be more fully developed in your family?
- *Mission*. This is what the extended family group intends to do in order to realize their vision.
  - What does the family want for their collective entity?
  - If the family were to accomplish all that is described in their mission, would it ensure that your vision is realized?

How Do You Get There?

- *Strategic Plan*. This is a written document that encompasses your mission and vision, and sets forth the plan to achieve your long-range goals. It includes such issues as
  - *Expected behavior and actions*. What is the behavior and actions we expect from each other? What do we feel constitutes inappropriate behavior?
  - *Family governance*. What is the process by which we will make decisions that affect our extended family group? What is the

leadership structure and how will our family leaders be selected in the future?

- o *Allocation of family resources.* How will family resources—financial, human, and intellectual capital—be allocated for the benefit of the extended family and individual members?
- o *Management of shared assets.* How will we manage and enjoy those assets in which we share legal ownership or beneficial interest?
- o *Family legacy.* What is our family's legacy and what is the process and structure by which we will enhance and perpetuate this legacy?
- o *Family philanthropy.* How will we organize and implement our collective and individual philanthropy and public responsibilities?
- o *Family communication.* How will we communicate with each other through the years and generations such that we will have the skill, freedom, and safety to express ourselves in a constructive, honest, and loving way?
- o *Conflict resolution.* We know we will disagree from time to time. What is the process and structure to ensure that we resolve our conflicts and convert our individual disagreements to collective wisdom?
- o *Estate planning.* We recognize that wealth will transfer through the generations. What are our appropriate expectations and how will we ensure that our wealth transfer planning remains consistent with our family mission, vision, and values?
- o *Extended family advisors.* What are the appropriate roles for our individual and collective family advisors? How do we effectively utilize outside resources to facilitate our planning and help us achieve our goals?
- *Family Constitution.* This is a written document containing the set of rules that you, as a family, agree upon to implement the strategic plan and cover such matters as:
  - o Governance
  - o Communication
  - o Code of conduct
  - o Confidentiality and rules of privacy
  - o Conflict resolution.
- *Action Items and Time Line.* A plan is only as good as its execution.
- *Measuring Success: Benchmarks.* How will you know if you are closer to your vision through the years than when you started?
- *Course Corrections.* Every plan will need to adjust due to time and circumstances and the addition of new family members whose ideas and opinions need to be considered.

Useful Tools: Sample Family Constitution

A. Purpose of the Family Constitution

The Family Constitution sets forth the definitive rules and procedures under which the Sample Extended Family shall be governed, operate its Shared Assets, allocate its joint resources, resolve conflicts, and conduct its collective affairs. This document shall, unless otherwise provided, override any inconsistencies that may arise between it and the Sample Extended Family Strategic Plan.

B. Definitions

The Sample Extended Family consists of Joe Sample and Mary Sample (referred to as the "Founders"), and the children of the Founders, their spouses, issue, and spouses of issue. There are four Family Groups, each of which is named after a child of the Founders (who are collectively referred to as "Generation Two"). These Family Groups are referred to collectively sometimes as the "Sample Extended Family" and sometimes as the "Extended Family."

1. Constitution" or "Family Constitution" shall be the document that formalizes and establishes the rules and structure of the Sample Extended Family. It shall be used to implement this Strategic Plan. If there is any inconsistency between this Plan and the Family Constitution, the latter document shall prevail.
2. "Family Group" shall consist of the Spouses, Issue and the Spouses of Issue of Generation Two. The four Family Groups shall known as the
   a. Tom Sample Family Group ("Tom")
   b. Carolyn Sample Family Group ("Carolyn")
   c. Carl Sample Family Group ("Carl")
   d. Lynn Sample Family Group ("Lynn")
3. "Family Member" shall include the members of Generation Two, their Spouses, Issue, and the Spouses of such Issue.
4. "Incapacity" shall mean that the individual is or has become substantially unable to manage his or her own financial resources or is

physically or mentally incapable of performing his or her duties as a Family Council Director or other services on behalf of the Extended Family. Such condition must be based on the written statement of a licensed physician, stating that (i) such physician is certified to practice medicine in the state in which the affected individual family member is living or being treated, (ii) the physician has examined the individual, and (iii) he or she has concluded that the individual is incapacitated as provided in this paragraph.

5. "Issue" shall mean the natural born child or children of any descendent of the Founders, or adopted child or children of such descendent, if the adoption occurs on or before the child attains age fifteen years and the child lives with the adopting parent for at least five years.

6. "Majority Vote" shall mean a vote of 51% of the quorum of the Directors serving on the Family Council. In the case of a six-member Family Council, this means that a vote of four is required to constitute a Majority Vote.

7. "Member" or "Members" shall refer to the legal or beneficial owners of the sample Family Investment Company, LLC.

8. "Quorum" shall mean a minimum of 50% of all Directors present at a meeting, either physically or by telephone or other electronic communication.

9. "Senior Generation" shall consist of the generation of the oldest living Issue of the Founders. So, for example, the members of Generation Two are the current Senior Generation. If one of them dies, leaving Issue surviving (who would be the grandchildren of the Founders), such Issue will constitute the Senior Generation. A spouse of a member of Generation Two is considered the Senior Generation for his or her Family Group, and, upon such spouse's death, the children will be considered the Senior Generation. If there are other living children of the Founders, they will be deemed the Senior Generation, and the living children of a deceased member of Generation Two will be considered the Senior Generation of that member's Family Group.

10. "Shared Asset" or "Shared Assets" shall mean that asset or those assets which are owned by more than one Family Group.

11. "Spouse" shall mean the lawfully married spouse of the individual, as determined by the state of such individual's residence, provided that the couple is not subject to legal separation, or temporary or permanent decree of marital dissolution or divorce. The status of "Spouse" as used in this Plan shall cease as long as such condition exists or continues.

12. "Super-Majority" shall mean a minimum two-thirds (66 2/3%) vote of all the Directors on the Family Council, excluding any such party who may be personally affected by the decision (e.g. removal or election).

13. "Unanimous Vote" shall mean the vote of all Directors of the Family Council who are not otherwise disqualified from voting on a specific issue or matter before the Council.

C. Family Governance

1. Family Council. The Extended Family shall be represented by a Family Council.
    a. The Family Council shall serve as the coordinating body for the Extended Family. It serves the purpose of organizing the collective family meetings, overseeing the management of its shared assets, and assisting each Family Member with fulfilling his or her own personal dreams and aspirations, as well as achieving the Extended Family's mission and vision.
    b. The Family Council shall consist of the Founders and one representative from each Family Group. Upon the death, incapacity, or resignation of the surviving Founder, at the option of the remaining members, it shall include one non–Family Member, who shall serve as the At–Large Director.
    c. For this purpose, a non–Family Member could include a step-child, foster child, or any other individual who does not meet the definition of a Family Member. It could also include a Family Member, if all the remaining Family Directors waive the criteria for a non–Family Member.
    d. The Family Group Director shall consist of the Issue of the Founders, unless all remaining Directors agree to waive this requirement, in which case it may include the Spouse of the Issue. The initial Family Group Directors shall be Tom, Carolyn, Carl, and Lynn.
    e. Except for the initial Family Directors, each must
        i. Be at least 30 years of age, unless all remaining Directors shall waive this requirement;
        ii. Demonstrate a high level of character, integrity, responsibility, judgment, and intelligence, as well as the ability and willingness to work as a collaborative and supportive member of the Extended Family. Such qualities may be reflected by the Candidate's completion of baccalaureate degree awarded by an accredited college or university, or life experience deemed commensurate with formal education, participation on the boards of nonprofit organizations or foundations, participation on committees or projects of the Sample Extended Family, and demonstrated actions within and for the Extended Family; and
        iii. Agree to perform the duties and responsibilities as a Director.
    f. In addition, the At–Large Director must provide needed or desirable skills, experience, independence, impartiality, and judgment to strengthen the Family Council to further the mission of the Sample Extended Family.

2. Election.
   a. A Family Group Director shall be elected by a Majority of the Qualified Members of the Senior Generation of such Family Group. A Qualified Member for purpose of electing a Director shall be any member of the Senior Generation of that Family Group who has attained the age of 18 years, has not been convicted of a felony, and has not been determined by the Family Council to be engaged in abuse of alcohol or narcotics. These criteria, except for age, may be waived by the Unanimous Vote of the remaining Directors of the Family Council.
   b. The At-Large Director shall be elected by a Majority of the remaining Directors.
   c. Notwithstanding the election by a Family Group, an individual may be barred from serving on the Family Council upon the Unanimous Vote of all remaining Directors, including the At-Large Director.
3. Tenure. A member of Generation Two, or the Spouse of a member of Generation Two, serving as a Director shall be entitled to serve until death, incapacity, resignation, or, if the Spouse, removal by the Generation Two member. All other Directors shall serve for three (3) years and may be reelected for one additional term. After serving two (2) consecutive terms, the Director may not serve again for three (3) years, unless the remaining Directors, by majority vote, waive this restriction because of the unavailability of any other qualified and interested candidate. Any Director other than Generation Two (or Spouse of Generation Two) may be removed by action of a Super-Majority of all remaining Directors.
   a. The initial term of office of any Director other than a Director who is a member of Generation Two shall be for one (1) year, during which time the Director shall serve in Provisional Capacity. This shall constitute a probationary period. At the end of the probationary period, the Director's term shall be extended to a full term upon the vote of a majority of the remaining Directors.
   b. If the Director fails to receive approval for the full term, then a new Director shall be elected by such Director's Family Group, as provided above, or by the remaining Directors, if such individual was serving as the At-Large Director.
   c. A Director may continue to serve until the earlier of the end of the term of office, resignation, death, or incapacity, as defined above.
4. Responsibilities and Authority. The Family Council shall be responsible for
   a. Providing oversight and review of the performance of the shared family assets;
   b. Approving the terms of the Strategic Plan;
   c. Approving the terms of the Family Constitution;
   d. Establishing and overseeing committees and boards as they determine are necessary and appropriate for the well-being of the

Extended Family and to achieve the Family Mission and Vision. This could include

  i. The Family Business Oversight Committee (or "Business Oversight Committee"). This Committee is intended to serve as the oversight entity for the Family's Shared Assets. This includes organizing periodic Extended Family Business Meetings, to discuss Issues related to the Shared Assets.

  ii. The Family Legacy Committee. This Committee is intended to develop projects and programs to strengthen the Extended Family's communication, interaction, education, and enjoyment. This includes planning and organizing periodic family meetings for education and training, as well as the annual Extended Family Retreat.

  e. Serving as a vehicle for conflict resolution among Family Members or to help choose a family representative to the Council if that branch is unable to do so.

  f. Serving as an advisor, trust protector, trustee, or special trustee on trusts established by Family Members.

  g. Setting a budget for the Family Council, in order for it to perform its responsibilities as required under the Strategic Plan and Family Constitution.

5. Compensation. Unless otherwise authorized by the Family Council, Family Members will not receive compensation for services provided to the Council. At-Large Directors will receive compensation for their service to the Family Council.

6. Alternates. The Senior Generation from each Family Group may also elect an alternate to serve contemporaneously with the Family Director. The alternate shall be subject to the same qualifications as a Director, except that the minimum age shall be twenty-one (21). The alternate shall be invited to attend all Board meetings and may, in the absence of the Director, represent the Family Group and exercise all such authority as delegated to the alternate by the Family Director.

7. Leadership roles. Opportunities will be extended to all qualified members of the Extended Family to assume leadership roles on both the Family Legacy Committee as well as on the Family Business Oversight Committee.

D. Shared Assets

Wherever practical, Family Shared Assets shall be managed by a written agreement that provides for governance, day-to-day management, financial management, allocation and distribution of profits, reporting and communication, exit alternatives, conflict resolution, termination, and liquidation.

F. Family Communication

1. Reporting on Shared Assets. The Family Council shall regularly, no less often than annually, review the status of Shared Assets.

2. Family meetings. The Family Council shall, either directly or through its approved committees, organize and host periodic Extended Family Meetings, designed to enhance the Mission and Vision, as well as provide specific education and mentoring Such meetings may be facilitated or not, focused on specific substantive Issues.

3. Family retreats. The Family Council will endeavor, subject to the circumstances of each Family Group, to organize an annual family retreat. The primary purpose of the retreat is to enjoy each other's company, but it may also be used to provide education for family members or other specific purposes.

G. *Code of Conduct*

Family Members commit to conduct themselves, with respect to each other, with

- Honesty, openness, and clarity;
- Sensitivity and discretion;
- Responsibility and accountability; and
- Mutual respect.

Family Members commit, with respect to outside third parties, to maintain the privacy and confidentiality of Extended Family matters, and to conduct themselves with

- Appropriate conduct and behavior;
- Honesty and integrity; and
- Responsibility and accountability.

H. *Conflict Resolution*

1. Informal process. The Extended Family encourages open, honest, and constructive discussion of Issues that affect family members. It shall attempt to resolve all conflicts and disagreements through informal discussions among the affected and interested parties.

2. Formal process. Any dispute that cannot be resolved in informal discussions shall be referred to the Family Council for resolution, unless the Family Council is a party to the disagreement or dispute. In that event, the Issue shall be referred to third party intervention. If the Family Council is unable to effect resolution of the dispute, the parties will then be requested to submit to mutually agreed upon third party intervention.

3. Third party intervention. The Family Council will utilize third party intervention, through mediation or arbitration as may be appropriate, if it is unable to resolve the dispute. If this step remains unsuccessful, the parties will then be free to pursue their own legal action or other recourse.

I. Review, Assessment, and Modification of Family Constitution

1. Statement of Values. The Family Constitution is the approved framework for the governance and guidance of the Sample Extended Family. The Family Members, as represented by the Family Council, agree to comply with the provisions of the Constitution, as this document may exist through the years. Nonetheless, the Constitution must be flexible and responsive to the needs of the Extended Family and, thus, may be amended as the Family Council wishes. It should, however, remain consistent to the Family's Mission, Vision, and Values, as those are expressed in this document.

2. Review Process. To ensure that the Constitution remains current and viable, the Family Council will, periodically but no later than every three (3) years, conduct a review of provisions of this document and receive input and advice from Family Members.

3. Third party review. The Family Council may, if it chooses, obtain input and guidance from outside third parties who are familiar with the concepts included and who may add insight and expertise that could be helpful to the Council.

4. Assessment of Benchmarks and Milestones. It is appropriate for the Family Council to establish realistic metrics with which to monitor and measure the success of the Extended Family's efforts to attain its Mission, Vision and Values. These benchmarks and milestones should always be a stretch, to encourage the Family to grow and improve, but not so ambitious that the very effort would appear fruitless and unattainable.

5. Process. The Council may establish a Governance Committee to focus on the Constitution and to seek the input from third parties. This Committee shall have such responsibility and authority as may be delegated to it by the Family Council.

6. Amendment Procedures. The Constitution may be amended upon the unanimous consent of each Director, including the At-Large Director, if then serving. Unanimity is important in this action because the interests and concerns of the minority are equally important and require greater protection from rules and procedures that might isolate or diminish its role within the Extended Family.

J. Adoption

This Family Constitution is deemed adopted on _____, 200_.

Joe: _____ Date:

Mary: _____ Date:

Tom: _____ Date:

Carolyn: _____ Date:

Carl: _____ Date:

Lynn: _____ Date:

Useful Tools: Sample Family Meeting Agenda and Topics

Sample Agenda

- Welcome
- Family Forum
  - ○ Personal updates
  - ○ Concerns and requests
- Family Strategic Plan
  - ○ Overview of family goals, needs, and expectations
  - ○ Family mission, vision, and values
- Family Business Matters
  - ○ Review of company performance
  - ○ Review of investment property performance
- Family Wealth Plan
  - ○ Review of current estate plan for G1—goals, structure, and operations
  - ○ Potential new strategies
- Family Foundation
  - ○ Grant requests
  - ○ Investment report
- Education Module based on the Four Capital accounts
- Action items and timeline
  - ○ Next meeting date

Sample Family Meeting Topics

- General Family Topics
  - ○ Tracing the family history
  - ○ Family story telling
  - ○ Web page

- Individual Family Group Topics
  - Travel and vacation planning
  - School and career update
  - Health and well-being update
- Financial Topics
  - Investment report
  - Investment planning
  - Financial education
- Business Topics
  - Performance report
  - Management transition plan
  - Succession plan
- Long Range Planning Topics
  - Family strategic plan
  - Family constitution
  - Family governance structure and staffing
  - Educational Topics
    Communication workshop
    Parenting/Grandparenting seminars
    Team building activities
    Building negotiating skills
    Recognizing diversity through the use of personality testing
    Goal setting

APPENDIX 4

Useful Tools: Common Feeling Words

Aggravated	Hopeless
Agile	Hurt
Angry	Inadequate
Annoyed	Incapable
Anxious	Irritated
Bored	Isolated
Burned out	Left out
Concerned	Lonely
Confused	Miserable
Defeated	Overwhelmed
Depressed	Oppressed
Disappointed	Put down
Discouraged	Rebuffed
Despair	Rejected
Disrespected	Sad
Distressed	Scared
Doubtful	Serious
Drained	Sorry
Embarrassed	Stifled
Enraged	Uncertain
Exhausted	Unfairly treated
Feel like giving up	Unhappy
Frustrated	Unloved
Furious	Worried
Hateful	Worthless

Useful Tools: Family Conflicts in Wealth Planning—Issues and Triggers Checklist

- Understanding the family dynamics
  - Sibling rivalry (incompatibility and distrust)
  - Favored child (jealousy and resentment)
  - Expectations
    - Wealth (lifestyle; influence)
    - Power (economic; social; political)
  - Family characteristics
    - Different leadership skills and expectations (age; intelligence; gender)
    - Right brain vs. left brain thinking process (quantitative vs. qualitative)
    - Different communication and learning styles (visual; auditory; analytical)
- Planning strategies
  - Allocation of assets (perceptions of fairness)
  - Timing of distributions (needs vs. expectations)
  - Conditions and criteria for distributions (clarity; ruling from grave; flexibility)
  - Controls and limitations (realistic and attainable vs. arbitrary and over controlling)
  - Selection of successor family leader (anointed vs. earned)
  - Selection of trustee (preparation and qualification)
- Ownership and management of shared assets
  - Decision making (consensus vs. imposed)
  - Financial obligations (capital calls; tax consequences)
  - Competing agendas (grow vs. spend)
  - Investment objectives (risk tolerances)

- o Compensation for management (how much, for what reason, to whom accountable)
- o Exit strategies (how, when, how much)
- Distribution of estate assets
  - o Equal vs. unequal allocations (actual or perceived)
  - o Cumulative lifetime gifts vs. estate gifts (makeup at original or current value)
  - o Selection of assets (sole ownership versus shared ownership)
  - o Valuation disparities (perceived vs. actual; market vs. discount)
  - o Rewarding success (more to the achiever)
  - o Rewarding failure (more to the failure)
  - o Timing and amounts (motivating vs. demoralizing; rewarding effort or encouraging dependency)
    - ▪ Distribution during career-building years (impact on work ethic and life style)
    - ▪ Controlling from the grave (delayed gratification; resentment)
  - o Ambiguities and abstract terms (tax term vs. practical meaning)
  - o Health (physical, mental, emotional; daily vs. emergency; insured vs. uninsured)
  - o Support (for whom and for what)
  - o Maintenance (at whose level)
  - o Education (formal vs. informal; expectations and standards)
- Financial competency and responsibility
  - o Expectations without preparation (risks, pressure, inefficiencies)
  - o Exposure to other family members (liability risk; creditor exposure)
  - o Family mooch (sibling expectations and resentment)
- Succession in family business
  - o Earned or inherited (expectations; resentment; preparation; drive)
  - o Accountability (to whom; with what consequence; sibling and cousin dynamics)
  - o Compensation and incentives (employee vs. owner)
  - o Communication and transparency (active vs. inactive owners)
- Selection and conduct of trustees
  - o Selection and qualifications (today, tomorrow, over time)
  - o Authority and responsibility vs. insight and expertise (family insight; fiduciary experience; impartiality)
  - o Compensation of family trustees (as a professional fiduciary vs. expectation of a family duty)
  - o Vagueness of distribution language (flexibility vs. uncertainty; perspective vs. expectations)
  - o Communication with beneficiaries (reactive vs. proactive; fiduciary vs. mentor)
  - o Conflicts of interest of fiduciary (distribute vs. accumulate)

- Prenuptials
  - Difficult conversation (timing; purpose; alternatives)
  - Communication from parent to child (demand vs. request; conditions and terms)
  - Communication from child to intended spouse (male vs. female factors; language and justification)
  - Justification and alternatives (contract vs. trusts)
- Advisory team perspectives and interaction
  - Different agendas (tax planning vs. goals planning; fees; control)
  - Inconsistent messages (goals; strategies; alternatives)
  - Mutual economic dependency (cross referrals and expected support)
  - Lack of collaboration (power conflict and control)

APPENDIX 6

Useful Tools: Sample Family Shared Asset Agreement—Topical Outline of Key Provisions

1   Definitions
2   Management of the Shared Assets
    2.1   Control by Manager
    2.2   Powers of Manager
    2.3   Management Rights and Powers of the Non-Managing Shared Owner(s)
    2.4   Election of Manager
    2.5   Removal of Manager
    2.6   Vacancy
    2.7   Manager Trustee
    2.8   Performance of Duties; Liabilities of Managers
    2.9   Compensation and Expenses of Manager
    2.10 Limited Liability
    2.11 Indemnification
3   Resolution of Deadlock
    3.1   Use of Intermediary
    3.2   Demand for Arbitration
    3.3   Selection of Arbitrator
    3.4   Costs
4   Additional Contributions
    4.1   Contributions to Save or Maintain Asset
    4.2   Failure to Make Contributions
5   Involuntary Buy-Out Events
    5.1   Transfer to Any Person or Entity Other than a Permitted Transferee
    5.2   Involuntary Bankruptcy
    5.3   Dissolution of Marriage

APPENDIX 7

Useful Tools: Comparisons between Private Foundations and Donor Advised Funds

Non-Tax Considerations	Donor Advised Fund	Private Foundation
Formation and Organization		
Advantages	The foundation is already established and tax qualified. The DAF is simple to establish. Very little paperwork required.	Can be designed to fit the circumstances and interests of the founder and family
Limitations	Many DAFs have specific formats and it may be difficult to change the structure or organization to fit the specific interests or needs of the founder, issue, and future generations	More complicated and expensive to set up and qualify
Size		
Advantages	The funding can be small. Some funds can be formed with $10,000. There is no maximum.	Can start at any size and grow through lifetime and deathbed funding. Most foundations take 15–20 years to fully fund.
Limitations	At some size, the costs of management will be similar to those of a private foundation.	If the cumulative funding does not reach a minimum level to offset the ongoing costs and burdens (which we believe is somewhere around $3.0 million), then this structure will be inefficient.
Management and Governance		
Advantages	The community foundation will have experienced and professional staff.	This enterprise creates opportunities to engage and train qualified family members in this field. Future generations have the opportunity to take on leadership roles.
Limitations	Depth and breath of experience varies widely among community and commercially sponsored foundations.	Family members may feel entitled, even though not qualified or experienced. There can be competition amongst family members and it can aggravate family rivalries.

Continued

Table Continued

Non–Tax Considerations	Donor Advised Fund	Private Foundation
Grant Making		
Advantages	Professional staff can provide experience, insight, research, implementation and follow up services. There is no legal obligation to distribute 5% of the annual fund, but many DAFs require this.	Much more flexible to meet the diverse goals of the founder and future generations, many of whom may live in other communities and parts of the world. Structured properly, grants can be given to individuals and non-U.S. charities.
Limitations	The quality and experience of the staff depends on the size, depth, and commitment of the foundation. Some DAFs provide very little expertise or assistance, and most do not permit grants to individuals or non-US charities.	Successful grant making requires preparation, organization, and process. A private foundation that does not prepare for this responsibility may make poor or ineffective grants.
Legacy		
Advantages	The philanthropic legacy of a family can be perpetuated forever.	The philanthropic legacy of a family can be perpetuated forever.
Limitations	If the DAF is subject to a limited duration, often two generations, perpetuating the legacy will be the responsibility of the institution, and not the family.	The legacy can last as long as the foundation lasts. But this may be left to the decision of future generations of the donor.
Costs		
Advantages	The management costs are shared and spread amongst many donors.	Many families absorb these costs and can actually eliminate most. In other cases, family members that perform real service can be compensated fairly.
Limitations	These costs are beyond family control and family members will not be compensated for services they perform on behalf of the DAF.	Some families abuse the rules by over-compensating themselves.
Investment Responsibilities Advantages	The combined assets of a community foundation facilitate diversification and assures outside controls.	Provides maximum family control and flexibility, and gives the directors the power to select amongst the best performing managers.
Limitations	Investment skills vary and managers may be predetermined or locked in, regardless of their performance. Certain assets, e.g. real estate, are often unwelcome in a DAF.	But, this flexibility is also vulnerable to inexperience and abuse.
Participation and continuity		
Advantages	Donor advice permits participation by the founder and selected representatives. Professional staff assures likelihood of due diligence.	The foundation will remain as long as the founder wished, or until a future board of directors determines.

| Limitations | Such advisory role may be limited to the first successor generation, and then the funds resort to the general wishes of the donor, but not subject to further advice by the family. | The strength of a family foundation is the family. It is also its potential weakness, if the family is ill-prepared. A strong board and governance structure is essential. |

Tax Considerations	Donor Advised Fund	Private Foundation
Deduction for Cash Gift	Limited to 50% of the donor's contribution base (usually the adjusted gross income).	Limited to 30% of the donor's contribution base (or AGI)
Deduction for Gifts of Appreciated Public Securities	Limited to 30% of the donor's contribution base (usually the adjusted gross income).	Limited to 20% of the donor's contribution base (usually the adjusted gross income).
Deduction for Gifts of Appreciated Real Estate or Closely Held Securities	Limited to 30% of the donor's contribution base (usually the adjusted gross income).	Limited to the donor's adjusted cost basis.
Carry-Over Deduction Available	5 years	5 years
Tax on Investment Income	None	2% of the realized gain and income (but may be reduced to 1% if certain levels of grant making are sustained).

APPENDIX 8

Useful Tools: Ten Frequently Asked Questions Regarding Governance and Management

1. Is there any advantage to a corporate form of foundation, compared to a trust form?

It is possible to operate a foundation in either legal form—corporate or trust. The choice depends on several factors. First, a corporate form offers better liability protection for the directors and officers than a trust form, although this difference can be mitigated through adequate Directors' and Officers' Insurance. Second, the corporate form is considerably more flexible than the trust form, since the Board of Directors of a corporation can adjust the structure and operations, as they may determine appropriate through the years. This is more difficult in a trust form, since only the trustee can make this decision, and only to the extent expressly permitted in the trust document. Often courts have to rule on any changes made to a perpetual trust. Sometimes the choice of structure is really the preference of the legal counsel, who may be more familiar with one variation or another, although this should not really be the overriding factor.

2. Is there a better state in which to establish my foundation than others?

It may depend on what activities you intend to engage in, how the foundation will be governed and what potential liabilities the directors or trustees might incur. This question can best be answered by experienced foundation legal counsel. It is not, however, as simple as looking to the state in which you or your family may currently be living. If your decision is to create a corporate structure, we prefer Delaware over most state jurisdictions. This is because Delaware has the most flexible corporate rules and offers the greatest protection for officers and directors. This is as true for foundations as it is for public companies. Virtually everything can be handled by facsimile and mail and you don't, of course, ever have to step foot in the state. But, ultimately, your legal counsel will guide you in this decision.

3. I've thought about forming a foundation, but want to compare this to a donor advised fund. Which is better and why?

The "best" choice depends on your short- and long-term goals, the family structure and dynamics, and even the size of the wealth that you anticipate contributing over time. Donor advised funds, whether operated under a traditional public charity, such as a community foundation or United Way, or under the auspices of a commercial for-profit company (like an investment firm or bank), serve an important function of providing relatively low-cost permanent endowments for charity. For the time being (and this issue is still under review by the Congress and Treasury Department), a donor can advise the sponsoring foundation regarding the founder's preference for distributions. It's not the same as having the power to direct the foundation, but the preference or request is routinely honored. In many cases, this power to advise will only continue for a limited period of time (e.g. two generations), after which the funds revert to the general endowment of the foundation, subject to its sole control and direction.

The obvious advantages include the avoidance of the cost of formation and the speed with which the process can be implemented. Perhaps the most important advantage is the tax benefit derived by contributing appreciated real estate to a public charity. In this situation, the donor is entitled to deduct the full fair market value of the property. When you contribute real estate to a private foundation, the deduction is limited to your adjusted cost basis. But, keep in mind, this is a one-time benefit, and the donor advised fund or foundation will continue for many years. So, while the contribution deduction is important, it's not the only factor to consider.

The community foundation usually has full-time, experienced professionals who can help guide the donors on their philanthropy, and the costs of the operations are often less, because it is shared with other donors and their funds. However, the role, authority, and responsibility of family members through the generations will clearly be very different in a donor advised fund than in a private family foundation. It's difficult for a large and growing family, not to mention two families, to share this "advisory" role. In addition, the limited authority the donor has over the foundation makes it very difficult to use this vehicle to teach the younger generations the concepts of governance, leadership, investment management and fiduciary responsibilities.

The choice should be based on a careful and impartial comparison of the benefits, burdens, costs, and overall economics of both approaches. In this area, as with so many others, the advice given may be affected by the way the advisor is paid. So proceed with care and prudence.

4. I've been advised to establish a supporting organization, because it has better tax advantages, than a private foundation. Is this true?

A supporting organization is actually a private foundation as well, but it is treated, for tax purposes, as a public charity. This is because, under the tax law, it is so closely connected to at least one public charity that it is almost a part of that organization. The connection can be achieved by having a majority of the foundation's board appointed by the public charity. Or, the purpose of the foundation can be to support specific projects of the public charity in such amounts that the government can be reasonably assured that the public charity will be supervising the activities of the foundation.

The special tax status is granted because Congress is comfortable that the public will be protected, through the oversight and control by a public charity. If you qualify, a contribution of appreciated real estate would be deductible at fair market value, instead of adjusted cost basis. Be careful, here, however, because the IRS has increasingly scrutinized both the applications of new supporting organizations, and their operations, just to be sure that there is such active oversight and control. There is recent legislation that makes this type of foundation considerably more difficult to qualify and maintain, and your legal counsel should advise you carefully on it.

5. How do I ensure that my family will always have a position on my foundation? I understand that there are no Ford family members on the Ford Foundation

By structuring the Bylaws (or Trust Agreement) to require, or at least reserve, a space on the foundation Board for a member of your family or that member's future issue, you can better protect the participation of future generations. This is particularly important if there is more than one family forming the foundation. Remember, however, that the term "family" should be defined clearly. Do you mean your natural born children, and their issue? How about spouses? Adopted children or issue? Domestic partners?

6. I have four children, but each of my children has a different number of children. How do I make it fair amongst my grandchildren? What happens as my family grows in numbers?

As the family grows in size, and spreads out around the country, it will become even more important to have a clear and fair transition plan in place. It may be important to maintain the balance amongst the different family groups, and it will certainly be important to establish the standards and criteria for Board participation, tenure in office, responsibilities and authority of each Board member. You should think about how your foundation will be governed three or four generations from now. If the plan is logical and fair, it will survive and thrive. If not, the future of the foundation could be tumultuous.

7. Can I pay my children for running my foundation?

Yes, but with several conditions to remember. First, if your corporate foundation is formed in California, then the Board must consist of a majority of "disinterested" directors, who are usually nonfamily and are not receiving compensation as officers or employees. Other states do not have this rule. Second, the compensation must be reasonably commensurate with the services provided, determined by independent directors, after consideration of the background, skill, time, and effort of the employee, as well as a review of the compensation provided by other foundations in similar circumstances. Don't be confused by compensation to board directors for services rendered in that policy-making capacity, with compensation paid to an employee for the day-to-day operations and administration. This is an area of high interest to the IRS. If you compensate family members, you will need to be very careful and conservative.

8. Can I pay the expenses of my children and their families to come to a foundation Board meeting?

The foundation may pay the reasonable expenses incurred by a Board member, or someone serving in an official capacity for the foundation, including travel and hotel accommodations, in connection with foundation business. However, this does not necessarily mean that other members of the Director's family can be reimbursed for their expenses. Be sure that everyone who receives some reimbursement is serving a real function for the foundation, and that the expenses are directly related to that function.

9. Can I rent a portion of my office building to my foundation?

The sale, lease or rental of property from a "disqualified person," which includes the founder and family members, to the foundation is prohibited. It would create "self-dealing," and cause both the foundation and the offending party to incur an excise tax. In some cases, the transgression could cause the loss of the foundation's tax-exempt status.

10. I want to have my young grandchildren become involved in the foundation, through its governance and grant-making activities. How do I do this?

Structured properly, a "junior board" of the younger generation can serve as a springboard for future leadership on the operating board of the foundation. You may find that children, as young as eight to ten years of age, can function well in an organized grant-making role. They can also participate on committees related to administration and even investments. This is an opportunity to mentor, educate, and inspire, but you may be surprised at how much the older generation will learn from and be inspired by these young adults and maturing children.

Useful Tools: Financial Competency Checklist

This is a checklist of your financial competency. Every young adult 18 or over should go through this exercise on a regular basis.

You are financially competent if you can score an average of 7 or above on the following questions. Mark yourself with a 10 for completely fluent, experienced, and knowledgeable. You're an expert at this level. Mark yourself with a 7 if you are experienced, knowledgeable, and proficient. You've mastered this question, even if you're not an expert in it. Give yourself a 5 if you're working on the topic, not yet in full command of it, but moving in the right direction. Give yourself a 3 if you haven't started, know you're not doing it right, and will get around to it one day. If all else fails, give yourself a 1 and go to a cheap movie. If you're somewhere in between these scores, pick your own number. Remember, fooling yourself won't help you win the game of life. Take the total score and divide by 18 (the number of sections). Your goal is to hit 7 in all areas, but you'll never have a final score until you're gone. This is a life-long quest. Good luck!

Managing Wealth

[ ] **Net Worth.** You are able to calculate and analyze your personal net worth and to create a personal balance sheet tied to realistic values of your assets and liabilities.

[ ] **Budget.** You have a monthly and yearly budget that properly identifies your sources of revenue, including earnings funds that come from employment and investments, as well as funds that are anticipated from gifts and other nontaxable sources. You demonstrate living within this budget on a consistent basis over time.

[ ] **Bill Paying.** You have a system for paying bills on time, whether electronically or otherwise, and a recordkeeping system that enables you to easily identify and access your information for tax and other purposes.

[ ] **Credit.** You regularly (perhaps annually) review credit report and you know your score. You are able to retain that score above 720 except for unforeseen and unanticipated circumstances.

[ ] **Major Purchases.** You are comfortable in using the Internet as well as print materials to research and conduct due diligence on major potential purchases, and you are comfortable in conducting negotiations, where appropriate, to obtain the best price and terms for those items.

[ ] **Income Tax.** You understand the concepts and can identify your own sources of taxable income and deductible expenses. You prepare or have a qualified tax preparer provide for you your annual federal and state income tax returns. You have adequately withheld or paid your quarterly installments sufficient to cover your tax obligations.

[ ] **Recordkeeping.** You have set up a personal filing system to retain your financial records for a minimum of three years, for those items that may affect your income tax returns, and longer if appropriate for your long-term investments and business.

Building Wealth

[ ] **Business.** If your life takes you into business or a profession, you will have completed your education and training, pursued your talents and demonstrated the drive, determination, responsibility, and commitment to be successful. There are many gradations of success. So you will need to set your sights on what will be personally and financially fulfilling to you. When you complete your career, you will have accomplished your goals and have considered this phase of your life *"a job well done."*

[ ] **Investing.** You have created an investment plan, through financial assets (including stocks, mutual funds, bonds, cash), real estate, or alternative investments (such as collectibles, private equity, hedge funds, and derivatives). You understand the principles of asset allocation, diversification, risk and return. You can read the appropriate economic indicators.

[ ] **Working with Advisors.** You have retained professional advisors to help you with your financial affairs, including investment advisors or managers, accountants, attorneys, and others who are experts in their respective fields. You have done your due diligence on the advisors before you retained them and you monitor their performance on a regular and consistent basis. You understand their scope of expertise and how they are compensated for such expertise.

[ ] **Planning for Retirement.** You have begun and are consistently building your personal retirement, through your employment or in other ways that will enable you to retire at the time and at the financial level that will then meet your personal objectives.

Protecting Wealth

[ ] **Risks and Risk Management.** You have identified and isolated, to the extent practical, your personal, business, and family risks. This may include how you own and manage assets.

[ ] **Insurance.** You have shifted as much risk as possible to third parties, including using sufficient insurance to cover the potential liabilities you may face. The risks may be due to accident, illness, death, personal negligence, or the negligence of others, theft of assets as well as identity, natural and man-made disasters.

Transferring Wealth

[ ] **Marriage, divorce, and cohabitation.** You have a clear understanding of the rules related to property, and the rights of a spouse, civil union partner, unmarried cohabitant, children, including step and adopted). You have obtained legal and tax advice on your responsibilities and benefits, risks and alternatives. You have provided for your dependents and others at least to the extent that you are required to do so but also to the extent you have chosen to do so, even if not required.

[ ] **Inheritance Laws.** You are familiar with the rules of inheritance wherever you reside or own property.

[ ] **Gift and Estate Taxes.** You are familiar with the tax rules related to transfers of wealth either during your lifetime or at death. You understand the consequences of such transfers that you may choose to make. You regularly (at least every five years) visit a tax or estate planning professional to review and update your planning.

[ ] **Estate Planning.** Your wills, trusts, beneficiary designations, advance directives, durable powers of attorney are up to date to meet your current goals and expectations, and are consistent with the tax law as it then exists. You regularly meet (at least every five years) with your advisors to review and update your strategies.

[ ] **Philanthropy.** You are contributing to your charities, donor advised fund, or foundation, consistent with your long-term goals and mindful of the impact such generosity has on your children and grandchildren. You have discussed this aspect of your life with your family so that they can appreciate and understand your goals and learn from your decision-making process.

Useful Tools: Reference Books and Reading List

Family and Wealth

Best Intentions: Ensuring Your Estate Plan Delivers Both Wealth and Wisdom
By: Colleen Barney and Victoria F. Collins (Dearborn Trade Publishing, 2002)

Beyond Success: Building a Personal, Financial, and Philanthropic Legacy
By: Randall Ottinger (McGraw-Hill, 2007)

The Dilemmas of Family Wealth: Insights on Succession, Cohesion, and Legacy
By: Judy Martel (Bloomberg, 2006)

Family Wealth—Keeping It in the Family: How Family Members and Their Advisers Preserve Human, Intellectual, and Financial Assets for Generations
By: James E. Hughes, Jr. (Bloomberg Press, 2004)

Family: The Compact Among Generations
By: James E. Hughes, Jr. (Bloomberg Press, 2008)

The Golden Ghetto
By: Jessie O'Neill (Hazelden, 1997)

Navigating the Dark Side of Wealth: A Life Guide for Inheritors
By: Thayer Cheatham Willis (New Concord Press, 2005)

The New Family Office
By: Lisa Gray, (Institutional Investor, 2004)

Preparing Heirs: Five Steps to a Successful Transition of Family Wealth and Values
By: Roy Williams (Robert Reed, 2003)

The Price of Privilege: How Parental Pressure and Material Advantage Are Creating a Generation of Disconnected and Unhappy Kids
By: Madeline Levine (Harper Collins, 2006)

The Ultimate Gift
By: Jim Stovall (Executive Books, 2000)

Unexpected Wealth
By: Bonnie Brown Hartley (Cultivating Change 2001)

Family Wealth Transition Planning
By: Bonnie Brown Hartley and Gwendolyn Giffith (Kogan Page, 2009)

Wealthy and Wise: Secrets About Money
Edited by: Heidi Steiger (Wiley, 2003)

For Parents and Grandparents

Are We Rich? Talking to Children About Money
By: Suzan Peterfriend and Barbara Hauser (Mesatop Press, 2001)

Children of Paradise ... Successful Parenting for Prosperous Families
By: Lee S. Hausner (2nd ed., Plaza Press 2005)

Dr Tightwad's Money- Smart Kids (and Parents Too)
By: Janet Bodnar (Kiplinger Washington Editors, 1993)

The Everything Kids' Money Book
By: Diane Mayr (Adams Media Corporation, 2006)

Mom, Can I Have That? (Dr. Tightwad Answers Your Kid's Questions about Money)
By: Janet Bodnar (Kiplinger 1994)

Raising Financially Fit Kids
By: Jolene Godfrey (Ten Speed Press, Berkeley 2003)

Wealth in Families
By: Charles Collier (Cambridge Press: 2006)

Financial Books

Beyond the Grave: The Right Way and the Wrong Way of Leaving Money to Your Children (and Others)
By: Gerald M. Condon (Harper Collins, 2001)

Cool Stuff They Should Teach You in School
By: Kent Healy and Kyle Healy (Cool Stuff Media, 2005)

Couples and Money
By: Victoria Collins, (Dearborn Trade Publishing, 2005)

Integrated Wealth Management: The New Direction for Portfolio Managers
By: Jean Brunel (Euromoney Institutional Investors, 2006)

Making the Most of Your Money
By: Jane Bryant Quinn (Simon and Schuster, 1997)

Money and the Meaning of Life
By: Jacob Needleman (Doubleday Business, 1991)

The Quarterlife Crisis
By: Abby Wilner and Cathy Stocker (Tarcher, 2001)

Standard and Poor's Guide to Money & Investing
By: Virginia M. Morris and Kenneth M. Morris (Lightbulb Press, 2004)

Standard and Poor's Guide to Understanding Personal Finance
By: Virginia M. Morris and Kenneth M. Morris (Lightbulb Press, 2006).

Business Succession

Generation to Generation: Life Cycles of a Family Business
By: Kelin Gersick, John A. Davis, Marion McCollom Hampton and Ivan Lansberg (Harvard Business School Press, 1997)

Hats Off to You: Balancing Roles and Creating Success in Family Business
By: Ernest A. Doud, Jr., and Lee Hausner (Doud/Hausner, 2000)

Perpetuating the Family Business: 50 Lessons Learned from Long Lasting, Successful Families in Business
By: John Ward (Palgrave Macmillan, 2004)

Reweaving the Family Tapestry
By: Fredda Hertz Brown (W.W. Norton and Company, 1991)

Generation to Generation: Life Cycle of Family Business
By: Ivan Lansberg, Kelin Gersick,. John Davis (Owner Managed Business Institute, 1997)

Working With the Ones You Love
By: Dennis Jaffe (Red Wheel/Weiser, 1991)

Family Business Leadership Series
By: John Ward and Craig Aronoff (Family Enterprise Publishers, 1997)

Negotiating

Getting to Yes
By: Roger Fisher and William Ury (Penguin, 1991)

Women's Focus

Ernst & Young's Financial Planning for Women: A Woman's Guide to Money for All of Life's Major Events
By: Ernst & Young LLP (Ernst & Young LLP, 2005)

Rich Woman: A Book on Investing for Women
By: Kim Kiyosaki (Rich Press 2006)

Smart Women Finish Rich: 9 Steps to Achieving Financial Security and Funding Your Dreams
By: David Bach (Broadway, 2002)

Women in Family Business: What Keeps you up at Night
By: Patricia Annino JD, Thomas Davidow EdD, Lisbeth Davidow EdM
   (Booksurge, 2009)

Communication

Difficult Conversations: How to Discuss What Matters Most
By: Doug Stone (Penguin, 2000)

It Pays to Talk: How to have the Essential Conversations with Your Family About Money and Investing
By: Carrie Schwab-Pomerantz and Charles Schwab (Schwab, 2002)

Men are From Mars, Women are From Venus
By: John Grey (Harper Collins, 2004)

Philanthropy and Foundations

Founder's Guide to the Family Foundation . . . How to Use, Enjoy, and Govern Your Family Foundation
By: Douglas K. Freeman and Lee Hausner (2nd ed.,Council on
   Foundations, 2005)

Generations of Giving: Leadership and Continuity in Family Foundations
By: Kelin E. Gersick (Lexington Books, 2006)

The Giving Family
By: Susan Crites Price (Council on Foundations, 2001)

Inspired Philanthropy: Your Step by Step Guide to Creating a Giving Plan
By: Tracy Gary (Inspired Legacy, 2007)

Splendid Legacy: The Guide to Creating Your Family Foundation
By: Virginia M. Esposito (National Center for Family Philanthropy, 2002)

INDEX